S0-BNY-700

REA's Practical Help for
PRE-ALGEBRA

Authors

Sally H. Spetz
for U.S. Department of Education

Robert A. Bell, Ph.D.
Mathematics Instructor
The Cooper-Union School of Engineering,
New York, NY

Diane Bohannon, Ed.S.
Chairperson of Mathematics Department
Halls High School, Knoxville, TN

Roger C. Fryer, M.A.T.
Mathematics Instructor
Cosumnes River College, Sacramento, CA

Elaine M. Klett, M.S.
Mathematics Instructor
Brookdale Community College, Lincroft, NJ

Lutfi A. Lutfiyya, Ph.D.
Associate Professor of Mathematics
Kearney State College, Kearney, NE

John S. Robertson, Ph.D.
Associate Professor of Mathematics
U.S. Military Academy, West Point, NY

Vijay K. Rohatgi, Ph.D.
Professor of Mathematics
Bowling Green State University,
Bowling Green, OH

Jerry R. Shipman, Ph.D.
Professor & Chairperson of Mathematics
Alabama A&M University, Normal, AL

Ricardo Simpson-Rivera, M.S.
Visiting Scientist
Oregon State University, Corvallis, OR

Walter Smulson, M.A.
Chairperson of Mathematics Department
Loyola College, Wilmette, IL

Ron Walters, M.Ed.
Chairperson of Mathematics Department
Meade County High School, Bradenburg, KY

Ernest Woodward, Ed.D.
Professor of Mathematics
Austin Peay State University, Clarksville, TN

**and the Staff of
Research & Education Association**

 *Research & Education Association*

REA's PRACTICAL HELP
FOR PRE-ALGEBRA

Copyright © 2002, 1998 by Research & Education Association. All rights reserved. No part of this book may be reproduced in any form without permission of the publisher.

Printed in the United States of America

Library of Congress Control Number 2002106270

International Standard Book Number 0-87891-761-6

Research & Education Association
61 Ethel Road West
Piscataway, New Jersey 08854

TABLE OF CONTENTS

4. Formulas And Tables

5. Answers To Tests And Exercises In Chapters 1 - 4

6. Practicing To Take Standardized Tests In Arithmetic

7. Practicing To Take Standardized Tests In Geometry

Glossary

Words/Terms

1. *Arithmetic Operations* A term which refers to the four operations: addition, subtraction, multiplication and division.
2. *Carry* To retain a portion of the results of a step in addition or multiplication and include it in the results from the next step. The term also refers to the number that is retained or "carried" to the next step.
3. *Common Factor* A number which divides into two or more other numbers with no remainders.
4. *Common Fraction* A fraction written as the number of parts (numerator) over the total parts in the whole (denominator), for example, ¾, ⁹⁄10, or ⁹⁄100.
5. *Decimal Fraction* A fraction with a denominator being a power of 10 (10, 100, 1000, and so on). Only the numerator is written, with the denominator indicated by the position of a decimal point, for example, .75, .9 or .09.
6. *Denominator* The part of a fraction that indicates the total parts in a whole. In the fraction, ¾, 4 is the denominator.
7. *Dividend* One of the parts in a division problem. This is the number divided *into*. In the problem, $24 \div 8$ or $8 \overline{)24}$, *24* is the dividend.
8. *Divisor* One of the parts in a division problem. This is the number divided *by*. In the problem, $24 \div 8$ or $8 \overline{)24}$, *8* is the divisor.
9. *Improper Fraction* A common fraction in which the numerator is larger than the denominator, for example, ¹³⁄8.
10. *Intersect* To cross or meet.
11. *Invert* To turn a fraction upside-down, writing the denominator over the numerator.
12. *Lowest Common Denominator (LCD)* The smallest common factor that will divide evenly into the denominators of two or more fractions.
13. *Lowest Terms* A form of a fraction where the numerator and denominator have no common factor.
14. *Magnitude* An amount, size or extent.
15. *Mixed number* A number that contains a whole number and a fraction, for example 8⅘.
16. *Multiplier* One of the parts of a multiplication problem, usually the smaller of two numbers being multiplied.
17. *Number Line* A line, somewhat like a ruler which shows the magnitudes and signs (negative or positive) of numbers on either side of a zero point.
18. *Numerator* The component of a fraction that tells how many parts of the whole are being dealt with in the fraction. In the fraction, ¾, *3* is the numerator.
19. *Place Holder* A function of zero, when it is used to indicate that a particular place value is empty. Zero as a place holder in the number 40,546 indicates that there are no one thousands.

20. *Place Value* The value of the location of a digit within a number.
21. *Proper Fraction* A fraction whose numerator is smaller than its denominator.
22. *Remainder* A part of a division problem that is the amount "left over" when the divisor does not divide evenly into the dividend.
23. *Whole Number* A common counting number that can have a + or − sign.

Signs/Symbols

+ A positive quantity. The symbol can also refer to the addition operation. Read as "plus."

− A negative quantity or the subtraction operation. Read as "minus."

× Indicates the multiplication operation. Read as "times."

÷ or $\overline{)}$ Indicates the division operation. Read as "divided by" (÷) or "divides into" ($\overline{)}$).

= An equal sign. Means that the quantity on the left of the sign is equivalent to the quantity on the right.

% A percent sign. A percent is a special fraction with a denominator of 100.

π The value, pi. A constant equal to approximately 3.14 that is used in computations dealing with circular figures.

° A sign used to mean degrees.

″ A sign used to represent inches.

′ A sign used to represent feet.

Abbreviations Used

cm centimeters (length measure)
ft   feet (length measure)
in   inches (length measure)
kwh kilowatt hours (measure of electricity usage)
lb   pounds (weight measure)
mm millimeters (length measure)
oz   ounces (weight measure)

1. How To Use This Book

This book simplifies the learning of pre-algebra math, and makes math interesting and fun.

The book teaches the subject without the complexities often considered scary by many students and others who need to acquire pre-algebra math.

Almost everyone pursuing a career or a course of study needs to know pre-algebra math. Also, almost all college entrance tests and professional exams require knowledge of at least pre-algebra math. The practicing of almost all crafts involves the use of pre-algebra math.

This book teaches pre-algebra math through practical problems which have been selected to reflect the daily activities that almost everyone encounters.

For example, homeowners use pre-algebra math in calculating curtain sizes, areas to be covered with carpets, mixing ingredients for cooking, and many other household activities. Pre-algebra math is necessary to check interest paid on loans and mortgages. Maintenance and operation of a car can involve many different math steps. To persons in trades such as carpenters, electricians, and contractors, for instance, math is particularly important for completing their tasks.

This book deals with mathematics as it is used in a variety of occupations. Practical problems illustrate each of the topics covered by the materials. Specific topics included are the following:

1. The four basic arithmetic operations (addition, subtraction, multiplication, and division)
2. Use of fractions, decimals, and percents
3. Use of formulas and tables
4. Practice tests to help you prepare for the arithmetic and geometry sections of standardized tests.

What Must I Do To Complete My Work In This Book?

Working your way through Chapters 2-5 of this book will require you to read the text, to answer the questions, to perform the exercises and to complete the pretest and posttest sections. Expect to spend about five hours working through the materials. The only resources you need to complete your work in this book are: (1) a pencil or pen; (2) a ruler; and (3) about five hours of time.

The materials are written in a self-instructional, programmed format. You may work through the text, examples, and questions at your own pace and leisure. You need not complete your work in the book at one sitting.

Each of Chapters 2-5 is devoted to a single skill, competency or unit of knowledge. The general format of the chapters is similar with the following parts:

1. A *chapter overview* containing all the necessary information you need to know in order to work through the chapter.
2. An *introduction* describing the knowledge or skill and the instructional objectives for the information.
3. *Principles, examples and applications* presenting and explaining the content as well as offering you practice opportunities to apply the information.
4. Additional sources of *information*.
5. *Self-test exercises* for applying the information under consideration.

Chapters 2-5 conclude with the answers to the Pretest, the Self-Test exercises from each chapter, and the Posttest.

How Much Do I Know About The Subject As I Begin?

Begin your work in this book by completing the self-assessment pretest that follows. When you have completed the pretest as directed in the assessment instructions and have finished reading the other materials in this introduction, continue your work in this book, one chapter at a time. Begin with Chapter 2, unless the results of your self-assessment indicate that you should do otherwise.

In each of Chapters 2-5, do the following:

1. Read:
   - Background information
   - Steps and procedures for performing skilled activities and explanations of major points and ideas
   - Examples illustrating use of information, performance or skill, or application of material
2. Consider the questions and exercises in the text. Work the questions and check your answers.
3. When you believe that you have mastered the material, take the Self-Test at the end of the chapter.
4. Check your answers with those provided in Chapter 5. If you achieve at least the minimum acceptable score, move to the next chapter. If your score is below acceptable levels, work through the chapter again.
5. After completing all the chapters, take the Posttest in Chapter 5.

To gain admission to college and professional programs, applicants are generally required to take standardized tests. You can prepare for taking such standardized tests in Arithmetic and Geometry by practicing with the materials given in Chapters 6 and 7. Chapter 6 is devoted to Arithmetic and Chapter 7 to Geometry. Each of these two Chapters includes practice tests and drills, and additional reviews that are pertinent to the practice tests. After reading the reviews and doing the practice tests, you should be well-equipped to take standardized tests in Arithmetic and/or Geometry.

Self-Assessment Pretest

Directions: The self-assessment will help you focus on specific strengths and limitations of your mathematics knowledge and skills. Select or calculate the best answer for each question and record it in the appropriate space. After you have worked through the entire pretest, score your test following the directions at the bottom of the test.

1. An electric meter reads 14725 KWH. What are the place values for each of the digits in the reading:

Digit	Place Value
1:	
4:	
7:	
2:	
5:	

2. The meter reading in question #1 was taken in March. If 839 KWH were used in the next month, what would the reading in April be?

3. If the same number of KWH were used in each month, what would be the meter reading next March (after 12 months)?

4. What is the length of the house in the figure below?

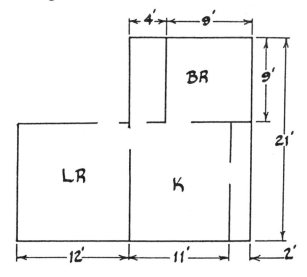

5. What is the width of the living room?

6. Metal rods measuring 156″ are to be cut into 6″ lengths. How many rods would be needed to cut 104 of the 6″ lengths?

7. A plumber has $458 in a checking account. If the plumber pays a $165 electric bill, how much would be left in the account?

8. A paperer has 18 rolls of wall paper on hand. If each roll covers 128 square feet, how many total square feet of wall can be covered with the paper on hand?

9. A machinist calculated a desired dimension to be 35.36864 mm. Round this measurement to the nearest thousandth mm.

10. Four parts of a component weighed as follows:

    6 ⅞ oz
    1 ⅔ oz
    4 ½ oz
    3 ¾ oz

    What is the total weight of the component? Reduce your answer to lowest terms.

11. Each adjustment on a 6 ¾″ circumference control moves the knob ⅜″. How many adjustments are required to move the knob one complete turn?

    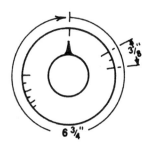

12. Parts which generally sold for $154.00/1,000 were being offered at a 25% discount. What is the disount price for 1000?

13. What would be the savings on an order of 8000 parts from Question 12?

14. A metal plate measured 5-⅝″. Convert this to a decimal.

15. A part is to be increased in size by ¼. What is the increased value for a dimension which measures 3-⅔″?

16. A rod measures 15-⅛ inches in length. If a work order requires a rod 14.25″ in length, how much needs to be cut off? Express your answer as a common fraction.

17. Write the following statement as a formula: The distance travelled by an object is equal to its velocity multiplied by the time travelled.

18. Write the following relationship as a formula: Perimeter of a rectangle is computed as the product of 2 times its length plus 2 times its width.

19. $R = E/I$. If the voltage (E) in a system is 220 and amperage (I) is 40, what is the resistance (R)?

20. Using the following formulas, calculate the area of a circle with a 7-½″ diameter (D):
    $$A = \pi \times R \times R$$
    $$R = D/2$$
    $$\pi = 3.14$$

21. Convert 25° Celsius to Fahrenheit using the table below.

°F	°C
70	21
72	22
74	23
76	24
77	25
79	26
81	27
83	28

22. The table below shows average monthly flow of waste from three sites into the City River for a six-month period. During which month did Site B have its greatest flow?

Average Monthly Flow of Waste
(liters/meter)

Month	Site		
	A	B	C
Jan	249	382	419
Feb	381	392	379
March	407	357	298
April	352	372	305
May	312	398	317
June	319	337	302

Scoring: *Check your answers with those provided in Chapter 5. Mark each answer right or wrong. Then, grouping the answers into the sets of questions listed below, count the number correct for each set. Enter the amount in the appropriate spot on the Chapter Overview Chart that introduces each chapter, beginning with Chapter 2.*

Questions 1-8, number correct is _____.
Questions 9-16, number correct is _____.
Questions 17-22, number correct is _____.

2. Arithmetic Operations

Chapter Overview

Purpose: To develop skills in basic arithmetic operations as applied to the trades. An apprentice will gain an understanding of how numbers are used to perform operations and an ability to solve work-related arithmetic problems.

Preassessment Score: Write in the following space the number of correct answers from Pretest questions 1-8: _____. If you answered seven or eight questions correctly, skip to Chapter 3. If you missed two or more questions, work through this chapter.

Prerequisites: Chapter 1 of this book.
Mastery of addition, subtraction, multiplication and division of one-digit numbers.

Resources: Time—about 2-3 hours to complete. You do not need to work through the chapter in one sitting.
Materials—paper, pencil.

Performance Measure: A thirty-minute paper-and-pencil Posttest, to be taken after completing the entire book.

Standards: To be successful, you must answer correctly 80% of the Posttest items.

Activities:
1. Read the text, examples and illustrations and commit information to memory.
2. Work questions, examples and problems.
3. Complete and check the Self-Test Exercises and the Posttest.

Introduction and Objectives

Four basic arithmetic operations form the foundation for much of mathematics: addition, subtraction, multiplication and division. These operations are involved in many of our everyday life activities, such as keeping a checkbook balance, comparative shopping, splitting a lunch tab or figuring your taxes. Moreover, they are extremely important because they are used in mathematical applications in virtually every apprenticeable trade. Applications range from calculating the pitch of a screw thread to determining the resistance of an auto starting motor to doubling the ingredients in a recipe. In each case, the fundamental arithmetic operations are critical to performing the task at hand. Thus, you should pay particular attention to this unit, either as a refresher for what you have learned before or a new way of looking at things you have had difficulty with in the past. After you have completed your work in this chapter, you will demonstrate your ability to:

1. Relate how characteristics of numbers are used to perform operations.
2. Solve work-related problems requiring addition.
3. Solve work-related problems requiring subtraction.
4. Solve work-related problems requiring multiplication.
5. Solve work-related problems requiring division.

Characteristics of Numbers

Whole Numbers

The everyday numbers you use for such things as counting, telling time and measuring temperature are called *whole numbers*. Often whole numbers are portrayed on a number line, something like a ruler. Look at the number line in Figure 1. It is used to illustrate the following principles which are basic to mastering arithmetic operations.

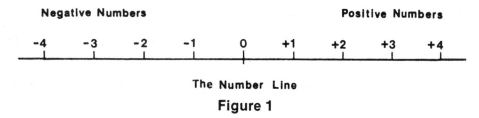

The Number Line

Figure 1

1. *Positive numbers become greater as you move away from zero. Negative numbers are smaller as you move away from zero.*

   For example, if you are running a business and you are operating in the black (making a profit), you want your balance to be a large number. If you are in the red, or losing money, however, a small balance would be better. This is because it is a negative number, and the closer it is to zero the less you would be in debt.

2. *Except for their signs, positive numbers and negative numbers behave in the same way.*

   On the number line, two is twice as far away from zero as one. Thus, two is two times as large as one, whether positive or negative.

   Starting at +1 on the line, move two units to the right. You end up at 3. Stated differently, one unit plus two units equals three units. The same principle could be applied using negative numbers.

Example

A carpenter has one 8-foot two-by-four. He needs the following pieces:

Two 3-foot sections

One 4-foot section

He can use the number line to determine if he has enough lumber. He starts at +8 on the number line, which represents the total length of the lumber. He moves to the left 3 units for the first 3-foot section and ends on +5. He then moves to the left 3 more units for the second 3-foot section and ends on +2. For the 4-foot section he moves four more to the left and ends on −2. How many feet short is he? If he went out and bought a two-foot length of 2×4, would he have enough lumber? Why not?*

---

* *Answer*

Since the carpenter ended on −2 on the number line, he would be 2 feet short of lumber. If he bought a 2-foot section, he still would not have enough. He would have two 2-foot sections when he needs one 4-foot section.

Exercises

Use the number line to complete the following exercises as illustrated in a, b, and c.

	Start At	*Move*	*End At*	*Write the Operation*
a.	3	+4	7	$3 + 4 = 7$
b.	6	−3	3	$6 - 3 = 3$
c.	−2	−3	−5	$-2 - 3 = -5$
d.	2	+1		
e.	3	−2		
f.	8	9		
g.	−5	+2		
h.	−4	−1		

Answers

	Start At	*Move*	*End At*	*Write the Operation*
d.	2	+1	3	$2 + 1 = 3$
e.	3	−2	1	$3 - 2 = 1$
f.	8	−9	−1	$8 - 9 = -1$
g.	−5	+2	−3	$-5 + 2 = -3$
h.	−4	−1	−5	$-4 - 1 = -5$

Place Values

A place value is the value of the location of a digit within a number. To see this, look at the place values of the following number.

Billions	Hundred-millions	Ten-millions	Millions	Hundred-thousands	Ten-thousands	Thousands	Hundreds	Tens	Ones
4,	3	0	8,	4	4	4,	5	1	2

Each place value is ten times the value to its right. For example, one hundred is ten times ten. One thousand is ten times one hundred. The example number could be read: Four billion, three hundred eight million, four hundred forty-four thousand, five hundred twelve. Each of the place values by itself would look like this:

4 Billions:	4,000,000,000
3 Hundred-millions:	300,000,000
0 Ten-millions:	00,000,000
8 Millions:	8,000,000
4 Hundred-thousands:	400,000
4 Ten-thousands:	40,000
4 Thousands:	4,000
5 Hundreds:	500
1 Tens:	10
2 Ones:	2
Added up, the place values equal:	4,308,444,512

Zero is used as a *place holder*, for ten-millions in this example. Be sure to remember to include the zero place holder. If your supervisor told you to place an order for one hundred eight (108) square feet of corrugated iron, how big would your order be if you forgot the zero place holder?* You surely would not want a zero left out of your paycheck.

Exercises

Use the illustration of an electric meter in Figure 2 to answer the questions. To read the meter you read dials from left to right, writing down the numbers pointed to on each dial. Write the smaller number when the pointer is between two figures.

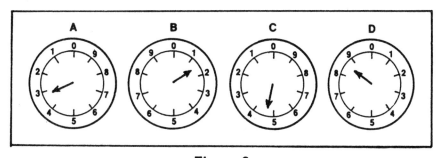

Figure 2

1. What is the reading on the meter? _____

2. Write the place value for each of the digits in the reading.

Dial	Reading	Place Value
A		
B		
C		
D		

3. If Dial **D** were to move clockwise past the zero reading, what effect would this have on the reading for Dial **C**?

---

*   *Answer*
    Your order for corrugated iron would be for 18 square feet instead of 108 square feet.

Answers

    1.   3148

    2.

Dial	Reading	Place Value
A	3	Thousands
B	1	Hundreds
C	4	Tens
D	8	Ones

    3.   Dial **C** (the tens column) would be increased by 1. Thus, it would read 5 instead of 4, until Dial **D** moves 10 values again.

Addition

If you had a very long number line, numbers could be added by starting at the location of one number and moving to the right the units of the numbers to be added. This is how you added numbers in the previous section. Keep this in mind when you are adding numbers because it gives you a feel for the magnitude of the numbers when they are combined. But there are easier ways to go about adding numbers together. Here are three steps for addition:

    1.   Write the numbers in a column. Be sure to line up the place values (ones, tens, hundreds, and so on) of each number one above the other.

        For example, suppose you had four plumbing jobs planned for the month and you wanted to determine if you could take on another assignment. Your estimates of the times for the jobs were: Smith job—23 hours, Meyers job—91 hours, Johnson job—9 hours, Lewin job—105 hours. To add up the total hours, you first write them in a column:

$$
\begin{array}{r}
23 \\
91 \\
9 \\
+105 \\
\hline
\end{array}
\quad \text{Job hours}
$$

    2.   Add up the digits in the ones column. Write the answer below the line. If it is greater than 9 only write the furthest digit to the right. Carry the rest of the results to the top of the tens column and write it there. This is exactly what the meter does when a dial passes zero—the extra is moved to the next higher dial. In the example above, we would do the following:

Example:	*Process:*
$Carry \rightarrow$ 1 23 91 9 105 ――― 8	a. $3+1+9+5=18$ b. Write the 8 in the ones column. c. Write the 1 above the tens column.

    3.   Continue the process for each column. The carried numbers are added into the column's sum.

Example

Process:

Carries → **11**
23
91
9
105

} *Job hours*

228   *Total hours*

Tens Column:
a. $1 + 2 + 9 + 0 = 12$
b.   Write the 2 in the tens column
c.   Write the 1 above the hundreds column

Hundreds Column:
a. $1 + 1 = 2$
b.   Write the two in the hundreds column

After adding up the job hours, you realize that you already will be overworked this month. Therefore, you decide not to take on another job, but give some thought to hiring an apprentice instead.

Example

An apprentice welder has an assignment of butt-welding five pieces of metal together. The lengths of the pieces are 55 cm, 89 cm, 7 cm, 10 cm, and 218 cm. She calculates what the total length of the metal after welding would be as follows:

Carries → **12**
55
89
7
10
+ 218

} *Lengths of individual pieces*

379 cm   *Total length or sum*

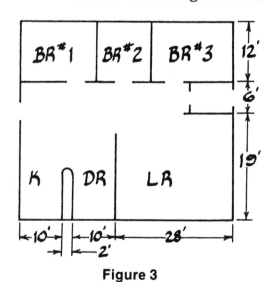

Figure 3

Exercises

1. Use the drawing in Figure 3 to answer the following:
    a.   What is the length of the house?
    b.   What is the width of the house?
    c.   What is the length of the kitchen/dining area (including the counter)?

2. Calculate what the length of the house would be if the dimensions were changed as follows:

	Kitchen	Counter	Dining Room	Living Room	Total Length
a.	12	3	12	20	
b.	15	0	16	22	
c.	8	2	10	25	
d.	18	3	14	31	

3. Five bins of scrap metal contain loads weighing 580 lbs, 614 lbs, 92 lbs, 108 lbs, and 379 lbs. What is the total weight of the scrap metal?

4. Calculate the total weight accumulated in the bins for each day of the week illustrated below. Which bin collected the most scrap for the entire week?

	Bin #1	Bin #2	Bin #3	Bin #4	Bin #5	Total Daily Weight
Monday	89	4	372	490	154	
Tuesday	93	28	207	377	117	
Wednesday	124	70	222	85	398	
Thursday	47	32	190	207	237	
Friday	188	55	308	229	174	

Answers

1. a. Length of the house would be equal to the sum of the lengths of the rooms:

Carries →	1
Kitchen:	10 feet
Counter:	2 feet
Dining Room:	10 feet
Living Room:	+ 28 feet
Total Length:	50 feet

b. Width of the house equals:

Living Room:	19
Bath:	6
BR #1:	+ 12
	37 feet

c. Kitchen-Dining Area length:

Kitchen:	10
Counter:	2
Dining Room:	+ 10
	22 feet

2. The total length again would equal the sum of the lengths. The answers should be:

	Total Length
a.	47
b.	53
c.	45
d.	66

If you answered incorrectly to any of these, first check that you set the problem up correctly. For "a", you should have set it up as:

$$
\begin{array}{r}
12 \\
3 \\
12 \\
+ 20 \\
\hline
\end{array}
$$

Next check that you copied the numbers correctly in setting up the problem. Finally, re-check your addition. If you still cannot find the error, review the steps for addition or get some help from your instructor.

3. Total weight equals:

Carries → **22**
580
614
92
108
+ 379
―――――
1773

4. To calculate the Total Daily Weight you should have totaled the weight in Bin 1, Bin 2, Bin 3, Bin 4 and Bin 5 for each day:

Day	Total Daily Weight
Monday	1109
Tuesday	822
Wednesday	899
Thursday	713
Friday	954

To find out which bin collected the most scrap in a week, you should have added down the columns for each Bin #:

Bin #	Total Weight
1	541
2	189
3	1299
4	1388
5	1080

Therefore Bin #4 collected the most waste in the week.

Subtraction

Subtraction involves taking away or removing something. This is represented by moving to the left on the number line. As with addition, you start subtraction by placing the numbers in a column, lining up the place values. But with subtraction, you can only work easily with two numbers at a time. The remaining steps in subtraction are:

1. Subtract the lower number in the ones place from the upper number. If the lower number is greater than the upper number, borrow 1 ten from the tens place. Record the result as shown below.

Example:

2
5$\cancel{3}$3
−147
―――
6

Process:

a. Borrow one ten from the tens column. This gives you 13 in the ones column.

b. Subtract 7 from 13 to get 6. Write this in the ones column.

c. Cross out the three and change it to a two in the tens column so you don't forget you borrowed 1.

2. Continue in the same way with the remaining columns, working from right to left.

Example:	*Process:*

Tens column:

$$
\begin{array}{r}
42 \\
\cancel{5}\cancel{3}3 \\
-147 \\
\hline
386
\end{array}
$$

a. Four is greater than 2, so borrow 1 hundred from the hundreds column. This gives you 12 tens.

b. Subtract 4 from 12 and write the result in the tens column.

c. Change the 5 in the hundreds column to 4 to record your borrow.

Hundreds column:

d. Subtract 1 from 4 and record the result (3) in the hundreds column.

Example

A self employed journeyman checked to see if the balance in his checking account was enough to pay some outstanding bills and still leave him enough to buy $540 worth of supplies he needed. His balance was $1,972. He itemized and totaled the bills as follows:

Electricity	$ 140
Gasoline Credit Card	97
Telephone	46
Rent	+ 750
	$ 1,033

To determine how much money he would have after paying the bills, he subtracted the total of the bills from his balance:

$$
\begin{array}{r}
6 \\
\$ \ 19\cancel{7}2 \\
-1033 \\
\hline
\$ \ \ 939
\end{array}
$$

Therefore, he would have plenty to buy the needed supplies. How much would be left after buying the supplies?*

* *Answer*

To determine how much would be left after buying supplies, subtract the amount of the supplies ($540) from the $939 remaining after paying bills:

$$
\begin{array}{r}
8 \\
\$ \ \ \ 9\cancel{3}9 \\
- 540 \\
\hline
\$399
\end{array}
$$

Exercises

1. A machinist makes 348 parts in a day. Of these, 23 are rejected by inspectors. How many good parts did she produce?

2. The machinist's weekly production figures are listed below. How many good parts did she make each day? What were her production figures for the week (Total produced, rejected, good parts)?

	Parts Produced	Parts Rejected	Good Parts
Monday	295	17	
Tuesday	303	19	
Wednesday	187	168	
Thursday	223	24	
Friday	352	33	

(On Wednesday, there was an error in the specifications which was not caught until late in the day. It was not the fault of the machinist).

3. The payroll figures for an industrial department are shown below. What is the take-home pay for each of the employees?

Employee ID	Gross Weekly Pay	Total Deductions	Take-Home Pay
210-62-4822	$ 424	$ 127	$
426-39-3001	392	107	
712-36-9143	519	185	
146-92-3242	358	81	
152-13-6491	387	96	
242-19-2990	525	114	

Answers

1. The number of good parts is determined by subtracting the number of bad parts from the total parts:

$$\begin{array}{r} 348 \\ -\ 23 \\ \hline 325 \end{array} \text{ good parts}$$

2.

Day	Good Parts
Monday	278
Tuesday	284
Wednesday	19
Thursday	199
Friday	319

If you missed one or more, try to find your error by:

a. Checking that you set the problem up correctly: Parts produced above parts rejected with the place values lined up.
b. Checking that you copied the figures correctly.

    c.   Re-checking your subtraction. Did you remember to reduce when you borrowed?

    d.   Rereading the steps for subtraction.

The total production figures would be found by adding down each of the columns:

Total Parts Produced	Total Parts Rejected	Total Good Parts
1360	261	1099

3.   Take-home pay is calculated by subtracting Deductions from Gross Pay. Answers are:

Employee ID	Take-Home Pay
210-62-4822	$ 297
426-39-3001	285
712-36-9143	334
146-92-3242	277
152-13-6491	291
242-19-2990	411

Multiplication

As an operation, multiplication is used to solve for a total amount when a particular amount occurs more than once. For example, suppose you had three bags of cement, each weighing 150 pounds. You are interested in determining the total weight of the cement on hand. One way to do this is to add the weights together:

$$Carry \rightarrow \quad 1$$
$$150$$
$$150$$
$$+ \ 150$$
$$\overline{}$$
$$450 \ lb$$

An alternative is to use multiplication:

$$Carry \rightarrow \quad 1$$
$$150$$
$$\times \ 3$$
$$\overline{}$$
$$450 \ lb$$

In this case, either approach provides a fairly simple solution to the problem. But, what if you had 33 bags of cement?*

---

*   *Answer*

    If you had 33 bags of cement each weighing 150 pounds, determining the total weight by addition would involve writing 150 thirty-three times and adding up the figures. Multiplication would be much easier in this case:

$$150$$
$$\times \quad 33$$
$$\overline{}$$
$$450$$
$$450$$
$$\overline{}$$
$$4950 \ lbs$$

Single-Digit Multiplication

In a typical employment situation, there are about 250 work days in a year. To find out how many hours are worked in a year, you would multiply the number of work hours in a day (usually 8) times the 250 work days. The following steps show how to solve such a problem.

1. Set up the problem, the larger number above the smaller (the multiplier).

    Example: *Process:*

    250   Line up the place
    × 8   values under each
    ───   other.
    ＼
    Multiplier

2. Multiply the digit in the ones column by the multiplier. Write the result in the ones column. If it is greater than 9, carry the extra to above the tens column.

    Example: *Process:*

    250   a. $8 \times 0 = 0$
    × 8   b. Write the zero in
    ───   the ones column.
    0

3. Multiply the digit in the tens column by the multiplier. Add the result to the carry, if there is one above the tens column. Write the result in the tens column. If it is greater than 9, carry the extra to above the hundreds column.

    Example: *Process:*

    Carry → **4**   a. $8 \times 5 = 40$
    250   b. Write the 0 in the
    × 8   tens column
    ───   c. Carry the 4 to above
    00   the hundreds col-
                umn.

4. Continue multiplying each place value by the multiplier and adding in the carry. When you reach the last place value, write the entire result of the operation (No need to carry).

    Example: *Process:*

    Carry → **4**   a. $8 \times 2 = 16$
    250   b. Add in the carry: 16
    × 8 $+ 4 = 20$
    ────   c. Write the result in
    2000   the hundreds and
                thousands columns.

Example

An electrician used 3,170 feet of wire on a job. He is interested in determining how much wire he would need for wiring 4 similar jobs. Therefore, he multiplies 3,170 by 4:

Process:

Carry → **2**
3170
× 4
─────
12680 ft.

1. $4 \times 0 = 0$
   Write the 0 in the ones column.
2. $4 \times 7 = 28$
   Write the 8 in the tens column
   Carry the 2 to above the hundreds column.
3. $4 \times 1 = 4$
   Add 4 to the carry: $4 + 2 = 6$
   Write the result in the hundreds column.
4. $4 \times 3 = 12$
   Write the result in the thousands and ten thousands column.

To wire 5 projects, he would need 3170 times 5 feet of wire:

$$Carry \rightarrow \mathbf{3}$$
$$3170$$
$$\times\ 5$$
$$\overline{15850\ \text{ft}}$$

Exercises

1. Suppose you are designing a bookcase that will hold a set of encyclopedias among other books. You would like the encyclopedias to fit on one shelf. If each volume is 4 cm wide and there are 28 volumes, how wide should your bookcase be?
2. A bid to print a 32-page booklet is $1740. How much would a bid to print 9 such booklets be?
3. A worker stamps 588 parts in an hour. How many parts would she produce in an 8-hour day?
4. The average hourly production of parts for all of the employees in a department are listed below. Calculate what their total production for the time periods listed would be.

	Average Hourly Production	Time Period	Total Production for Time Period
a.	492	4 hrs	
b.	387	5 hrs	
c.	405	6 hrs	
d.	519	3 hrs	
e.	538	7 hrs	
f.	456	9 hrs	

Answers

1. You determine total width by multiplying the width of one volume (4 cm) times the number of volumes (28):

   $$\mathbf{3} \qquad \leftarrow Carry$$
   $$28$$
   $$\times\ 4$$
   $$\overline{112\ \text{cm}}$$

2. $$\mathbf{63} \qquad \leftarrow Carries$$
   $$\$\ 1740$$
   $$\times\ 9$$
   $$\overline{\$15,660}$$

3. $$\mathbf{76} \qquad \leftarrow Carries$$
   $$588$$
   $$\times\ 8$$
   $$\overline{4704\ \text{parts}}$$

4.   To solve these problems you should have multiplied the hourly production times the number of hours (time period), giving you the total production for the time period:

	Total Production
a.	1968
b.	1935
c.	2430
d.	1557
e.	3766
f.	4104

Multiple-Digit Multiplication

If the multiplier in a problem has more than one digit, the procedures for multiplying are somewhat different. As an example, multiply the 250 work days times a daily salary of $78 to determine an annual income. Steps to follow in solving the problem are:

1.   Set up the problem. Place the larger number over the smaller number and line up the place values.

$$\begin{array}{r} 250 \\ \times\ \ 78 \\ \hline \end{array}$$

2.   Multiply the 250 by the number in the ones column of the multiplier: 8. This is done exactly the same way as was done for single-digit multiplication. Therefore the result of this step would be:

Carry →
$$\begin{array}{r} 4 \\ 250 \\ \times\ \ 78 \\ \hline 2000 \end{array}$$

3.   Next, multiply the 250 by the figure in the tens column: 7. Again use the same procedures, but record the results in a different location. Record them below the first result, beginning in the column under the multiplier and working right to left. Carries are recorded above those resulting from the first step.

Example:

Carries →
$$\begin{array}{r} 3 \\ 4 \\ 250 \\ \times\ \ 78 \\ \hline 2000 \\ 1750 \end{array}$$

Process:

a. $7 \times 0 = 0$; Record in the tens column.
b. $7 \times 5 = 35$; Record the five in the hundreds column.
c.   Write the carry above the 4 from Step 1.
d. $7 \times 2 = 14$
e.   Add in the carry: $14 + 3 = 17$
f.   Record the result to the left of the 5.

4. The final step in multiple-digit multiplication is addition. Add the results of the multiplications together to produce the final result:

$$
\begin{array}{r}
Carries \begin{array}{l} \rightarrow \\ \rightarrow \end{array} \quad \begin{array}{r} 3 \\ 4 \end{array} \\[4pt]
250 \\
\times \quad 78 \\
\hline
2000 \\
+1750 \\
\hline
\$\ 19500 \quad \leftarrow Final\ result
\end{array}
$$

Example

An apprentice was instructed to check the inventory of a particular part. Parts were stored by the gross (12 dozen), and he counted 138 gross. To determine the total number of parts, the apprentice first multiplied 12 times 12 to find the number of parts in a gross:

$$
\begin{array}{r}
12 \\
\times\ 12 \\
\hline
24 \\
12 \\
\hline
144
\end{array}
$$

He then multiplied the 144 parts in a gross times the 138 gross to get the total parts:

Process:

$$
\begin{array}{r}
Carries \begin{array}{l} \rightarrow \\ \rightarrow \end{array} \quad \begin{array}{r} 11 \\ 33 \end{array} \\[4pt]
144 \\
\times\ 138 \\
\hline
a \rightarrow \quad 1152 \\
b \rightarrow \quad 432 \\
c \rightarrow \quad 144 \\
\hline
d \rightarrow \quad 19872
\end{array}
$$

a. $8 \times 144 = 1152$; Record right to left starting in the ones column.
b. $3 \times 144 = 432$; Record right to left starting in the tens column.
c. $1 \times 144 = 144$; Record right to left starting in the hundreds column.
d. Add the results of the 3 single digit multiplication operations.

Exercises

1. One row of brick in a wall requires 118 bricks. How many bricks will be needed to lay 79 additional rows of brick?
2. How many bricks will be required to complete the following walls:

Number of Bricks In One Row	Number of Rows	Total Bricks
374	54	
2227	396	
99	88	
937	42	

3. A printing apprentice is preparing for a job to offset print 550 copies of a 75-page booklet. How much paper will she need?

4. An apprentice's wage scale for the next four years is shown below. If there are 250 work days in a year, what will his yearly gross income be for each of the four years.?

	Daily Rate	*Yearly Income*
Year 1	$55	
Year 2	$62	
Year 3	$69	
Year 4	$77	

Answers

1. The answer is found by multiplying the number of bricks in a row (118) times the number of rows (79):

   15   ← *Carries*
   17   ←
   118
   × 79
   ————
   1062
   826
   ————
   9322 bricks

2. Using the same procedure you should have found the following:

	Total Bricks
374 × 54	20,196
2227 × 396	881,892
99 × 88	8,712
937 × 42	39,354

   Try to find any errors by checking your copying and multiplying. Check your carries.

3. She will need 550 copies of each of 75 pages:

   3   ‾ *Carries*
   2   ‾
   550
   × 75
   ————
   2750
   3850
   ————
   41250 pages

4. Yearly income is determined by multiplying daily rate by 250 days per year.

	Yearly Income
Year 1	$13,750
Year 2	$15,500
Year 3	$17,250
Year 4	$19,250

Division

Division is the opposite of multiplication. In multiplication the purpose is to find a total for multiple cases of an occurrence. Division, on the other hand, involves determining a value associated with *one* occurrence when you have information on multiple happenings. For example, if a catalog gave price information for parts in quantities of 12, you would use division to find the price of one part (dividing the total price by 12). Or, if you needed to know how many 2′ lengths you could cut out of an 8′ length of lumber, you would divide 8 by 2 to find 4 pieces.

Single-Digit Division

A machinist produces 296 parts in an eight-hour day. To determine how many parts on the average were produced per hour, you would divide 296 by 8. The steps for performing this operation are as follows:

1. Set up the problem as shown below:

   divisor → 8)296 ← *dividend*

2. Divide the divisor into the first digit of the dividend. Write the result *above* the dividend.

   Example:

   ```
     0
   8)296
   ```

   Process:

   a. 2 cannot be divided by 8
   b. Write 0 above the 2 in the dividend

3. Multiply the result of this by the divisor. Write the result *below* the dividend. Subtract to find a remainder, or how much is left after the division.

   Example:

   ```
       0
     8)296
       0
       ‾
   remainder → 2
   ```

   Process:

   a. $0 \times 8 = 0$
   b. Write 0 below 2 in the dividend
   c. Subtract 0 from 2 to get the remainder

4. Write the next digit in the dividend next to the remainder. Divide this figure by the divisor.

   Example:

   ```
     03
   8)296
     0
     ‾
    29
    24
    ‾
     5
   ```

   Process:

   a. Bring down the 9 and write next to the 2 remainder
   b. Divide 8 into 29
   c. Write the result (3) above the 9
   d. Multiply 3×8
   e. Write the result below the 29
   f. Subtract to find the remainder

5. Continue Step 4 until there are no more digits to bring down.

   Example:

   ```
      037
    8)296
      0
      ‾
     29
     24
     ‾
     56
     56
     ‾
      0
   ```

   Process:

   a. Bring down the 6 next to the 5 remainder
   b. Divide 56 by 8
   c. Write the result (7) above the 6
   d. Multiply 7×8
   e. Write the result below the 56
   f. Subtract to find the remainder

Some Other Guidelines

a. The zero in the result above has no value as a place holder. That is, $037 = 37$. You can drop the 0 and write the result 37.

b. If there is a remainder after you have finished dividing, you can include it as part of the result. For example, suppose we had divided 297 by 8:

   ```
        037 ⅛
      8)297
        0
        ‾
       29
       24
       ‾
       57
       56
       ‾
        1
   ```

The remainder can be written above the divisor as a fraction and included with the result.

In the example, the fraction is created by putting 1 over 8. Thus, the solution to this problem would be 37-⅛. More on fractions is provided in the next chapter.

c. Sometimes you will not be interested in retaining the remainder. For example, if you wanted to know how many 8mm lengths you could get out of a piece of stock 297mm long, 37 would be the appropriate answer. The extra ⅛ of a piece does you no benefit—it is scrap.

d. On the other hand, if you were interested in knowing how long each piece would be if you cut a 297 mm long sheet into 8 equal length pieces, the correct answer would be 37-⅛. To measure and cut correctly and utilize the entire sheet, you would need to retain the ⅛.

Exercises

1. A 261″ length of extruded aluminum is to be cut into 6″ sections. How many sections would result?

2. A stack of 3mm-thick sheets of plastic is 252mm high. How many sheets are in the stack?

3. Two wholesale catalogs have the following price listings for 10-inch carbide-tipped saw blades.

Catalog A	Catalog B
8 blades for $192	6 blades for $138

   Which catalog has the lowest priced saw blades?

Answers

1. The number of sections is calculated by dividing the total length by the length per section:

```
      043
   6)261        43 Sections
      0
     ___
      26
      24
     ___
      21
      18
     ___
```

2.
```
      084
   3)252        84 Sheets
      0
     ___
      25
      24
     ___
      12
      12
     ___
```

3. *Price for one blade*

   Catalog A:
```
      $24
   8)192
      16
     ___
      32
      32
     ___
```

   Catalog B:
```
      $23
   6)138
      12
     ___
      18
      18
     ___
```

   Blades in Catalog B are less expensive.

Multiple-Digit Division

Multiple-digit division operates in the same manner as single-digit division. However, since more than one digit is used, the operation requires more estimation, or trial and error on your part. Suppose you want to cut an 840mm piece of dowel into 36mm lengths. To determine how many pieces you would have, divide as follows:

Example: *Process:*

```
          3
        024
    36) 840
          0
        ——
         84
         72
        ——
        120
        144
        108
        ——
         12
```

Remainder →

a. 8 is not divisible by 36, so write a 0
b. Estimate how many times 36 will go into 84. A rule of thumb is to use the first digits: 8 divided by 3 is 2. So try 2.
c. Multipy 2×36. Subtract. Bring down the zero.
d. Estimate the next figure: 12 divided by three is 4. Try 4. Multiply 4×36.
e. 4 was too large since 144 is greater than the remainder (120). Try 3.
f. Multiply 3×36. The remainder is scrap. The answer is 23 pieces of dowel.

Exercises

1. Twelve inches is equal to one foot. How many feet are in 408 inches?
2. A farmer is planning to plant a block of pepper plants. He wants the plants to be 12″ apart. How many plants will he need to plant one row 25′ (300″) long? How many will he need for 14 such rows?
3. An incremental adjustment on a control knob moves a dial pointer 15°. How many adjustments will have to be made to move the dial 345°?
4. The following is a task order for cutting steel pipe into segments. Calculate how many segments you would get from each piece. Also write in the remainder. All measurements are in millimeters.

	Pipe Length	Length of Each Cut Segment	Number of Segments	Remainder
a.	2498	127		
b.	1924	88		
c.	983	62		
d.	624	48		

Answers

1. To determine the number of feet, you divide the number of inches by the number of inches in one foot.

```
        34 feet
    12)408
        36
        ——
         48
         48
        ——
```

2.
```
        25 plants
    12)300
        24
        ——
         60
         60
        ——
```

For 14 such rows he would need 14×25 plants or 350 plants.

3.
$$\begin{array}{r} 23 \text{ adjustments} \\ 15\overline{)345} \\ 30 \\ \hline 45 \\ 45 \\ \hline \end{array}$$

4. To find the number of segments, divide the pipe length by the length of each cut segment. The remainder is scrap.

	Number of Segments	*Remainder*
a.	19	85
b.	21	76
c.	15	53
d.	13	0

Chapter Example

The four operations do not have to be used alone, as some of the exercises illustrated. Some problems require use of multiplication, division and addition, division and subtraction or other combinations of operations. The following example shows how multiple operations are used to solve a problem.

The Problem

A painter is planning to paint a room—the walls and closet Robin's Egg Blue and the ceiling Desert Sand. She planned to use one coat on both walls and ceilings, with no primer. The dimensions of the room are as follows:

	Area (Square Feet)
Three Walls	128 (each)
One Wall	114
Ceiling	272
Closet	96

Prices for the paints by the quart and gallon, and the areas covered by the quantities are below:

Paint	*Size*	*Price*	*Coverage (Sq Ft)*
Robin's Egg Blue	Gallon	$12	480
	Quart	$ 4	120
Desert Sand	Gallon	$11	360
	Quart	$ 4	80

The painter has allowed $45 to buy paint. How much money will she have left over to do the trim?

The Solution

The problem can be divided into five steps that lead to the solution:

1. Determine what the total square footage to be painted in each color will be.
2. Based on total square footage and the coverage of the paints, find out how much paint is required.
3. Decide what size and how many cans to buy (The larger sizes are more economical, but there may be more waste).
4. Determine the price of the paint.
5. Calculate how much money would be left over.

Step 1

To calculate total square footage:

a. *Walls*:
   - There are 3 walls with 128 sq ft each. The total of these would be $128 \times 3 = 384$.
   - Add in the other wall areas:

$$384$$
$$114$$
$$+\ 96$$
$$\overline{}$$
Total sq ft: 594

b. *Ceiling*: Total is 272 sq ft

Step 2

To determine the amount of paint required, divide the total square footage by the amount covered per gallon of paint. This gives the total gallons and/or portions of gallons.

a. *Walls*:

$$\begin{array}{r} 1 \text{ gallon} \\ 480\overline{)594} \\ 480 \\ \hline 114 \end{array}$$

The remainder is the square footage *not* covered by the 1 gallon.

Divide the remainder by the amount covered by a quart to determine the number of quarts needed.

$$120\overline{)114}$$

Since 114 is not divisible by 120, 1 quart should be enough to cover the remainder.

b. *Ceiling*:

$$350\overline{)272}$$

One gallon would be enough to cover.

Now see if it would be less expensive to buy quarts:

$$\begin{array}{r} 3 \\ 80\overline{)272} \\ 240 \\ \hline 32 \end{array}$$

Three quarts would *not* be enough to cover. 32 sq ft remainder.

Step 3

Based on the division in Step 2, you decide that the following paint is needed:

a. *Robin's Egg Blue*: 1 Gallon
    1 Quart

Since the painter is planning to use a roller, and the 120 sq. ft. coverage of a quart is not a great deal larger than the 114 sq. ft. to be covered, she decides to purchase an extra quart.

b. *Desert Sand*: 1 Gallon

Step 4

The price of the paint is determined from the price list and the quantities desired:

a. *Robin's Egg Blue*:
              1 Gallon = $12.00
              2 Quarts = $4 × 2 =   8.00

b. *Desert Sand*:
              1 Gallon =   11.00
          Total Price = $31.00

Step 5

To find out how much money would be left over for the trim, subtract the total price of the paint from the amount allocated:

$$\begin{array}{r} \$\ 45 \\ -31 \\ \hline \$\ 14 \end{array}$$

There would be $14 left.

Self-Test Exercises

Answer the following questions and problems. Check your answers with those in Chapter 5. If you answer less than 7 items correctly, repeat your work in this chapter. If you answer 7 or 8 correctly you have mastered basic mathematical operations using whole numbers. Go on to the next chapter.

1. Find a seven-digit whole number somewhere at work or at home. (For example, a telephone number, serial number, or a bank balance if you're lucky). Write the number below. Identify the place values for each of the digits of your number.

2. How much would you have to add to the ones column of your number from question 1 to make the digit in the tens column increase by 1? What would be the value in the ones column?

Use the illustration in Figure 4 to answer questions 3 and 4.

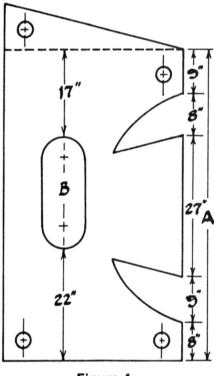

Figure 4

3. What is the length of dimension **A**?

4. What is the length of slot **B**?

Read the following situation to answer questions 5-7.

A plumber is estimating what his total expenditures for gasoline this year will be. He uses the following estimates in his calculations:

> Average distance driven per week: 247 miles
> Number of weeks worked per year: 50 weeks
> Average mileage: 17 miles per gallon
> Average price of gas: 95¢/gallon

5. Estimate the number of miles he will drive this year.

6. Approximately how many gallons of gas will he use this year?

7. About how much will he spend on gas this year? (Your answer will be in cents. To change it to dollars, divide by 100).

8. A carpenter needs the following lengths of two-by-fours:

Quantity	Length
3	72″
4	18″
3	40″
5	12″
3	32″

There are 6 eight-foot long (96″) two-by-fours on site. Does she have enough lumber to make the required cuts?

3. Fractions

Chapter Overview

Purpose: To develop skills in working with fractions in work-related problems. You will develop an understanding of what fractions are and an ability to solve problems using common and decimal fractions and percents.

Preassessment Score: Write in the following space the number of correct answers from Pretest questions 9-16: _____. If you answered seven or eight questions correctly, skip to Chapter 4. If you missed two or more questions, work through this book.

Prerequisites: Chapter 1 and Chapter 2.

Resources: Time—about 3-4 hours to complete. You do not need to work through the chapter in one sitting.
Materials—paper, pencil.

Performance Measure: A thirty-minute paper-and-pencil Posttest, to be taken after completing the entire book.

Standards: To be successful, you must answer correctly 80% of the Posttest items.

Activities:
1. Read the text, examples and illustrations and commit information to memory.
2. Work questions, examples and problems.
3. Complete and check the Self-Test Exercises and the Posttest.

Introduction and Objectives

In Chapter 2 the operations you used dealt solely with whole numbers. However, you will be exposed to fractions and be required to perform the arithmetic operations on both common and decimal fractions. For example, many measurements you make will not be in whole feet and inches, but in fractions: 2' 1-3/16". You most likely will be required to work with decimals if you perform any calculations involving money. Paychecks and bills generally are not whole numbers-for example a bill for $10.46. Even our car odometers usually display in decimals. The wheel that goes around the fastest is tenths (1/10's) of a mile. If you think about it, you can probably come up with numerous uses of fractions in your everyday work and home activities. This Chapter will help you deal with problems that involve the use of fractions. After completing the chapter, you will demonstrate your ability to:

1. Reduce and expand common fractions.
2. Find the least common denominator.
3. Perform the four basic operations using common fractions.
4. Convert common fractions to decimal fractions and decimals to common fractions.
5. Round decimals to a desired number of places.
6. Perform the four basic operations using decimal fractions.
7. Compute percents.

Fractions as Parts of a Whole

If something were divided into two equal parts, each part would be one-half of the total. One-half is a fraction and is written as ½. Fractions are numbers used to describe parts of a whole. For example, a circle could be divided into four equal parts, as shown in Figure 5. Each part represents ¼ of the total circle. The fraction ¼ is called a common fraction.

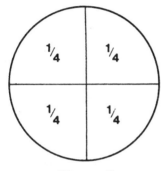

Figure 5

As you can see, a common fraction has two numbers. The number on top is called a numerator. The number on the bottom is called a denominator.

- The *numerator* tells how many parts are in the fraction.
- The *denominator* is the total number of parts in the whole.

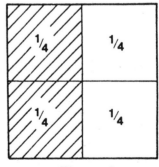

Figure 6

In Figure 6, each part is ¼ of the total square. If you only considered the shaded portion of the square, you would have 2 of the total 4 parts. This would be written ²⁄₄. If you used three parts, how would the fraction be written?*

A whole number can be divided into as many parts as desired. You could take the square above and divide each part into four parts. This is illustrated in Figure 7. Now the total number of parts is 16. Each individual part has a value of ¹⁄₁₆. Two parts would be written ²⁄₁₆, and so on.

---

*   *Answer*

The fraction is written ¾. This is because you used 3 parts (the numerator) of the total 4 parts (denominator). Since you write the numerator over the denominator you have ¾.

A whole number can be divided into as many parts as desired. You could take the square above and divide each part into four parts. This is illustrated in Figure 7. Now the total number of parts is 16. Each individual part has a value of ¹⁄₁₆. Two parts would be written ²⁄₁₆, and so on.

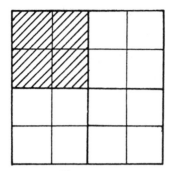

Figure 7

If you took the shaded portion of the square, this would be ⁴⁄₁₆ of the total. Notice that the shaded portion is the same size as one part in Figure 6. Thus, the same portion can be represented in different ways, ⁴⁄₁₆ or ¼. It also could be written as ²⁄₈. Can you draw a figure that would show that ²⁄₈ is the same as ¼? First, trace Figure 6, then divide your figure into 8 equal parts.

Reducing Fractions

The fractions ⁴⁄₁₆ and ¼ are called *equivalent fractions* because they represent the same portion of the whole. You can change ¼ to ⁴⁄₁₆ and it would not change its value. This is done by multiplying both the numerator and the denominator by 4:

$$\frac{1 \times 4}{4 \times 4} = \frac{4}{16}$$

You can change it back by dividing both numbers by 4:

$$\frac{4 \div 4}{16 \div 4} = \frac{1}{4}$$

This second operation is called *reducing* the fraction. To reduce a fraction you divide both the numerator and denominator by a *common factor*. This is a number which divides into both terms with no remainder. In the example above, the common factor divided into both terms was 4. Would 2 also be a common factor of ⁴⁄₁₆? Try dividing both terms by 2. What is the result?*

When no common factor exists, the fraction is *reduced to lowest terms*. Generally, fractions are used in their lowest terms. For example, if you measured the length of a room you would probably record it as 26-½′ instead of 26-¹⁶⁄₃₂′. Fractions in their lowest terms are easier to work with.

---

*   *Answer*

Two is also a common factor of ⁴⁄₁₆. Dividing both terms by 2 would give you:

$$\frac{4 \div 2}{16 \div 2} = \frac{2}{8}$$

This shows mathematically what you have already shown with a drawing—that ⁴⁄₁₆ and ²⁄₈ are equivalent fractions.

Example

A scale measures weight in ounces, which are sixteenths of a pound. Five measurements obtained from the scale were ⁸⁄₁₆, ⁷⁄₁₆, ²⁄₁₆, ¹²⁄₁₆ and ¹³⁄₁₆. It was an apprentices' task to reduce the weights to lowest terms before recording them in a log. She did this by:

1. Identifying a common factor in the terms
2. Dividing the common factor into both the numerator and the denominator
3. Checking to see if the terms share another common factor. If so, repeating steps 2 and 3.

⁸⁄₁₆: Step 1. Both numbers are divisible by 8.

Step 2. $\dfrac{8 \div 8}{16 \div 8} = \dfrac{1}{2}$

Step 3. No common factor exists.

⁷⁄₁₆: Step 1. There is no common factor. It is reduced to lowest terms.

²⁄₁₆: Step 1. Two is a common factor.

Step 2. $\dfrac{2 \div 2}{16 \div 2} = \dfrac{1}{8}$

Step 3. No common factor exists.

¹²⁄₁₆: Step 1. Both numbers are divisible by 2.

Step 2. $\dfrac{12 \div 2}{16 \div 2} = \dfrac{6}{8}$

Step 3. Two is a common factor again.

Step 2. $\dfrac{6 \div 2}{8 \div 2} = \dfrac{3}{4}$

Step 3. No common factor exists.

¹³⁄₁₆: Step 1. The fraction is in lowest terms.

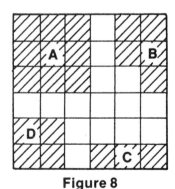

Figure 8

Exercises

1. Refer to Figure 8. Write the fractions which represent the following shaded areas:

    A.
    B.
    C.
    D.

2. Reduce the fractions to the lowest terms:

    A.
    B.
    C.
    D.

3. Write an equivalent fraction for each of your answers to Exercise 2 by multiplying both terms by 4. Are any of your results the same as you wrote for Exercise 1? Why or why not?

    A.
    B.
    C.
    D.

Answers

1.   **A.** $\frac{9}{36}$ **B.** $\frac{5}{36}$ **C.** $\frac{3}{36}$ **D.** $\frac{4}{36}$

2.   **A.** $\dfrac{9 \div 9}{36 \div 9} = \dfrac{1}{4}$ **B.** $\frac{5}{36}$ is in lowest terms

     C. $\dfrac{3 \div 3}{36 \div 3} = \dfrac{1}{12}$ **D.** $\dfrac{4 \div 4}{36 \div 4} = \dfrac{1}{9}$

3.   **A.** $\dfrac{1 \times 4}{4 \times 4} = \dfrac{4}{16}$ **B.** $\dfrac{5 \times 4}{36 \times 4} = \dfrac{20}{144}$

     C. $\dfrac{1 \times 4}{12 \times 4} = \dfrac{4}{48}$ **D.** $\dfrac{1 \times 4}{9 \times 4} = \dfrac{4}{36}$

D has the same answer as in Exercise 1. This is because to reduce the answer you divided by 4. In multiplying by 4 it brings you back to where you started.

Mixed Numbers

When a number contains a whole number and a fraction, it is called a *mixed number*. An example of this is 8-¾ or 5-⅔. Another way to write mixed numbers is as improper fractions. In an *improper fraction*, the numerator is larger than the denominator. In a *proper fraction*, the numerator is smaller than the denominator. For example, 8-¾ could be written as $^{35}/_{4}$—they are equivalent. Divide 35 by 4 to check that this is true. Be sure to keep the remainder.*

For some operations, such as multiplication and division, you need to write mixed numbers as improper fractions. But, when you obtain the result of an operation, such as summing the lengths of a series of copper pipe segments, you generally want to record it as a mixed number. Therefore, you will need to know how to change the form of the fraction.

---

*   *Answer*

$$\begin{array}{r} 8\,¾ \\ 4\overline{)35} \\ \underline{32} \\ 3 \end{array}$$

*To Change a Mixed Number to an
Improper Fraction*   *Example*: 9-⅘

1. Multiply the denominator of the fraction by the whole number $5 \times 9 = 45$

2. Add the result to the numerator. $45 + 4 = 49$

3. Write the result over the denominator.

$$\frac{49}{5}$$

*To Change an Improper Fraction
to a Mixed Number*   *Example*: ⁴⁹⁄₅

1. Divide the numerator by the denominator.

$$\begin{array}{r} 9 \\ 5\overline{)49} \\ 45 \\ \hline 4 \end{array}$$

2. Write the remainder as a fraction   ⅘

3. Combine the results   9-⅘

Exercises

1. A work specification for cutting lengths from aluminum bar is outlined below. Write each length as an improper fraction so that total length required can be determined.

	Number of Pieces	*Length*	*Improper Fraction*
a.	5	5-⅜″	
b.	4	12-⁵⁄₁₆″	
c.	2	8-¼″	
d.	8	7-⅞″	

2. Change the following measurements to mixed numbers:

a. $\dfrac{19''}{4}$ c. $\dfrac{83''}{9}$

b. $\dfrac{27''}{12}$ d. $\dfrac{48''}{16}$

Answers

1. a.   5-⅜″: 1. $8 \times 5 = 40$
                 2. $40 + 3 = 43$
                 3. ⁴³⁄₈″ is the improper fraction

    c.   8-¼″: 1. $4 \times 8 = 32$
                 2. $32 + 1 = 33$
                 3. ³³⁄₄″ is the improper fraction

    b.   12-⁵⁄₁₆″: 1. $12 \times 16 = 192$
                 2. $192 + 5 = 197$
                 3. ¹⁹⁷⁄₁₆″ is the improper fraction

    d.   7-⅞″: 1. $8 \times 7 = 56$
                 2. $56 + 7 = 63$
                 3. ⁶³⁄₈″ is the improper fraction

2. a. $\quad$ 4
$\qquad$ 4)19
$\qquad$ 16
$\qquad$ ——
$\qquad\quad$ 3

4-¾ is the mixed number

$\quad$ b. $\quad$ 2
$\qquad$ 12)27
$\qquad$ 24
$\qquad$ ——
$\qquad\quad$ 3

2-³/₁₂ or 2-¼ is the mixed number

$\quad$ c. $\quad$ 9
$\qquad$ 9)83
$\qquad$ 81
$\qquad$ ——
$\qquad\quad$ 2

9-²/₉ is the mixed number

$\quad$ d. $\quad$ 3
$\qquad$ 16)48
$\qquad$ 48
$\qquad$ ——
$\qquad\quad$ 0

The result is a whole number since there is no remainder.

Addition With Fractions

Adding Fractions with the Same Denominators

When fractions to be added have the same number in their denominators, addition involves three steps:

Steps:	*Example*:
	⅜ + ⅝ + ⅞
1. Add the numbers in the numerators	3 + 5 + 7 = 15
2. Write the result over the denominator	¹⁵⁄₈
3. Change improper fractions to mixed numbers	1-⅞

Adding Fractions with Different Denominators

When fractions to be added have different denominators it is necessary to find a denominator that they can share in common before adding. For example, you could not add ⅜ + ¼ in the form they are in. As you can see in Figure 9, their parts are fractions of different wholes. But by giving them the same denominator, as in Figure 10, it makes sense to add them: ²⁄₈ + ⅜ = ⅝.

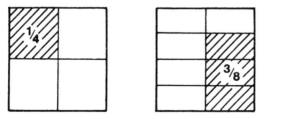

Figure 9

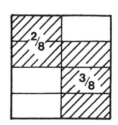

Figure 10

Therefore, the first step in adding fractions is to find the *lowest common denominator* or *LCD*. The LCD is the smallest number that is evenly divisible by all the denominators. To find the LCD for a set of fractions, use the following steps:

Steps:	*Example:*
	¼ + ⅓ + ⅜

1. Try the largest denominator as an LCD. If it is divisible by the other denominators, it is the LCD

2. Multiply the largest denominator by 2. Try this as the LCD.

3. Multiply the largest denominator by 3. Try this as the LCD. Continue multiplying the largest denominator by 4, 5, 6 and so on until you find a LCD.

1. 8 is divisible by 4, but not by 3. 8 is not the LCD.

2. 8 × 2 = 16. 16 is divisible by 4 but not by 3. 16 is not the LCD.

3. 8 × 3 = 24. 24 is divisible by 4 and by 3. 24 is the LCD.

After finding the LCD, change the fractions to equivalent fractions having common denominators. This is what was done in Figure 10, changing the ¼ to ⁶⁄₈. Do this by dividing the denominator of each fraction into the LCD and multiplying the result times the fraction's numerator. This result is placed over the LCD. For the example, you would do the following:

¼: a. Divide 24 by 4 = 6
      b. Multiply 6 times 1 = 6
      c. ⁶⁄₂₄ is the equivalent fraction

⅓: a. Divide 24 by 3 = 8
      b. Multiply 8 × 1 = 8
      c. ⁸⁄₂₄ is the equivalent fraction

⅜: a. Divide 24 by 8 = 3
      b. Multiply 3 × 3 = 9
      c. ⁹⁄₂₄ is the equivalent fraction

Reduce the three equivalent fractions to show that they are equivalent.* Since you now have common denominators, you are able to add the fractions using the three-step process:

$$⁶⁄₂₄ + ⁸⁄₂₄ + ⁹⁄₂₄ = \frac{6+8+9}{24} = ²³⁄₂₄$$

* *Answers*

$$\frac{6 \div 6}{24 \div 6} = \frac{1}{4} \qquad \frac{8 \div 8}{24 \div 8} = \frac{1}{3} \qquad \frac{9 \div 3}{24 \div 3} = \frac{3}{8}$$

Example

The dimensions of a sheet metal utility box are shown in Figure 11. What is the total length of metal needed to make the box?

The total length is equal to the sum of the dimensions:

$$\text{⅜} + 2\text{-¾} + 6\text{-½} + 2\text{-¾} + \text{⅜}$$

To solve the problem:

1. Find the LCD. First try the largest denominator, 8, as the LCD. Since 8 is divisible by 4 and 2, 8 is the LCD.
2. Write the fractions in terms of the LCD:

$$\begin{aligned} \text{⅜} &= \quad\text{⅜} \\ 2\text{-¾} &= 2\text{-⁶⁄₈} \\ 6\text{-½} &= 6\text{-⁴⁄₈} \\ 2\text{-¾} &= 2\text{-⁶⁄₈} \\ \text{⅜} &= \quad\text{⅜} \end{aligned}$$

3. Add up the fractions:

$$\text{⅜} + \text{⁶⁄₈} + \text{⁴⁄₈} + \text{⁶⁄₈} + \text{⅜} = \text{²²⁄₈}$$

4. Add up the whole numbers:

$$2 + 6 + 2 = 10$$

5. Change the improper fraction, reduce terms, and combine with the whole number:

$$\begin{aligned} \text{²²⁄₈} &= 2\text{-⁶⁄₈} = 2\text{-¾} \\ 10 + 2\text{-¾} &= 12\text{-¾} \end{aligned}$$

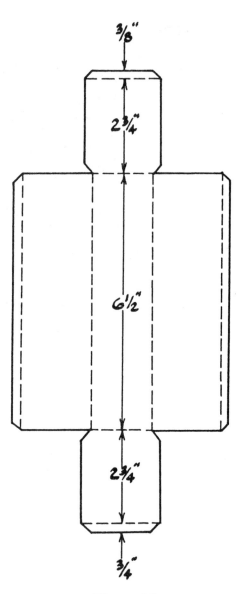

Figure 11

Exercises

1. Find the LCD for the following groups of fractions:

a.	³⁄₁₆	⅝	¾	⅔
b.	⅗	¼	½	
c.	²⁄₉	⅙	½	¾
d.	½	¾	⁵⁄₁₂	

2. What is the length of the pin in Figure 12?
3. Thicknesses of materials used in an exterior wall are as follows:

Brick:	2-⅔″
Insulation:	⅝″
Studs:	3-¾″
Sheetrock:	½″
Wallcovering:	¹⁄₁₆″

   What is the total thickness of the wall?

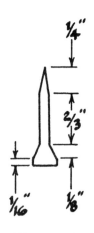

Figure 12

Answers

1. a. First try 16. It is not divisible by 3.
        Try $16 \times 2 = 32$. It is not divisible by 3.
        Try $16 \times 3 = 48$. It is divisible by all four denominators and is the LCD.
    b. First try 5. Not divisible by 4 or 2.
        Try $5 \times 2 = 10$. Not divisible by 4.
        Try $5 \times 3 = 15$. Not divisible by 4 or 2.
        Try $5 \times 4 = 20$. 20 is the LCD.
    c. Try 9.
        Try $9 \times 2 = 18$.
        Try $9 \times 3 = 27$.
        Try $9 \times 4 = 36$. 36 is the LCD.
    d. Try 12. 12 is the LCD.

2. The length of the pin is the sum of the lengths:

    $$\frac{1}{4} + \frac{2}{3} + \frac{1}{8} + \frac{1}{16}.$$

    - The LCD is 48

    - Convert the fractions:

    $$\frac{1}{4} = \frac{12}{48} \qquad \frac{1}{8} = \frac{6}{48}$$

    $$\frac{2}{3} = \frac{32}{48} \qquad \frac{1}{16} = \frac{3}{48}$$

    - Add the numerators and write over the LCD.

    $$\frac{12 + 32 + 6 + 3}{48} = \frac{53}{48} = 1\text{-}\frac{5}{48}$$

3. The thickness of the wall is equal to the sum of the widths of the materials:

    $$2\text{-}\frac{2}{3} + \frac{5}{8} + 3\text{-}\frac{3}{4} + \frac{1}{2} + \frac{1}{16}$$

    - The LCD is 48

    Convert the fractions:

    $2\text{-}\frac{2}{3} = 2\text{-}\frac{32}{48}$ $\qquad$ $\frac{1}{2} = \frac{24}{48}$
    $\frac{5}{8} = \frac{30}{48}$ $\qquad$ $\frac{1}{16} = \frac{3}{48}$
    $3\text{-}\frac{3}{4} = 3\text{-}\frac{36}{48}$

    - Add the whole numbers: $2 + 3 = 5$

    - Add the fractions:

    $$\frac{32 + 30 + 36 + 24 + 3}{48} = \frac{125}{48} = 2\text{-}\frac{29}{48}$$

    - Combine the whole number and fraction

    $5 + 2\text{-}\frac{29}{48} = 7\text{-}\frac{29}{48}''$ thick

Subtraction With Fractions

The process for subtracting fractions is similar to addition. The following steps show you how to subtract fractions.

Steps:	*Example:* ¾ − ⅜

1. Find the lowest common denominator

1. $6 \times 2 = 12$; 12 is the LCD

2. Write the fractions in terms of the LCD

2. ¾ = ⁹⁄₁₂
    ⅜ = ⁶⁄₁₂

3. Subtract the numerators of the fractions and write above the denominator

3. $\dfrac{9 - 6}{12} = ³⁄₁₂$

4. Write the result as a proper fraction reduced to lowest terms.

4. ³⁄₁₂ = ¼

Example

A bolt is to be used to attach a plate to an undercarriage. The combined width of the metal and washers is 2-⅞″. The length of the bolt is 3-³⁄₁₆″. An apprentice was told to find the length of the bolt that would be exposed to hold a nut. To do this, he subtracted 2-⅞″ from the total length of the bolt (3-³⁄₁₆″). He used the following steps:

1. Find the LCD: 16 is divisible by both denominators.

2. Write the fractions in terms of the LCD: 2-⅞ = 2-¹⁴⁄₁₆
    3-³⁄₁₆ = 3-³⁄₁₆

3. Subtract the fractions: ³⁄₁₆ − ¹⁴⁄₁₆. Since ³⁄₁₆ is less than ¹⁴⁄₁₆, the apprentice needed to *borrow* from the whole number. This is just like borrowing 10 when subtracting whole numbers. In this case it means taking 1 or ¹⁶⁄₁₆ from the whole number and combining it with the fraction:

    3-³⁄₁₆ = 2 + 1-³⁄₁₆ = 2-¹⁹⁄₁₆

    Then, the fractions can be subtracted:

    ¹⁹⁄₁₆ − ¹⁴⁄₁₆ = ⁵⁄₁₆

4. Subtract the whole numbers: Since 1 was borrowed from the 3, only 2 remains.

    2 − 2 = 0

5. Combine the results and reduce to lowest terms.

    0 + ⁵⁄₁₆ = ⁵⁄₁₆

    which is in lowest terms.

Exercises

1. A carpenter is planning to cut 5 two-by-fours to 18-¾″. The lengths of the lumber are in the table below. Find out how much of each of the two-by-fours will be left after she makes the cuts.

	Total Length	*Length Remaining After Making Cut*
a.	27-⅞″	
b.	36″	
c.	42-⁵⁄₁₆″	
d.	50-⁹⁄₁₀″	
e.	65-½″	

2. An operator moved a control knob clockwise ⅝ of a complete turn. He had only wanted to move it ⅗ of a complete turn. How far should he move the knob counter-clockwise to make the proper adjustment? (See Figure 13)

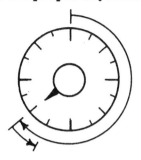

Figure 13

3. Find dimensions **A**, **B** and **C** in Figure 14.

   A.
   B.
   C.

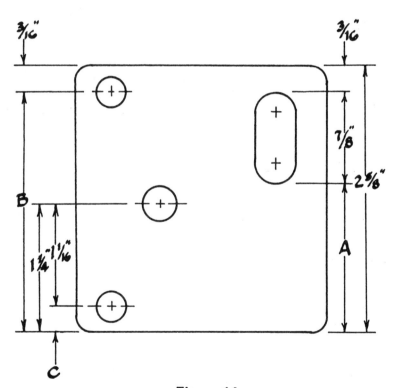

Figure 14

Answers

1. a. 27-⅞ − 18-¾
    - The LCD is 8: 27-⅞ − 18-⁶⁄₈
    -
        Subtract the fraction: $\dfrac{7-6}{8} = \dfrac{1}{8}$
    - Subtract the whole numbers: 27 − 18 = 9
    - Write the results together: 9-⅛″

b. $36 - 18\text{-}\frac{3}{4}$
  - The LCD is 4
  - Borrow 1 from the 36 to be able to subtract the fractions: $36 = 35\text{-}\frac{4}{4}$ (writing the 1 in terms of the LCD)
  - Subtract the fractions: $\frac{4}{4} - \frac{3}{4} = \frac{1}{4}$
  - Subtract the whole numbers: $35 - 18 = 17$
  - Write the result: $17\text{-}\frac{1}{4}$

c. $42\text{-}\frac{5}{16} - 18\text{-}\frac{3}{4}$
  - The LCD is 16: $42\text{-}\frac{5}{16} - 18\text{-}\frac{12}{16}$
  - Borrow 1 from 42: $42\text{-}\frac{5}{16} = 41 + 1\text{-}\frac{5}{16} = 41\text{-}\frac{21}{16}$
  - Subtract the fractions: $\frac{21}{16} - \frac{12}{16} = \frac{9}{16}$
  - Subtract the whole numbers: $41 - 18 = 23$
  - Write the result: $23\text{-}\frac{9}{16}$

d. $50\text{-}\frac{9}{10} - 18\text{-}\frac{3}{4}$
  - The LCD is 20 $50\text{-}\frac{18}{20} - 18\text{-}\frac{15}{20}$
  - Subtract the fractions: $\frac{18}{20} - \frac{15}{20} = \frac{3}{20}$
  - Subtract the whole numbers: $50 - 18 = 32$
  - Write the result: $32\text{-}\frac{3}{20}''$

e. $65\text{-}\frac{1}{2} - 18\text{-}\frac{3}{4}$
  - The LCD is 4: $65\text{-}\frac{2}{4} - 18\text{-}\frac{3}{4}$
  - Borrow one from 65: $65\text{-}\frac{2}{4} = 64 + 1\text{-}\frac{2}{4} = 64\text{-}\frac{6}{4}$
  - Subtract the fractions: $\frac{6}{4} - \frac{3}{4} = \frac{3}{4}$
  - Subtract the whole numbers: $64 - 18 = 46$
  - Write the result: $46\text{-}\frac{3}{4}$

2. He would move it back $\frac{5}{8} - \frac{3}{5}$ of a turn
  - The LCD is 40: $\frac{25}{40} - \frac{24}{40} = \frac{1}{40}$ of a turn

3. A would equal $2\text{-}\frac{5}{8}$ minus the lengths $\frac{7}{8}$ and $\frac{3}{16}$. So first add $\frac{7}{8}$ and $\frac{3}{16}$:

$$\tfrac{14}{16} + \tfrac{3}{16} = \tfrac{17}{16} = 1\text{-}\tfrac{1}{16}$$

Next subtract this dimension from the total length:

$$2\text{-}\tfrac{5}{8} - 1\text{-}\tfrac{1}{16} = 2\text{-}\tfrac{10}{16} - 1\text{-}\tfrac{1}{16} = 1\text{-}\tfrac{9}{16}$$

B would equal $2\text{-}\frac{5}{8} - \frac{3}{16} = 2\text{-}\frac{10}{16} - \frac{3}{16} = 2\text{-}\frac{7}{16}$
C would equal $1\text{-}\frac{1}{4} - 1\text{-}\frac{1}{16} = 1\text{-}\frac{4}{16} - 1\text{-}\frac{1}{16} = \frac{3}{16}$

Multiplication With Fractions

Multiplying numbers with fractions involves three steps:

Steps:

1. Change any mixed numbers to improper fractions.

2. Multiply together the numerators. Then multiply the denominators. Write the numerator result over the denominator result.

3. Change to a mixed number and reduce to lowest terms.

Example: $2\text{-}\frac{3}{4} \times \frac{7}{8}$

1. $2\text{-}\frac{3}{4} = \frac{11}{4}$, so the problem becomes $\frac{11}{4} \times \frac{7}{8}$

2. $\dfrac{11 \times 7}{4 \times 8} = \dfrac{77}{32}$

3. $\begin{array}{r} 2\text{-}\frac{13}{32} \\ 32\overline{)77} \\ 64 \\ \overline{13} \end{array}$

Example

In a certain week a grader operator worked 6-½ hours a day for 4-⅔ days. How many total hours did he work that week? To solve the problem, you would multiply the hours worked per day times the total days worked:

1. First, change the mixed numbers to improper fractions:

    $$6\text{-}\tfrac{1}{2} = \tfrac{13}{2}$$
    $$4\text{-}\tfrac{2}{3} = \tfrac{14}{3}$$

2. Next, multiply numerators together and denominators together:

    $$\tfrac{13}{2} \times \tfrac{14}{3} = \frac{13 \times 14}{2 \times 3} = \frac{182}{6}$$

3. Then, change the result to a mixed number and reduce it:

    $$
    \begin{array}{r}
    30\text{-}\tfrac{2}{6} \\
    6\overline{)182} \\
    18 \\
    \hline
    2 \\
    0 \\
    \hline
    2
    \end{array}
    $$

Since the numerator and denominator are both divisible by 2, ⅖ can be reduced to ⅓. Therefore, the answer is 30-⅓.

a. A short-cut to this step is to use *cancellation*. This is similar to reducing fractions. Taking the fractions,

    $$\frac{13 \times 14}{2 \times 3},$$

    you would cancel out terms that divide into one of the numerators and one of the denominators. In this example, 14 is divisible by 2 and 2 is divisible by 2. So, you cancel 2 out of both terms:

    $$\frac{13 \times \overset{7}{\cancel{14}}}{\underset{1}{\cancel{2}} \times 3} = \frac{91}{3}$$

    This step simplifies your multiplication and also the next step.

b. Using the simplied, cancelled fraction, you would obtain:

    $$
    \begin{array}{r}
    30\text{-}\tfrac{1}{3} \\
    3\overline{)91} \\
    9 \\
    \hline
    1 \\
    0 \\
    \hline
    1
    \end{array}
    $$

Exercises

1. An inexpensive machine component is subject to 1-$\frac{3}{4}$ times as many breakdowns as the normal component used. If the breakdown rate of the normal component is 2-$\frac{3}{5}$ times per month, how many breakdowns in a month would you expect using the inexpensive component?

2. The capacity of an oil drum is 31-$\frac{1}{2}$ gallons. If the drum is $\frac{5}{8}$ full, how many gallons are there?

3. A carpenter can saw through 1″ of one-inch thick pine in $\frac{1}{6}$ of a minute. How long would it take him to cut through 12″ of pine. (A whole number can be written as a fraction by using 1 as a denominator, for example, $\frac{12}{1}$).

   The following are his times to saw 1″ of other types of lumber. Calculate the total time required to cut through the widths listed.

	Minutes Per 1″	*Width in Inches*	*Total Time Required*
Plywood	$\frac{1}{8}$	48	
Maple	$\frac{2}{5}$	10	
Oak	$\frac{3}{4}$	7-$\frac{2}{3}$	
Ash	1-$\frac{1}{8}$	5-$\frac{3}{4}$	
Hickory	1-$\frac{1}{3}$	12	

Answers

1. The breakdown rate would equal:

$$1\text{-}\tfrac{3}{4} \times 2\text{-}\tfrac{3}{5} = \tfrac{7}{4} \times \tfrac{13}{5} = \frac{7 \times 13}{4 \times 5} = \frac{91}{20}$$

   This reduces to 4-$\frac{11}{20}$ breakdowns.

2. $$31\text{-}\tfrac{1}{2} \times \tfrac{5}{8} = \tfrac{63}{2} \times \tfrac{5}{8} = \frac{63 \times 5}{2 \times 8} = \frac{315}{16}$$

   This reduces to 19-$\frac{11}{16}$ gallons of oil in a drum $\frac{5}{8}$ full.

3. Multiply the time to cut 1″ times the total inches:

$$\text{Pine: } \tfrac{1}{6} \times 12 = \frac{1 \times \overset{2}{\cancel{12}}}{\underset{1}{\cancel{6}} \times 1} = \frac{2}{1} = 2 \text{ minutes}$$

$$\text{Plywood: } \tfrac{1}{8} \times 48 = \frac{1 \times 48}{8 \times 1} = \frac{48}{8} = 6 \text{ minutes}$$

$$\text{Maple: } \tfrac{2}{5} \times 10 = \frac{2 \times 10}{5 \times 1} = \frac{20}{5} = 4 \text{ minutes}$$

$$\text{Oak: } \tfrac{3}{4} \times 7\text{-}\tfrac{2}{3} = \tfrac{3}{4} \times \tfrac{23}{3} = \frac{\overset{1}{\cancel{3}} \times 23}{4 \times \underset{1}{\cancel{3}}} = \frac{23}{4} =$$

   5-$\frac{3}{4}$ minutes

$$\text{Ash } 1\text{-}\tfrac{1}{8} \times 5\text{-}\tfrac{3}{4} = \tfrac{9}{8} \times \tfrac{23}{4} = \frac{9 \times 23}{8 \times 4} = \frac{207}{32} =$$

   6-$\frac{15}{32}$ minutes

$$\text{Hickory: } 1\text{-}\tfrac{1}{3} \times 12 = \frac{4 \times \overset{4}{\cancel{12}}}{\underset{1}{\cancel{3}} \times 1} = 16 \text{ minutes}$$

Division With Fractions

Dividing using fractions is very similar to multiplication. It involves three steps:

Steps:

1. Change any mixed numbers to improper fractions.
2. Invert the divisor. Invert means to turn upside-down.

Example: 1-$\frac{2}{3} \div \frac{3}{4}$

1. 1-$\frac{2}{3}$ = $\frac{5}{3}$, so the problem becomes $\frac{5}{3} \div \frac{3}{4}$
2. Invert $\frac{3}{4}$ to $\frac{4}{3}$

3. Using the inverted divisor, proceed as if it was a multiplication problem.

3. a. ⅝ ÷ ¾ is the same as ⅝ × ⁴⁄₃

    b. $\dfrac{5 \times 4}{3 \times 3} = \dfrac{20}{9}$

    c. $\begin{array}{r} 2 \\ 9\overline{)20} \\ 18 \\ \hline 2 \end{array}$ The result is 2-²⁄₉

Example

A 72″ steel bar is to be cut into 3-⁵⁄₁₆″ lengths. An apprentice determines how many pieces she can cut from the bar using the following steps.

1. She sets up the problem as:

    72″ ÷ 3-⁵⁄₁₆″ per piece = total number of pieces

2. Then, converting mixed numbers to fractions:

    $$\frac{72}{1} \div \frac{53}{16}$$

3. Next, the apprentice inverts the divisor:

    $$\frac{72}{1} \div \frac{53}{16} = \frac{72}{1} \times \frac{16}{53}$$

4. And she calculates the result:

    $$\frac{72 \times 16}{1 \times 53} = \frac{1152}{53}$$

$\begin{array}{r} 21 \\ 53\overline{)1152} \\ 106 \\ \hline 92 \\ 53 \\ \hline 39 \end{array}$ 21 total pieces could be cut from the bar

Exercises

1. The cutting tool on a lathe is set to move automatically ⅞″ every minute. How long would the turning of a 12-⅔″ rod take?

2. For each ½ turn of a small gear, a large gear moves ⅛ of a turn. How many times would the small gear rotate for one full turn of the large gear?

3. The following lengths of sheet metal are to be cut into equal sized pieces. Calculate the total number of pieces that can be cut from each length.

	Total Length	Length Per Piece	Number of Pieces Per Length
a.	48″	2-⅔″	
b.	25-⅞″	6-¼″	
c.	17-⅕″	½″	
d.	64-⅔″	2-⅓″	

Answers

1. The time required would equal the total length divided by the length moved each minute:

$$12\text{-}\tfrac{2}{3} \div \tfrac{7}{8} = \tfrac{38}{3} \div \tfrac{7}{8} = \tfrac{38}{3} \times \tfrac{8}{7} = \frac{38 \times 8}{3 \times 7} = \frac{304}{21} = 14\text{-}\tfrac{10}{21} \text{ minutes.}$$

2. The number of turns would equal the amount moved by the small gear divided by the amount moved by the large gear:

$$\tfrac{1}{2} \div \tfrac{1}{8} = \tfrac{1}{\cancel{2}_1} \times \tfrac{\cancel{8}^4}{1} = 4 \text{ turns}$$

3. a. $48'' \div 2\text{-}\tfrac{2}{3}'' = \dfrac{48}{1} \div \dfrac{8}{3} = \dfrac{\overset{6}{\cancel{48}} \times 3}{1 \times \underset{1}{\cancel{8}}} = 18 \text{ lengths}$

    b. $25\text{-}\tfrac{7}{8}'' \div 6\text{-}\tfrac{1}{4}'' = \dfrac{207}{8} \div \dfrac{25}{4} = \dfrac{207}{8} \times \dfrac{\overset{1}{\cancel{4}}}{25} = \dfrac{207}{50} = 4 \text{ lengths}$

    c. $17\text{-}\tfrac{1}{5}'' \div \tfrac{1}{2}'' = \dfrac{86}{5} \div \dfrac{1}{2} = \dfrac{86}{5} \times \dfrac{2}{1} = \dfrac{172}{5} = 34 \text{ lengths}$

    d. $64\text{-}\tfrac{2}{3}'' \div 2\text{-}\tfrac{1}{3}'' = \dfrac{194}{3} \div \dfrac{7}{3} = \dfrac{194}{\underset{1}{\cancel{3}}} \times \dfrac{\overset{1}{\cancel{3}}}{7} = \dfrac{194}{7} = 27 \text{ lengths}$

Decimal Fractions

Decimals are fractions whose denominators are multiples of 10, that is 10, 100, 1000, and so on. Instead of writing the denominator, its value is indicated by the position of a *decimal point*. For example, ⁹⁄₁₀ is written as .9 and said "nine-tenths." Also, ³³⁄₁₀₀ is .33, meaning thirty-three one-hundredths. The rules for writing decimals are the following:

-   Only the numerator of the fraction is written.
-   A decimal point indicating the value of the denominator precedes the numerator of the fraction.
-   The number of zeros in the denominator determines the number of place values to the right of the decimal.

To write ⁹⁄₁₀₀, we would:

1. Write the numerator.   9
2. Place a decimal point.   .9
3. Determine the number of place values—this is 2 since 100 has 2
   zeros. So, we have to insert a place holder, which is 0.   .09

To write ²⁷⁄₁₀,₀₀₀, we would:

1. Write the numerator.   27
2. Place a decimal point.   .27
3. Add 2 place holders (so we have a total of 4 digits).   .0027

How would you write the following fractions as decimals?*

   a. ¹⁷⁄₁₀₀   b. ³⁄₁₀   c. ²⁄₁₀₀₀   d. ⁴³⁷⁄₁₀₀₀

Changing Fractions To Decimals

Oftentimes it is necessary to change the results of your calculations to decimals so the results will be consistent with measures or other figures that are expressed in decimals. For example, suppose you calculated that the length of a particular rod was to be ¹⁷⁄₂₀″. Using a machinist's scale, which is divided into hundredths, it would be impossible to make the necessary measurement. Therefore, you must be able to change your result to a decimal for this and many other applications.

To convert a common fraction to a decimal fraction, divide the numerator by the denominator. This is done by following these steps:

Steps:	*Example*: ¹⁷⁄₂₀
1. Set up the division problem as you learned in the last unit.	$20\overline{)17}$
2. Place a decimal point after the number under the sign. Then put a zero next to the decimal. Placing zeros to the right of the decimal does not change the value of a number. But it does enable you to divide a larger number into a smaller one.	$20\overline{)17.0}$
3. Place the decimal point above the sign in the same position it is beneath the sign.	$20\overline{)17.0}^{\,.}$
4. Divide as you would with whole numbers. Add zeros to continue the operation until there is no remainder.	$\begin{array}{r} .85 \\ 20\overline{)17.00} \\ 16\,0 \\ \hline 1\,00 \\ 1\,00 \\ \hline \end{array}$

---

* *Answers:*

   a. .17   b. .3   c. .002   d. .437

Change the following fractions to decimals:*

a. ⅗   b. ⅜   c. ¹⁴/₄₀   d. ¹/₂₅

Rounding Decimals

Sometimes in changing a fraction to a decimal you will find that no matter how many zeros are added you still have a remainder. Take for example the fraction ⅓:

$$
\begin{array}{r}
.3333 \\
3\overline{)1.0000} \\
\underline{9} \\
10 \\
\underline{9} \\
10 \\
\underline{9} \\
10 \\
\underline{9} \\
1
\end{array}
$$

As you can see, the division process would go on forever. So, in cases such as this, you need to stop dividing when your answer has a desired amount of accuracy. The more decimal places in the answer, the greater the accuracy will be. If you are dealing with micrometer measurements, you may need accuracy to three decimal places (thousandths). When working with a ruler, tenths may be accurate enough for your purposes.

Based on the degree of accuracy you need in an answer, you can *round the number to the nearest decimal*. Rounding involves the following steps:

Steps:	*Examples:*
1. Drop all of the digits to the right of your desired cut-off point.	a. Round .33333333 to the nearest thousandths
	b. Round .4567 to the nearest hundredths
2. Compare the digit to the right of the number you saved with the number 5.	
a. If it is less than 5, retain the number as you have it	a. .333
b. If it is equal to or greater than 5, add one to the last digit in your retained number.	b. .46

*   *Answers*

a.
$$
\begin{array}{r}
.6 \\
5\overline{)3.0}
\end{array}
$$

b.
$$
\begin{array}{r}
.375 \\
8\overline{)3.0} \\
\underline{2\,4} \\
60 \\
\underline{56} \\
40 \\
\underline{40}
\end{array}
$$

c.
$$
\begin{array}{r}
.35 \\
40\overline{)14.00} \\
\underline{12\,0} \\
2\,00 \\
\underline{2\,00}
\end{array}
$$

d.
$$
\begin{array}{r}
.04 \\
25\overline{)1.00} \\
\underline{1\,00}
\end{array}
$$

Example

A 2″ metal rod was to be taken down to ⅚ of its diameter. This would be:

$$\frac{\overset{1}{\cancel{2}}}{1} \times \frac{5}{\underset{3}{\cancel{6}}} = \text{⁵⁄₃} = 1\text{-}\text{⅔}''.$$

The accuracy of the finished product would be checked with a micrometer. Therefore, it was necessary to change the final diameter to a decimal fraction, accurate to three decimal places. The apprentice solving the problem used the following steps:

1. First, he set up the problem as a division problem:

   $3\overline{)2.0}$

2. He added a decimal point and zero to start the division

3. Next, a decimal point was placed above the sign and the apprentice proceeded with the division problem. He added 4 zeros so that he would have enough digits to round his answer to 3 places.

   $$\begin{array}{r} .6666 \\ 3\overline{)2.0000} \\ 18 \\ \hline 20 \\ 18 \\ \hline 20 \\ 18 \\ \hline 20 \\ 18 \\ \hline 20 \\ 18 \\ \hline 2 \end{array}$$

4. The final step was to combine the decimal fraction with the whole number and round 1.6666 to the nearest thousandths. He kept 1.666. Since the next digit (6) was greater than 5, the number was rounded up to 1.667. Therefore, the diameter to check was 1.667″.

Exercises

1. The following measurements are expressed as common fractions. Change the measurements to decimal form and round them as instructed.
   a. ³⁄₁₆″, round to the nearest thousandth
   b. 2-⅝″, round to the nearest hundredth
   c. 5-⅞″, round to the nearest tenth
   d. 17-⁹⁄₁₆′, round to the nearest thousandth

2. In exercise d above, you were instructed to round 17-⁹⁄₁₆′ to the nearest thousandth. Does this seem like an unusual request? Why?

Answers

1. a. ³⁄₁₆ = .1875 = .188
   b. 2-⅝ = 2.625 = 2.63
   c. 5-⅞ = 5.87 = 5.9
   d. 17-⁹⁄₁₆ = 17.5625 = 17.563

2. This is an unusual request because the measurement is in feet. You generally do not require such high accuracy as thousandths when you are working with such large measures as feet.

Addition And Subtraction Using Decimals

Adding and subtracting decimals follow the same rules or steps that apply to working with whole numbers. But you must be careful to *line up the decimals of each figure* when you set up the problem. This assures that all the place values will be lined up.

Example

Various components of a product weigh .345 lb, 2.1 lb, .012 lb, 13 lb, and .07 lb. What will be the total weight of the assembled product?

To solve this problem, set up the figures in a column, aligning the decimals.

$$
\begin{array}{r}
.345 \\
2.1 \\
.012 \\
13. \\
.07 \\
\hline
\end{array}
$$

↑
Line up
decimals

To make addition easier you may fill in the blank spaces with zeros. This does not change any of the values.

$$
\begin{array}{r}
00.345 \\
02.100 \\
00.012 \\
13.000 \\
+\ 00.070 \\
\hline
\end{array}
$$

Next, proceed with addition. Numbers may be carried and borrowed just as they are in adding and subtracting whole numbers.

$$
\begin{array}{r}
00.345 \\
02.100 \\
00.012 \\
13.000 \\
+\ 00.070 \\
\hline
15.527 \quad \text{lb}
\end{array}
$$

Exercises:

1. A metal bar is 8.167 cm wide. If the desired width of the bar is 7.85 cm, how much should be removed?

2. The prices of supplies needed to install a gutter on portions of a roof are listed below. What will be the total cost of the supplies?

3 ten-foot gutter sections @ $5.99 each	$17.97
2 caps @ $.49 each	.98
2 corners @ $2.69 each	5.38
1 drop outlet	2.49
1 elbow	1.19
1 downspout	6.49
1 can touch-up paint	2.79
2 tubes caulk @ $1.99 each	3.98

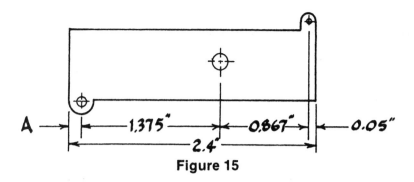

Figure 15

3. Refer to the drawing in Figure 15. What is the length of dimension **A**?

Answers

1.
$$
\begin{array}{r}
8.167 \\
-\ 7.850 \\
\hline
.317 \text{ cm}
\end{array}
$$

2.
$$
\begin{array}{r}
17.97 \\
.98 \\
5.38 \\
2.49 \\
1.19 \\
6.49 \\
2.79 \\
+\ 3.98 \\
\hline
\$41.27
\end{array}
$$

3. Dimension **A** would equal the total length minus the sum of the remaining dimensions. First, add the length segments:

$$
\begin{array}{r}
\mathbf{11} \ \leftarrow Carries \\
1.375 \\
.867 \\
+\ .050 \\
\hline
2.292
\end{array}
$$

Then, subtract this from the total:

$$
\begin{array}{r}
\mathbf{39} \\
2.\cancel{4}\cancel{0}\cancel{0} \\
-2.292 \\
\hline
.108''
\end{array}
$$

Multiplying And Dividing With Decimals

Multiplication with decimals is the same process as used with whole numbers. However, you must pay particular attention to placing the decimal point in your answer. This involves two steps:

Steps:	*Example:*

1. Count the number of digits to the right of the decimals in both of the numbers you are multiplying. Total them.

$$
\begin{array}{r}
4.67 \\
\times\ \ 3.5 \\
\hline
2335 \\
1401 \\
\hline
16345
\end{array}
\qquad
\begin{array}{l}
\textit{2 digits} \\
+\ \textit{1 digit} \\
\hline
\textit{3 digits}
\end{array}
$$

2. In the answer, count from the right of the total number of digits you counted above. Place the decimal there.

$$16.345 \ \leftarrow 3 \text{ digits}$$

Division is also the same as with whole numbers, but the trick is in placing the decimal point. If the only decimal point in the problem is under the division sign, then simply place the decimal in the answer directly above the point under the sign.

Example: 12)$\overline{24.782}$
                    ↑

Line up the decimals when the only decimal is under the sign.

If the divisor has a decimal, the process is a little more complicated, but not too bad. Follow these steps:

Steps:	*Examples:*
1. Count the number of digits to the right of the decimal in the divisor.	1. a. 12.12)$\overline{24.782}$ ↑ 2 digits b. .12)$\overline{24}$ ↑ 2 digits
2. Count that number of digits to the right of the decimal in the number under the sign. Add zeros if there are not enough places. That is where the decimal in the answer is placed.	2. a. 12.12)$\overline{24.782}$ b. .12)$\overline{24.00}$

Example

A metal plate is 16.5 cm in length. Holes are to be drilled in the plate at a distance of 1.45 cm on center. Is the plate large enough for 10 holes?

To solve this problem first make a rough sketch of the problem, as in Figure 16. You want each of the distances, D, to equal 1.45 cm.

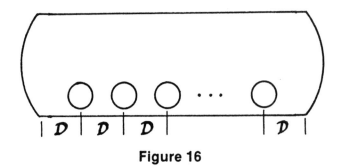

Figure 16

Next, find out how many D's you have in the total length. You do this by dividing 16.5 by 1.45. To fit 10 holes on the plate you need at least 11 D's. This is because there is a D at each end of the plate. Draw in 10 holes and count the D's to see how this works.

The results of the division gives the following:

```
        11.379
1.45)16.50 000
     14 5
     ────
      2 00
      1 45
      ────
        55 0
        43 5
        ────
        11 50
        10 15
        ─────
         1 350
         1 305
         ─────
```

There are 11 distances (D's) on the plate so the holes will fit. By continuing the division, you can determine how much excess length there is. Two-digit accuracy is sufficient for our purposes. .379 can be rounded to .38 cm, which is the amount of excess.

Exercises

1. The following work order is to cut aluminimum rods into equal length segments. Determine how many segments you could cut from each rod. Also, find the amount of scrap, by continuing the division, and round to 2 places.

	Rod Length	Length Per Segment	Total Segments	Scrap
a.	62.85 cm	12.5 cm		
b.	48 in	5.685 in		
c.	12 ft	1.8 ft		
d.	120.5 cm	10 cm		

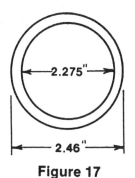

Figure 17

2. The outside diameter of a pipe is 2.46″. The inside diameter is 2.275″. a. What is the difference between the inside and outside diameters? b. What is the thickness of the pipe? (See Fig. 17).

3. The diameter of the head on a countersunk screw is 1.74 times the diameter of the screw. a. If the diameter of the screw is .435 cm, what is the diameter of the head? b. What would be the diameter of the head if the screw were .265 cm in diameter? Round your answers to three places.

Answers

		Result of Division	Total Segments	Scrap
1.	a.	5.028	5	.03 of a segment
	b.	8.443	8	.44 of a segment
	c.	6.666	6	.67 of a segment
	d.	12.05	12	.05 of a segment

2. a.
$$\begin{array}{r} 35 \\ 2.460 \\ -2.275 \\ \hline .185 \end{array}$$

   b. The thickness of the pipe is ½ of the difference between the diameters. If you do not understand this, look closely at Figure 17. By subtracting the diameters, we find the measurement of 2 thicknesses.

$$.185 \times \frac{1}{2} = \frac{.185}{2} = .0925''$$

3. a. $.435 \times 1.74 = .75690 = .757$
    b. $.265 \times 1.74 = .46110 = .461$

Using Percents

Percents are special types of fractions where the denominator of the fraction is 100. Instead of writing the denominator as 100, a percent sign is used. For example:

$$^{12}\!/_{100} = 12 \text{ percent or } 12\%$$
$$^{50}\!/_{100} = 50 \text{ percent or } 50\%$$
$$^{2}\!/_{10} = {}^{20}\!/_{100} = 20 \text{ percent or } 20\%$$
$$^{3}\!/_{5} = {}^{60}\!/_{100} = 60 \text{ percent or } 60\%$$

Percents are used often in most work situations. For example, a supervisor may request, "Give me 80% power." Or you may be asked, "What percent of that is scrap." You may complain each week that the government takes 25 percent of your paycheck (or even more).

Generally, there are three different calculations you may need to perform with percents.

1.   Change common or decimal fractions to percents.
2.   Calculate a percentage of a total amount.
3.   Determine what percent an amount is of a total amount.

Change Fractions to Percents

It is easy to work with percents because they have a built-in common denominator. Therefore, it is simple to make comparisons and to perform basic operations. For example it is clear that 60% is greater than 58%. Would it be that easy to see that ⅗ is greater than ²⁹⁄₅₀?

To change fractions to percents, first put them in decimal form, then:

•   Move the decimal two places to the right
•   Add a percent sign

To change a percent to a fraction:

- Move the decimal two places to the left, adding zeros if necessary
- Drop the percent sign
- Change to a common fraction if you like

Examples

.23 = 23%
.476 = 47.6% or 47-³/₅%
³/₅   = .60 = 60%
18% = .18
25% = .25 or ¼

Exercises

1. A fuel gauge reads ¾ full. What percent of the fuel has been burned?

2. Listed below are the hours that various production machines were not operating in a 24-hour day. What is the percentage of time that each of the machines was down in a day? Round your decimals to the nearest hundredths.

Machine	Hours down	% Down time
1	2	
2	.5	
3	3.6	
4	8	

Answers

1. Change ¾ to a decimal:

$$\begin{array}{r} .75 \\ 4\overline{)3.00} \\ 2\,8 \\ \hline 20 \\ 20 \\ \hline \end{array}$$

    Therefore, the tank is 75% full. To find out how much has been burned, subtract the amount remaining from the total capacity (100%):

    $$100 - 75 = 25\% \text{ of the fuel has been burned}$$

2. To find % down time, divide hours down by total hours (24), and move the decimal 2 places to the right.

Machine	% Down Time
1	
2	8.33 %
3	2.08 %
4	15.00 %
	33.33 %

Calculate Percentage of a Total Amount

Oftentimes it will be necessary to compute a percentage of a number. For example, in ordering raw materials you frequently will have to include an additional percentage for waste allowance. Calculating amount of sales tax is another example of taking a percentage of a total.

Wherever you have a problem that involves determining a certain percentage of a total amount, use the following steps:

1. Convert the percentage to a decimal.
2. Multiply the decimal times the total amount.

Example

A parts catalog advertised a 20% savings on all the company's merchandise. To calculate what the savings would be on an order of $128.95, you would:

1. Change 20% to .20 or .2
2. Multiply:
3. Count off 3 places from right in   **1 1 1**   ← *Carries*
    answer and place decimal there.   128.95
                                         $\times$ .2
                                         ———————
                                         $25.790

The savings would be $25.79

Exercises

1. The employees listed below each pay 6.6% of their weekly earnings to social security. How much do they pay per week?

Employee	Weekly Earnings	Social Security Payment
Howard	$ 435.86	
Engles	$ 298.42	
Johnson	$ 347.33	
Murdock	$ 369.27	

2. Two companies had comparable 5-piece sets of drawing instruments on sale. One company originally priced the sets at $39.95 and was offering a 25% reduction. The second company had a 30% reduction, but the sets were originally $42.50. Which company offered the lowest sale price?

Answers

1. First, change 6.6% to a decimal—.066. Multiply weekly earnings by .066 to get the SS payment.

Employee	Social Security Payment
Howard	$28.77
Engles	$19.70
Johnson	$22.92
Murdock	$24.37

    The answers are rounded to hundredths of dollars since that is the smallest American currency (cents).

2. The first company's reduction is $39.95 times .25 which equals $9.99. So, the sales price is $39.95 − 9.99 = $29.96. For the second company the reduction is $42.50 × .30 = $12.75. The sales price is $42.50 − 12.75 = $29.75. The second company had the lower price.

Determine What Percent An Amount Is

A third frequent use of percentages is to find out what percent one amount is of another. This is what you do to figure out what percent of your paycheck goes to the government. To determine the percent in this case, you would first divide the amount taken out by the total amount and then change the resulting decimal to a percent. This is the same way you would handle all similar problems:

1. Form a fraction by putting the part over the total amount.
2. Divide the fraction to change it to a decimal.
3. Change the decimal to a percent.

Example

The basement in a set of house plans is 900 square feet. The total area of the house is 2600 square feet. Assuming the basement will not be heated, what percentage of the house will be heated space?

To solve this, first determine how many square feet will be heated. This is found by subtracting the unheated area from the total area:

$$\begin{array}{r} 2600 \\ -900 \\ \hline 1700 \text{ heated square feet} \end{array}$$

Next create a fraction by putting the heated area over the total area: $^{17\cancel{00}}/_{26\cancel{00}}$ (cancelling out 100).

Dividing, you would find the decimal equivalent:

$$\begin{array}{r} .6538 \\ 26\overline{)17.0000} \\ 15\ 6 \\ \hline 1\ 40 \\ 1\ 30 \\ \hline 100 \\ 78 \\ \hline 220 \\ 208 \\ \hline \end{array}$$

And lastly, change the decimal to a percent:

.654 = about 65% of the house would be heated space.

Exercises

1. The total production and amount of scrap produced by four machines is listed below. Which machine produced the highest percentage of scrap? Round answers to the nearest tenths.

	Total		
Machine #1	*Production*	*Scrap*	*% Scrap*
1	5433	389	
2	1794	180	
3	4876	340	
4	3944	295	

2. A painter had three gallons of paint, each of which would cover 420 square feet of area. If the job was 1800 square feet, what percentage of the job could the painter finish with the paint on hand?

Answers

1. Percent scrap is calculated by dividing scrap by the total production and moving the decimal two places to the right.

Machine #	*% Scrap*
1	7.2
2	10.0
3	7.0
4	7.5

2. The total space the painter could paint is 420 square feet/gallon times 3 gallons = 1260 sq. ft. To determine the percentage of the job this would complete, divide 1260 by 1800 and convert to %.

$$\frac{1260}{1800} = .7 = 70\%$$

Self-Test Exercises

Answer the following questions and problems. Check your answers with those in Chapter 5. If you answer less than 7 items correctly, repeat your work in this Chapter. If you answer 7 or 8 of the problems or questions correctly, you have mastered the use of fractions in solving problems. Go on to the next chapter.

Refer to Figure 18 to answer questions 1-4.

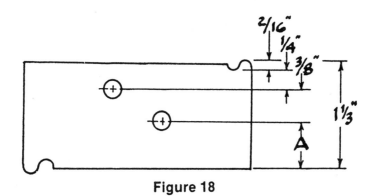

Figure 18

1. Determine the dimension A, reducing to lowest terms.

2. Convert A to a decimal fraction. Round to nearest thousandth.

3. If you had a work order to produce the plate at ⅔ of its size in Fig. 18, what would be the size of dimension **A**?

4. What percent of its full size would this reduction be?

Use the following situation to answer questions 5 and 6.

A landscaper needed the following supplies:

		Catalog Price
12 dozen leaf bags		$3.99 per dozen
50# 8-8-8 fertilizer		8.50
100 feet mulch sheeting		3.98
25 feet border wire		8.79
motor oil		5.65

5. What is the total cost of the supplies?

6. Being a regular customer, the landscaper receives a 20% discount off the regular catalog prices for most supplies. What will be his reduced price for the 50# of fertilizer?

7. Each setting on a control moved a cutting blade .175 inches. How many settings would an operator need to adjust the control to move the blade a total of 2.275 inches?

8. Eight-foot pine planks measuring 5-¾″ wide are to be used to panel an 8 foot by 8 foot wall. Assuming that the panels will overlap by ½″, how many planks will be needed to panel the wall? (8 feet is equal to 96 inches).

4. Formulas And Tables

Chapter Overview

Purpose: To develop skills in using tables and formulas. You will gain an understanding of how formulas represent rules and relationships and an ability to determine values of unknowns using formulas and tables.

Preassessment Score: Write in the following space the number of correct answers from Pretest questions 17-22: _____. If you answered five or six questions correctly, skip to the Posttest in Chapter 5. If you missed two or more questions, work through this chapter.

Prerequisites: Chapter 1 of this book.
Chapters 2 and 3 of this book or mastery of the four basic arithmetic operations using whole numbers, fractions, decimals and percents.

Resources: Time—About 1-1½ hours to complete.
Materials—paper, pencil

Performance Measure: A thirty-minute paper-and-pencil Posttest, to be taken after completing the entire book.

Standards: To be successful, you must answer correctly 80% of the Posttest items.

Activities:
1. Read the text, examples and illustrations and commit information to memory.
2. Work questions, examples and problems.
3. Complete and check the Self-Test Exercises and the Posttest.

Introduction And Objectives

Formulas and tables are ways of showing relationships among the parts of a problem. A formula is written to describe the rules governing various calculations. For example, the diameter of a circle is equal to twice the radius of the same circle. This general rule could be written as:

$$D = 2 \times r$$

where **D** is the diameter and **r** is the radius. Then if you had a circle whose radius was 3″, you could solve for the diameter:

$$D = 2 \times 3'' = 6''$$

Another way this relationship could be represented is in a table:

D = 2 × r	
D	**r**
2	1
4	2
6	3
8	4
10	5
12	6

In this case, values of **r** are listed along with the associated value of **D**. Rather than compute the value of **D** as you did with the formula, you would look in the table. First, you would read down the column marked **r** until you find the appropriate value (3). Then reading across to the associated value of **D**, you would find it to be 6.

Both formulas and tables are very useful tools in most trades. They show relationships among such things as:

- Pitch of a screw and threads per inch
- Length, width and area of a floor plan
- Inches and centimeters
- Resistance, current and voltage in a circuit
- Gravel, sand and cement mix
- Feed, cutting speed and diameter of milling cutters

As you work through the unit, you will most likely recognize a number of opportunities where you can make use of formulas and tables in your work. After completing the chapter you will demonstrate your competence by being able to:

1. Write formulas to represent rules and relationships.
2. Solve formulas for unknowns.
3. Read tables to determine the value of an unknown.

Writing Formulas For Rules

Writing rules or relationships as formulas involves assigning letters or symbols to the quantities and combining them into an expression. The steps for writing formulas are listed below, using the following relationship as an example:

The area of a triangle is equal to one-half of the base of the triangle times the height of the triangle.

Steps:

1. Identify the quantities that are involved in the relationship.

Example:

1. In the example the rule describes a relationship among:

   a. area
   b. base
   c. height

2. Assign letters or symbols to represent unknown amounts of the quantity. Use standardized terms if you are aware of any. A useful rule is to use the first letter of the quantity.

2. For each of the quantities you would assign:

   area   — A
   base   — b
   height — h

   These are standard terms as well as the first letters of the quantities.

3. Define the operations that are involved. It is often useful to draw an illustration such as Figure 19 to help you picture the relationships.

3. First, draw a figure to show the relationship:

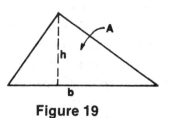

Figure 19

A formula would define the relationship between (1) the area (A) of a triangle and (2) its base and height (b,h). Operations involved are:

- taking ½ of the base, which means ½ × b
- multiplying this times the height

4. Write the formula form. Use the equals sign to separate one quantity from those it is being related to.

4. First, write from Step 3:

   A =

   Then, on the right side of the equals sign, write the other quantities and operations involved:

   A = ½ × b × h

Writing a problem in formula form can be useful to you for two reasons:

1. The process helps you define in your own mind what calculations will be involved in solving the problem.
2. Once you have written the formula, often you can use it to solve future problems involving the same quantities and unknowns.

The example which follows will show you one way formulas can be used.

Example

An apprentice needed to determine the total distance around a house site to plan for laying the footings. From the floor plans for the house, he found the dimensions in Figure 20.

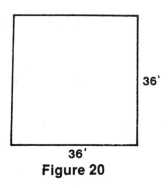

36'

36'

Figure 20

So, to find the distance around or the *perimeter* of the planned house, he added up the lengths of the sides: 36' + 36' + 36' + 36' = 144'.

In doing this, the apprentice noticed that this was equal to 4 × 36' = 144'. A more general rule from this problem is that the perimeter of a square (because it has equal length sides) is equal to 4 times the length of one side. This can be written as P = 4 × S. This formula can be used to determine the perimeter of *any* square, by simply measuring the length of one side and substituting this in place of S in the formula.

Exercises

Write a formula for each of the relationships below.

1. The gas mileage of an automobile is equal to the number of miles traveled divided by the number of gallons used.

2. The number of feet is equal to the number of inches divided by 12.

3. The perimeter of a rectangle is equal to 2 times the length of the rectangle plus 2 times the width of the rectangle.

4. One kilogram equals 2.2 pounds. (This could also be written: the number of pounds equals 2.2 times the number of kilograms).

Answers

1. MPG = m/g

2. f = i/12

3. P = (2 × l) + (2 × w). The parentheses mean that you would do the multiplication operations before you add the results together.

4. p = 2.2 × k

Solving Formulas For Unknowns

Once a formula is written, you are able to solve for unknowns by substituting values of known quantities in the formula. Look at the formula for the area of a triangle:

$$A = \frac{1}{2} \times b \times h.$$

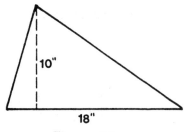

Figure 21

If you measured the dimensions in Figure 21, you could solve for the area of the triangle. First, substitute the known values of 18 for b and 10 for h in the formula:

$$A = \frac{1}{2} \times 18 \times 10.$$

This allows you to *solve for the unknown* quantity A by performing the calculations:

$$A = \frac{1}{2} \times 18 \times 10$$

$$A = \frac{1}{2} \times 180 = 90 \text{ square inches}$$

Example

A builder faced the problem of raising a number of fixtures to the second floor of a construction job. She decided to rig up a pulley system to move the fixtures. The number of strands in the pulley system is equal to the load divided by the amount of force that can be applied to lift the weight. So she had a formula:

$$N = \frac{W}{F}$$

N = Number of ropes
W = Weight of load
F = Force applied

Drawing a figure of the problem would produce something like Figure 22.

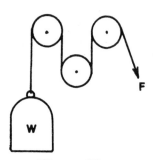

Figure 22

Since the builder knew the heaviest fixture weighed 275 pounds, she had a value for W. She assumed that the force applied by someone pulling on the ropes would be 75-100 pounds. Therefore she tried both of these values for F:

For F = 75:

$$N = \frac{275}{75}$$

N = 3.67 or about 4 ropes

For F = 100:

$$N = \frac{275}{100}$$

N = 2.75 or about 3 ropes

So the builder could rig a pulley using 3 or 4 ropes, depending on the strength of the person moving the fixtures.

Exercises

1. The voltage (E) in an electrical circuit is equal to the current times the resistance. This is written as $E = I \times R$. What voltage is required for a circuit with a resistance of 15 ohms (R) and a current of 3 amperes (I).

2. Use the formulas you wrote in the last set of exercises to solve the following:

   a. Calculate mileage for:

   miles   = 247.6

   gallons =   8.5

   (Round to the nearest hundredth)

   b. How long in feet is a 36″ rule?

   c. Find the perimeter of the rectangle in Figure 23.

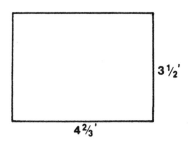

Figure 23

   d. What would be the weight in pounds of a 3½ kg component?

Answers

1. $E = I \times R$: $I = 3$

                        $R = 15$

   $E = 3 \times 15$

   $E = 45$ volts

2. a. $MPG = m/g$

   $MPG = {}^{247.6}\!/_{8.5}$

   $MPG = 29.13$ miles per gallon

   b. $f = {}^{i}\!/_{12}$

   $f = {}^{36}\!/_{12}$

   $f = 3$ feet

   c. $p = (2 \times l) + (2 \times w)$

   $p = (2 \times 4\text{-}\!{}^{2}\!/_{3}) + (2 \times 3\text{-}\!{}^{1}\!/_{2})$

   $p = (2 \times {}^{14}\!/_{3}) + (2 \times {}^{7}\!/_{2})$

   $p = ({}^{28}\!/_{3}) + 7$

   $p = 9\text{-}\!{}^{1}\!/_{3} + 7 = 16\text{-}\!{}^{1}\!/_{3}{}'$

   d. $p = 2.2 \times k$

   $p = 2.2 \times 3\text{-}\!{}^{1}\!/_{2}$

   $p = 2.2 \times 3.5$

   $p = 7.70$ pounds

Reading Tables

Tables present values of quantities in a relationship. Therefore, you can look up values of known quantities in the table to identify the associated value of an unknown. This is an alternative to solving for an unknown when (1) an appropriate table is available and (2) when you don't have a formula relating quantities. Using the area of a triangle as an example (see Figure 24), steps for reading a table are presented below.

Steps:

1. Identify the known values of quantities.

Example:

1. You want to find the area of a triangular foyer. You measure the dimensions of 6 ft. and 9 ft. $b = 6$; $h = 9$.

2. Find the value of one of the known quantities on the table. This could involve reading across or down a row or column.

3. Find the values of other known quantities in the same manner.

4. Find the associated value of the unknown.

2. Look for values of 6. They run down the left column of the table. Read down the column until you find 6.

3. h runs across the top of this table. Read across until you find 9. There are only 2 known values in this example, but other tables may have more.

4. To find the value for the area, identify where the associated b and h values cross or intersect. On the table, run your finger across the row where b is 6. Run your other hand down the column where h is 9. They cross at a point where the value is 27. This is the area of the triangle.

Table of Values for A = ½ b × h

b\h	1	2	3	4	5	6	7	8	⑨
1	.5	1	1.5	2	2.5	3	3.5	4	4.5
2	1	2	3	4	5	6	7	8	9
3	1.5	3	4.5	6	7.5	9	10.5	12	13.5
4	2	4	6	8	10	12	14	16	18
5	2.5	5	7.5	10	12.5	15	17.5	20	22.5
⑥	3	6	9	12	15	18	21	24	㉗
7	3.5	7	10.5	14	17.5	21	24.5	28	31.5
8	4	8	12	16	20	24	28	32	36
9	4.5	9	13.5	18	22.5	27	31.5	36	40.5
10	5	10	15	20	25	30	35	40	45
11	5.5	11	16.5	22	27.5	33	38.5	44	49.5

Figure 24. Sample Table of Values for the Area of a Triangle

Exercises

Substitute the values of b = 6 and h = 9 in the formula for area to verify that the table gave us the correct answer. Using Figure 24, find the area of triangles with the following measurements:

	b	h	A
1.	2″	7″	
2.	8″	3″	
3.	5″	8″	

Check your answers by using the formula for area.

Answers

$$A = \frac{1}{2} \times b \times h$$

$$A = \frac{1}{2} \times \overset{3}{\underset{1}{6}} \times 9$$

$$A = 27 \text{ square feet}$$

1. 7 $A = \frac{1}{2} \times \overset{1}{\underset{1}{2}} \times 7 = 7 \text{ square inches}$

2. 12 $A = \frac{1}{2} \times \overset{4}{\underset{1}{8}} \times 3 = 12 \text{ square inches}$

3. 20 $a = \frac{1}{2} \times 5 \times \overset{4}{\underset{1}{8}} = 20 \text{ square inches}$

Reading the Table Backwards

You can also use the table to find the value of b or h. Take for example a situation where you know the area and one dimension of a triangle. This could be a job where you are commissioned to build a triangular-shaped pool of 28 square feet. Assuming that you are limited to one side of 7 feet, you need to determine the other dimension. This problem is illustrated in Figure 25.

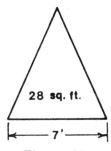

28 sq. ft.

7'

Figure 25

To find the height, first find the value b = 7 ft in the table. Reading across that row, you find the area of the pool—28 sq ft. The appropriate height for the triangluar pool is found by reading up the column from 28. You read the value of h to be 8 ft.

Exercises

Find the value of h for the following triangles:

	b	A	h
1.	3 ft	10.5 sq ft	
2.	8 ft	12 sq ft	
3.	9 ft	22.5 sq ft	

Answers

1. 7 ft

2. 3 ft

3. 5 ft

Other Table Formats

Tabular information can be presented in a number of different formats. But the steps you would follow to read the tables are basically the same. The values for area of a triangle are presented in two different ways in Figures 26 and 27. An example is shown in each of the tables for locating area when b = 5 and h = 3.

Exercises

After looking at the examples, find the areas of the following triangles:

Using Figure 26:

	b	h	A
1.	1′	5′	
2.	4′	2′	
3.	7′	3′	

Table of Values for A = 1/2 b × h

b	h	A	b	h	A	b	h	A	b	h	A	b	h	A
1	1	.5	1	2	1	1	3	1.5	1	4	2	1	5	2.5
2	1	1	2	2	2	2	3	3	2	4	4	2	5	5
3	1	1.5	3	2	3	3	3	4.5	3	4	6	3	5	7.5
4	1	2	4	2	4	4	3	6	4	4	8	4	5	10
5	1	2.5	5	2	5	⑤	③	⑦.5	5	4	10	5	5	12.5
6	1	3	6	2	6	6	3	9	6	4	12	6	5	15
7	1	3.5	7	2	7	7	3	10.5	7	4	14	7	5	17.5
8	1	4	8	2	8	8	3	12	8	4	16	8	5	20
9	1	4.5	9	2	9	9	3	13.5	9	4	18	9	5	22.5
10	1	5	10	2	10	10	3	15	10	4	20	10	5	25
11	1	5.5	11	2	11	11	3	16.5	11	4	22	11	5	27.5

Figure 26. Sample Table (#2) of Values for the Area of a Triangle

Using Figure 27:

	b	h	A
4.	3″	2″	
5.	4″	4″	
6.	6″	1″	

Table of Values for A = 1/2 b × h

h = 1		h = 2		h = ③		h = 4		h = 5	
b	A	b	A	b	A	b	A	b	A
1	.5	1	1	1	1.5	1	2	1	2.5
2	1	2	2	2	3	2	4	2	5
3	1.5	3	3	3	4.5	3	6	3	7.5
4	2	4	4	4	6	4	8	4	10
5	2.5	5	5	⑤	(7.5)	5	10	5	12.5
6	3	6	6	6	9	6	12	6	15
7	3.5	7	7	7	10.5	7	14	7	17.5
8	4	8	8	8	12	8	16	8	20
9	4.5	9	9	9	13.5	9	18	9	22.5
10	5	10	10	10	15	10	20	10	25
11	5.5	11	11	11	16.5	11	22	11	27.5

Figure 27. Sample Table (#3) of Values for the Area of a Triangle

Answers

1. 2.5 sq ft
2. 4 sq ft
3. 10.5 sq ft

4. 3 sq in
5. 8 sq in
6. 3 sq in

Self-Test Exercises

Answer the following questions and problems. Check your answers with those in Chapter 5. If you answer less than 7 items correctly, repeat your work in this chapter. If you answer 7 or 8 correctly, you have mastered the application of formulas and tables in solving work-related problems. Take the Posttest that is contained in Chapter 5.

Write formulas to represent the relationships in questions 1 and 2.

1. The number of centimeters equals the number of inches times 2.5.

2. The discount price of a product is equal to the regular price minus the product of the regular price times the percent discounted divided by 100.

3. The circumference of a metal disk is equal to the diameter times the value pi (π). This is written:

$$C = \pi \times D$$

π is always equal to 3.14. Find the circumference of the disk when D = 4.5 inches.

4. A plumber has an appointment to install new fixtures in a house located 35 miles away. The formula for calculating travel time is

$$T = \frac{D}{R}$$

where D is the distance travelled and R is the rate of speed. How long should the plumber allow for travel time (going and coming) if he can drive 55 miles per hour?

5. The amount of profit you can make on a job equals the price charged minus the cost of doing the job. How much profit would you make if you charged $475 for a job that cost you $387.49?

6. The tempering temperature for hammer faces is 232° Celsius (C). To measure that temperature using a Fahrenheit (F) thermometer you would need to convert the degrees C to F. Use the table in Figure 28 to find the temperature in Fahrenheit.

Temperature Conversion Table	
C°	°F
224	435
226	438
228	442
230	445
232	449
234	453
236	456
238	460

Figure 28

Figure 29 shows the size of bits needed to drill shank holes and pilot holes for different screw sizes. Use it to answer questions 7 and 8.

7. What size bit would you need to drill a shank hole for a size 6 screw?

8. What size bit would be needed to drill a pilot hole in hardwood for a number 3 screw?

Drill Bit Sizes			
For Screw Size	Shank Hole	For Pilot Hole	
		Softwood	Hardwood
0	$\frac{1}{16}$	$\frac{1}{64}$	$\frac{1}{32}$
1	$\frac{5}{64}$	$\frac{1}{32}$	$\frac{1}{32}$
2	$\frac{3}{32}$	$\frac{1}{32}$	$\frac{3}{64}$
3	$\frac{7}{64}$	$\frac{3}{64}$	$\frac{1}{16}$
4	$\frac{7}{64}$	$\frac{3}{64}$	$\frac{1}{16}$
5	$\frac{1}{8}$	$\frac{1}{16}$	$\frac{5}{64}$
6	$\frac{9}{64}$	$\frac{1}{16}$	$\frac{5}{64}$

Figure 29

5. Answers

Answers To Pretest

1. 1 : ten thousands
   4 : thousands
   7 : hundreds
   2 : tens
   5 : ones
2. 15564
3. 24793
4. 25′
5. 12′
6. 4 (26 lengths can be cut per rod)
7. $293
8. 2304 square feet
9. 35.369 mm.
10. 16-$\frac{19}{24}$ oz.
11. 18
12. $115.50
13. $308.00
14. 5.625″
15. 4-$\frac{7}{12}$″
16. $\frac{7}{8}$ in.
17. $D = V \times T$
18. $P = 2 \times L + 2 \times W$
19. 5.5
20. 44.16 square inches
21. 77 degrees fahrenheit
22. May

Answers To Self-Test Exercises

Chapter 2: Arithmetic Operations

1.

Millions	Hundred Thousands	Ten Thousands	Thousands	Hundreds	Tens	Ones
7	6	5	4	3	2	1

You should have ← identified these place values

2. Find your digit in Column A. Check your Answer in Column B.

Column A *If the digit in your ones column was:*	Column B *You would have to add the following to increase the tens column by 1*
0	10
1	9
2	8
3	7
4	6
5	5
6	4
7	3
8	2
9	1

The value in the ones column would be zero. For example:

```
      1  ← Carry
7863284
    + 6
-------
7863290
```

3. Dimension A = **61"**:

$$
\begin{array}{r}
\mathbf{4} \\
9 \\
8 \\
27 \\
9 \\
+8 \\
\hline
61
\end{array}
$$

Using multiplication:

$$
\begin{array}{rr}
 & \mathbf{2} \\
9 \times 2 = & 18 \\
8 \times 2 = & 16 \\
 & + 27 \\
\hline
 & 61
\end{array}
$$

4. To find out the length of Slot B, you would subtract out 17" and 22" from the length of Dimension A:

$$
\begin{array}{r}
17 \\
+\ 22 \\
\hline
39
\end{array}
\qquad
\begin{array}{r}
5 \\
\cancel{6}1 \\
-\ 17 \\
\hline
44
\end{array}
$$

-or-

$$
\begin{array}{r}
5 \\
\cancel{6}1 \\
-\ 39 \\
\hline
\mathbf{22''}
\end{array}
\qquad
\begin{array}{r}
44 \\
-\ 22 \\
\hline
\mathbf{22''}
\end{array}
$$

5. The number of miles he would drive this year would equal the miles per week times the weeks per year:

$$
\begin{array}{r}
\mathbf{23} \\
247 \\
\times\ \ 50 \\
\hline
000 \\
1235 \\
\hline
\mathbf{12{,}350}\ \text{miles}
\end{array}
$$

6. Gallons of gas would equal the miles driven divided by the average miles per gallon:

$$
\begin{array}{r}
\mathbf{726}\ \text{gallons} \\
17\overline{)12350} \\
119 \\
\hline
45 \\
34 \\
\hline
110 \\
102 \\
\hline
8
\end{array}
$$

Since we are estimating, we don't worry about the remainder.

7. The cost of gas this year equals the number of gallons times the cost per gallon:

$$
\begin{array}{r}
\mathbf{25}\ \leftarrow \\
\mathbf{13}\ \leftarrow \quad Carries \\
726 \\
\times\ \ 95 \\
\hline
3630 \\
6534 \\
\hline
\mathbf{68970¢}
\end{array}
$$

or in dollars

$$
\begin{array}{r}
\mathbf{\$\ 689} \\
100\overline{)68970} \\
600 \\
\hline
897 \\
800 \\
\hline
970 \\
900 \\
\hline
70
\end{array}
$$

8. **Yes.** One way she could cut the lengths would be:

		Scrap
1.	3 - 32" lengths = 96"	0
2.	1 - 72" + 2 - 12" = 96"	0
3.	1 - 72" + 2 - 12" = 96"	0
4.	1 - 72" + 1 - 18" = 90"	6"
5.	1 - 40" + 3 - 18" = 90"	2"
6.	2 - 40" + 1 - 12" = 92"	4"

Chapter 3: Fractions

1. **A** is equal to the total width minus the sum of the other dimensions. The LCD is 48:

$$\frac{2}{16} = \frac{6}{48} \qquad \frac{1}{4} = \frac{12}{48}$$

$$\frac{3}{8} = \frac{18}{48} \qquad 1\text{-}\frac{1}{3} = \frac{64}{48}$$

$$\frac{6+12+18}{48} = \frac{36}{48} \ \text{(sum of dimensions)}$$

$$\frac{64}{48} - \frac{36}{48} = \frac{28}{48} \ \text{(which reduces to } \frac{7}{12}\text{")}$$

2.

$$12\overline{)7.0000} \quad \frac{.5833}{} \qquad 7/12'' = \textbf{.583}''$$

```
        .5833
  12)7.0000
     6 0
     ───
     1 00
       96
     ───
       40
       36
     ───
       40
       36
     ───
```

3. $7/\overset{1}{\underset{6}{12}} \times 2/3 = 7/18''$

4. A 2/3 reduction would be about **67%** of full-size. (Determined by dividing 2 by 3 and rounding it to the nearest percent).

5. Cost of bags = $3.99 × 12 =

```
            47.88
             8.50
             3.98
             8.79
          +  5.65
          ────────
Total cost $74.80
```

6.

```
   $  8.50
   ×   .20
   ───────
   $1.7000
```

The discount is $1.70, so the reduced price is $8.50 − 1.70 = **$6.80**

7. The number of settings equals the total inches divided by the inches per setting:

```
            13. settings
  .175)2.275
       1 75
       ────
        525
        525
```

8. Since the planks overlap by ½″, the total space covered by each plank would be 5-¾″ − ½″ = 5-¼″. The number of planks equals the total height of the wall divided by the space covered by each plank:

$$96 \div 5\text{-}\tfrac14 = \frac{96}{1} \div \frac{21}{4} = \frac{\overset{32}{\cancel{96}}}{1} \times \frac{4}{\underset{7}{\cancel{21}}} = \frac{128}{7} =$$

18-2/7

19 planks would be needed.

Chapter 4: Formulas and Tables

1. **C = 2.5 × I** (you could have used different letters to represent centimeters and inches, for example: cm = 2.5 × in)

2. **DP = RP − (RP × D/100)**.
   DP = Discount price
   RP = Regular price
   D = Discount

3. C = π D
   C = 3.14 × 4.5
   C = 14.13 inches

4. The total distance (D) coming and going is equal to 2 × 35 or 70 miles. The rate (R) equals 55 miles per hour.
   T = D/R
   T = 70/55
   T = 1.27 hours

5. P = Pr − C
   P = $475 − $387.49
   P = $87.51

6. **449°F**

7. **9/64**

8. **1/16**

Posttest

Directions: *Answer the following questions. Place your answers in the space provided or use a separate sheet to perform your calculations and record your answers. After completing all of the questions, check your answers with the answers that follow. If you score 80% or better, you have successfully completed the material. If you score less than 80%, repeat the portions of the module with which you had difficulty.*

For questions 1–5 indicate the arithmetic operation you would use to solve the problem:

      a. Addition   c. Multiplication
      b. Subtraction   d. Division

1. A machinist produces 317 parts in an eight hour day. How would you determine the machinist's average production for one hour? _____

2. Fabric costs $4.97 per yard. How would you determine the price for 23 yards of fabric required for a job? _____

3. An apprentice is to weld six lengths of iron rod of varying sizes end to end. How would the apprentice determine the length of the finished product? _____

4. If the six rods in question 3 were equal in length, how would the apprentice determine the total length? _____

5. A mason contractor writes a check for $1,078.49 for supplies. How would the mason determine the balance of the checking account? _____

6. An apprentice is instructed to buy wallpaper for a room with the following wall areas:

         East Wall: 72 square feet
         West Wall: 72 square feet
         North Wall: 96 square feet
         South Wall: 96 square feet

   Windows took up 32 square feet of space that would not need papering. How many square feet of wallpaper would be needed for the room?

7. A contractor is building a subdivision of homes, 13 of which will have the same wallpaper requirements as the room in question 6. How much paper will be needed for all 13 houses?

8. How many rows of corn can be planted in a 576 foot wide field if the rows are planted about 3 feet apart?

9. Solve the problem in question 2.

10. How would the measurement 12.75″ be written as a common fraction?

11. A pipefitter needs 24 sections of ⅝″ pipe, each measuring 14-½″ in length. The pipe can be purchased in 96″ lengths. How many 96″ lengths will the pipefitter need to buy?

12. Of 438 parts produced in a day, 28 were rejects. What percent of the daily production were rejects? Round your answer to the nearest hundredth.

13. What is the length of dimension **A** in the figure below?

14. What is the length of dimension **B** in the figure below?

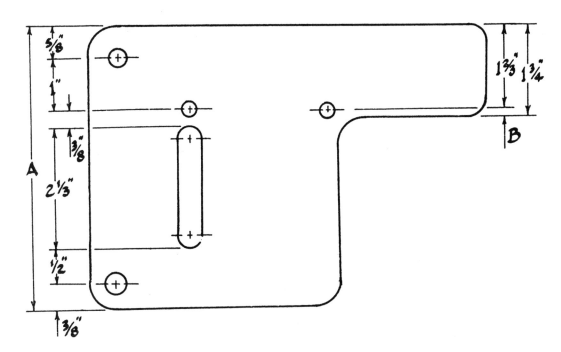

15. Cost of weekly supplies are listed below. What is the total cost for the week's supplies?

$249.59
  10.00
  17.49
   2.29
   2.29
  87.64

16. If State tax on the supplies listed above is 5%, how much tax would be paid on the week's supplies?

17. Write a formula to represent the distance around the figure pictured below:

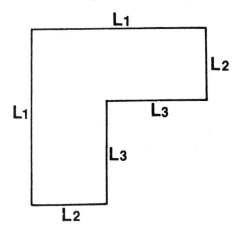

18. Write a formula for the following rule:

    Degrees Fahrenheit is equal to 9/5 times degrees Celsius, plus 32.

19. Determine the Fahrenheit equivalent of 30° Celsius.

20. One gallon is equal to 3.79 liters ($l = 3.79 \times G$). How many liters can fit in a 50 gallon drum.

21. An apprentice's gross wages for one month are $937.48. How much income tax should be withheld from the employee's check if the number of allowances claimed is 3. Use the table below.

Single Persons—Monthly Payroll Period

Wages		Number of Withholding Allowances Claimed					
At Least	Less Than	0	1	2	3	4	5
		Income Tax Withheld					
840	880	117.70	101.00	86.30	72.90	59.60	46.30
880	920	125.70	109.00	92.70	79.30	66.00	52.70
920	960	133.70	117.00	100.30	85.70	72.40	59.10
960	1000	141.70	125.00	108.30	92.10	78.80	65.50
1000	1040	149.70	133.00	116.30	99.70	85.20	71.90
1040	1080	158.40	141.00	124.30	107.70	91.60	78.30

22. If your employer withheld $133.00 in income tax from your check, what were your approximate wages and the number of allowances claimed? Use the table above.

Answers To Posttest

1. d. Division
2. c. Multiplication
3. a. Addition
4. c. Multiplication
5. b. Subtraction
6. 304 sq. ft.
7. 3952 sq. ft.
8. 192 rows
9. $114.31
10. 12-¾″
11. 4

12. 6.39%
13. 5-5/24″
14. 1/12″
15. $369.30
16. $18.47
17. $2 \times L_1 + 2 \times L_2 + 2 \times L_3$
18. $°F = \frac{9}{5} °C + 32$
19. 86° F
20. 189.5 liters
21. $85.70
22. Wages range from $1000–1040
    Allowances claimed is 1

Items 1–8 test material covered in Chapter 2, items 9–16 test material in Chapter 3 and items 17–22 test material in Chapter 4.

Practice tests to help you prepare for the
Arithmetic & Geometry
sections of the following
standardized tests:

PSAT • SAT I • ACT • PRAXIS • PPST
CBEST • GRE • GMAT • GED
CLEP • ELM

═══════════════

CHAPTER 6

Practicing to take Standardized Tests in Arithmetic

- ➤ *Answer Sheet*
- ➤ *Arithmetic Diagnostic Test*
- ➤ *Answer Key*
- ➤ *Detailed Explanations of Answers*
- ➤ *Arithmetic Review and Drills*
- ➤ *Answer Key to Drills*
- ➤ *Arithmetic Glossary*

ARITHMETIC DIAGNOSTIC TEST

1. Ⓐ Ⓑ Ⓒ Ⓓ Ⓔ		26. Ⓐ Ⓑ Ⓒ Ⓓ Ⓔ
2. Ⓐ Ⓑ Ⓒ Ⓓ Ⓔ		27. Ⓐ Ⓑ Ⓒ Ⓓ Ⓔ
3. Ⓐ Ⓑ Ⓒ Ⓓ Ⓔ		28. Ⓐ Ⓑ Ⓒ Ⓓ Ⓔ
4. Ⓐ Ⓑ Ⓒ Ⓓ Ⓔ		29. Ⓐ Ⓑ Ⓒ Ⓓ Ⓔ
5. Ⓐ Ⓑ Ⓒ Ⓓ Ⓔ		30. Ⓐ Ⓑ Ⓒ Ⓓ Ⓔ
6. Ⓐ Ⓑ Ⓒ Ⓓ Ⓔ		31. Ⓐ Ⓑ Ⓒ Ⓓ Ⓔ
7. Ⓐ Ⓑ Ⓒ Ⓓ Ⓔ		32. Ⓐ Ⓑ Ⓒ Ⓓ Ⓔ
8. Ⓐ Ⓑ Ⓒ Ⓓ Ⓔ		33. Ⓐ Ⓑ Ⓒ Ⓓ Ⓔ
9. Ⓐ Ⓑ Ⓒ Ⓓ Ⓔ		34. Ⓐ Ⓑ Ⓒ Ⓓ Ⓔ
10. Ⓐ Ⓑ Ⓒ Ⓓ Ⓔ		35. Ⓐ Ⓑ Ⓒ Ⓓ Ⓔ
11. Ⓐ Ⓑ Ⓒ Ⓓ Ⓔ		36. Ⓐ Ⓑ Ⓒ Ⓓ Ⓔ
12. Ⓐ Ⓑ Ⓒ Ⓓ Ⓔ		37. Ⓐ Ⓑ Ⓒ Ⓓ Ⓔ
13. Ⓐ Ⓑ Ⓒ Ⓓ Ⓔ		38. Ⓐ Ⓑ Ⓒ Ⓓ Ⓔ
14. Ⓐ Ⓑ Ⓒ Ⓓ Ⓔ		39. Ⓐ Ⓑ Ⓒ Ⓓ Ⓔ
15. Ⓐ Ⓑ Ⓒ Ⓓ Ⓔ		40. Ⓐ Ⓑ Ⓒ Ⓓ Ⓔ
16. Ⓐ Ⓑ Ⓒ Ⓓ Ⓔ		41. Ⓐ Ⓑ Ⓒ Ⓓ Ⓔ
17. Ⓐ Ⓑ Ⓒ Ⓓ Ⓔ		42. Ⓐ Ⓑ Ⓒ Ⓓ Ⓔ
18. Ⓐ Ⓑ Ⓒ Ⓓ Ⓔ		43. Ⓐ Ⓑ Ⓒ Ⓓ Ⓔ
19. Ⓐ Ⓑ Ⓒ Ⓓ Ⓔ		44. Ⓐ Ⓑ Ⓒ Ⓓ Ⓔ
20. Ⓐ Ⓑ Ⓒ Ⓓ Ⓔ		45. Ⓐ Ⓑ Ⓒ Ⓓ Ⓔ
21. Ⓐ Ⓑ Ⓒ Ⓓ Ⓔ		46. Ⓐ Ⓑ Ⓒ Ⓓ Ⓔ
22. Ⓐ Ⓑ Ⓒ Ⓓ Ⓔ		47. Ⓐ Ⓑ Ⓒ Ⓓ Ⓔ
23. Ⓐ Ⓑ Ⓒ Ⓓ Ⓔ		48. Ⓐ Ⓑ Ⓒ Ⓓ Ⓔ
24. Ⓐ Ⓑ Ⓒ Ⓓ Ⓔ		49. Ⓐ Ⓑ Ⓒ Ⓓ Ⓔ
25. Ⓐ Ⓑ Ⓒ Ⓓ Ⓔ		50. Ⓐ Ⓑ Ⓒ Ⓓ Ⓔ

ARITHMETIC DIAGNOSTIC TEST

This diagnostic test is designed to help you determine your strengths and your weaknesses in arithmetic. Follow the directions for each part and check your answers.

50 Questions

DIRECTIONS: Choose the correct answer for each of the following problems. Fill in each answer on the answer sheet.

1. What part of three fourths is one tenth?

    (A) $^1/_8$ (B) $^{15}/_2$ (C) $^2/_{15}$

    (D) $^3/_{40}$ (E) None of the above

2. One number is 2 more than 3 times another. Their sum is 22. Find the numbers.

    (A) 8, 14   (B) 2, 20   (C) 5, 17

    (D) 4, 18   (E) 10, 12

3. What is the median of the following group of scores?

    27, 27, 26, 26, 26, 26, 18, 13, 36, 36, 30, 30, 30, 27, 29

    (A) 30   (B) 26   (C) 25.4

    (D) 27   (E) 36

4. What percent of 260 is 13?

    (A) .05%   (B) 5%   (C) 50%

    (D) .5%   (E) 20%

5. Subtract: $4 \, ^1/_3 - 1 \, ^5/_6$

    (A) $3 \, ^2/_3$ (B) $2^1/_2$ (C) $3^1/_2$

    (D) $2 \, ^1/_6$ (E) None of the above

6.   What is the product of $(\sqrt{3}+6)$ and $(\sqrt{3}-2)$?

   (A) $9+4\sqrt{3}$ (B) -9 (C) $-9+4\sqrt{3}$

   (D) $-9+2\sqrt{3}$ (E) 9

7.   The number missing in the series, 2, 6, 12, 20, x, 42, 56 is:

   (A) 36   (B) 24   (C) 30

   (D) 38   (E) 40

8.   What is the value of the following expression: $\dfrac{1}{1+\dfrac{1}{1+\dfrac{1}{4}}}$

   (A) $^9/_5$ (B) $^5/_9$ (C) $^1/_2$

   (D) 2   (E) 4

9.   Which of the following has the smallest value?

   (A) $^1/_{0.2}$ (B) $^{0.1}/_2$ (C) $^{0.2}/_1$

   (D) $^{0.2}/_{0.1}$ (E) $^2/_{0.1}$

10. Which is the smallest number?

   (A) $5 \cdot 10^{-3} / 3 \cdot 10^{-3}$ (B) $.3 / .2$

   (C) $.3 / 3 \cdot 10^{-3}$ (D) $5 \cdot 10^{-2} / .1$

   (E) $.3 / 3 \cdot 10^{-1}$

11. $10^3 + 10^5 =$

   (A) 10^8 (B) 10^{15} (C) 20^8

   (D) 2^{15} (E) 101,000

12. How many digits are in the standard numeral for $2^{31} \cdot 5^{27}$?

   (A) 31   (B) 29   (C) 28

   (D) 26   (E) 25

13. $475,826 \cdot 521,653 + 524,174 \cdot 521,653 =$

(A) 621,592,047,600   (B) 519,697,450,000

(C) 495,652,831,520   (D) 521,653,000,000

(E) 524,174,000,000

14. How many ways can you make change for a quarter?

(A) 8   (B) 9   (C) 10

(D) 12   (E) 14

15. The sixtieth digit in the decimal representation of $^1/_7$ is

(A) 1   (B) 4   (C) 2

(D) 5   (E) 7

16. What is the least prime number which is a divisor of $7^9 + 11^{25}$?

(A) 1   (B) 2   (C) 3

(D) 5   (E) $7^9 + 11^{25}$

17. Evaluate $10 - 5[2^3 + 27 \div 3 - 2(8 - 10)]$

(A) -95 (B) 105   (C) 65

(D) -55 (E) -85

18. Fifteen percent of what number is 60?

(A) 9   (B) 51   (C) 69

(D) 200   (E) 400

19. Which is the largest fraction: $^1/_5$, $^2/_9$, $^2/_{11}$, $^4/_{19}$, $^4/_{17}$?

(A) $^1/_5$ (B) $^2/_9$ (C) $^2/_{11}$

(D) $^4/_{19}$ (E) $^4/_{17}$

20. How many of the scores 10, 20, 30, 35, 55 are larger than their arithmetic mean score?

(A) None   (B) One   (C) Two

(D) Three   (E) Four

21. Evaluate $\left(2^{1-\sqrt{3}}\right)^{1+\sqrt{3}}$

    (A) 4   (B) – 4   (C) 16

    (D) $^{1}/_{2}$ (E) $^{1}/_{4}$

22. $\dfrac{2^{100} + 2^{98}}{2^{100} - 2^{98}} =$

    (A) 2^{198} (B) 2^{99} (C) 64

    (D) 4   (E) $^{5}/_{3}$

23. What is the least natural number which is a multiple of each number from 1 to 10?

    (A) 3,628,800   (B) 5040   (C) 840

    (D) 1,260   (E) 2,520

24. If in $\triangle ABC$, $AB = BC$ and angle A has measure 46°, then angle B has measure

    (A) 46°   (B) 92°   (C) 88°

    (D) 56°   (E) 23°

25. What is the last digit in the number 3^{2000}?

    (A) 0   (B) 1   (C) 3

    (D) 7   (E) 9

26. In the set of integers 1000, 1001, 1002, ..., 9998, 9999, how many of the numbers do not contain the digit 5?

    (A) 6,561   (B) 5,000   (C) 9,000

    (D) 4,500   (E) 5,832

27. $15,561 + 25 + 9,439 + 25 =$

    (A) 997   (B) 1,000   (C) 1,002

    (D) 1,005   (E) 1,005.08

28. What is the units digit for 4^{891}?

    (A) 4   (B) 6   (C) 8

    (D) 0   (E) 1

29. $\dfrac{1}{1\cdot2}+\dfrac{1}{2\cdot3}+\dfrac{1}{3\cdot4}+\ldots+\dfrac{1}{99\cdot100} =$

    (A) $^{49}/_{50}$ (B) $^{74}/_{75}$ (C) $^{98}/_{99}$

    (D) $^{99}/_{100}$ (E) $^{101}/_{100}$

30. $1 + 2 + 3 + 4 + \ldots + 99 =$

    (A) 4,700   (B) 4,750   (C) 4,850

    (D) 4,900   (E) 4,950

31. The decimal $.24\overline{24}$ expressed as a fraction is

    (A) $^{8}/_{33}$ (B) $^{6}/_{25}$ (C) $^{1}/_{4}$

    (D) $^{303}/_{1250}$ (E) $^{121}/_{500}$

32. $\dfrac{2^{-4} + 2^{-1}}{2^{-3}}$

    (A) $9/2^7$ (B) $9/2^{-1}$ (C) $1/2$

    (D) 2^{-3} (E) $9/2$

33. What is the smallest positive number that leaves a remainder of 2 when the number is divided by 3, 4 or 5?

    (A) 22   (B) 42   (C) 62

    (D) 122   (E) 182

34. What part of three eights is one tenth?

    (A) $^{1}/_{8}$ (B) $^{15}/_{2}$ (C) $^{4}/_{15}$

    (D) $^{3}/_{40}$ (E) None of the above

35. $(^{2}/_{3}) + (^{5}/_{9}) =$

    (A) $^{7}/_{12}$ (B) $^{11}/_{9}$ (C) $^{7}/_{3}$

    (D) $^{7}/_{9}$ (E) $^{11}/_{3}$

36. Add $^3/_6 + ^2/_6$

    (A) $^1/_{12}$ (B) $^5/_6$ (C) $^5/_{12}$

    (D) $^8/_9$ (E) $^9/_8$

37. Change 125.937% to a decimal

    (A) 1.25937   (B) 12.5937   (C) 125.937

    (D) 1259.37   (E) 12593.7

38. What is the ratio of 8 feet to 28 inches?

    (A) $^1/_7$ (B) $^7/_1$ (C) $^{24}/_7$

    (D) $^6/_7$ (E) $^7/_2$

39. Using order of operations, solve: 3 * 6 – 12/2 =

    (A) – 9   (B) 3   (C) 6

    (D) 12   (E) 18

40. The most economical price among the following prices is

    (A) 10 oz. for 16¢   (B) 2 oz. for 3¢

    (C) 4 oz. for 7¢   (D) 20 oz. for 34¢

    (E) 8 oz. for 13¢

41. Change $4^5/_6$ to an improper fraction.

    (A) $^5/_{24}$ (B) $^9/_6$ (C) $^{29}/_6$

    (D) $^{30}/_4$ (E) $^{120}/_6$

42. If the sum of four consecutive integers is 226, then the smallest of these numbers is

    (A) 55   (B) 56   (C) 57

    (D) 58   (E) 59

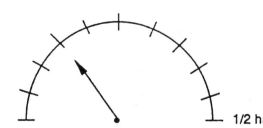

1/2 hr.

43. How much time is left on the parking meter shown on the previous page?

    (A) 8 minutes   (B) 9 minutes   (C) 10 minutes

    (D) 12 minutes   (E) 15 minutes

44. $15,561 + 25 - 9,561 + 25 =$

    (A) 997   (B) 240   (C) 1,002

    (D) 1,005   (E) 1,005.08

45. $4\% \cdot 4\% =$

    (A) 0.0016%   (B) 0.16%   (C) 1.6%

    (D) 16%   (E) 160%

46. Which of the following numbers is not between $.\overline{85}$ and $.\overline{86}$?

    (A) $.\overline{851}$ (B) $.\overline{859}$ (C) .859

    (D) $.\overline{861}$ (E) .861

47. Change the fraction $^7/_8$ to a decimal.

    (A) .666   (B) .75   (C) .777

    (D) .875   (E) 1.142

48. $\sqrt{75} - 3\sqrt{48} + \sqrt{147} =$

    (A) $3\sqrt{3}$ (B) $7\sqrt{3}$ (C) 0

    (D) 3   (E) $\sqrt{3}$

49. The following ratio: 40 seconds : $1^1/_2$ minutes : $^1/_6$ hour, can be expressed in lowest terms as

    (A) $4:9:60$ (B) $4:9:6$ (C) $40:90:60$

    (D) $^2/_3 : 1^1/_2 : 10$ (E) $60:9:4$

50. Simplify $6\sqrt{7} + 4\sqrt{7} - \sqrt{5} + 5\sqrt{7}$

    (A) $10\sqrt{7}$ (B) $15\sqrt{7} - \sqrt{5}$ (C) $15\sqrt{21} - \sqrt{5}$

    (D) $15\sqrt{16}$ (E) 60

ARITHMETIC DIAGNOSTIC TEST

ANSWER KEY

1. (C)	11. (E)	21. (E)	31. (A)	41. (C)
2. (C)	12. (B)	22. (E)	32. (E)	42. (A)
3. (D)	13. (D)	23. (E)	33. (C)	43. (B)
4. (B)	14. (D)	24. (C)	34. (C)	44. (B)
5. (B)	15. (E)	25. (B)	35. (B)	45. (B)
6. (C)	16. (B)	26. (E)	36. (B)	46. (A)
7. (C)	17. (A)	27. (B)	37. (A)	47. (D)
8. (B)	18. (E)	28. (A)	38. (C)	48. (C)
9. (B)	19. (E)	29. (D)	39. (D)	49. (A)
10. (D)	20. (C)	30. (E)	40. (B)	50. (B)

DETAILED EXPLANATIONS
OF ANSWERS

1.   **(C)**   First, observe that three fourths is $^3/_4$ and one tenth is $^1/_{10}$. Let x be the unknown part which must be found. Then, one can write from the statement of the problem that the x part of three fourths is given by:

$$\frac{3}{4}x.$$

The equation for the problem is given by

$$\frac{3}{4}x = \frac{1}{10}.$$

Multiplying both sides of the equation by the reciprocal of $^3/_4$ one obtains the following:

$$\frac{4}{3}\frac{3}{4}x = \frac{4}{3}\frac{1}{10} \text{ or } x = \frac{4}{30} \text{ or } x = \frac{2}{15}$$

which is choice (C).

   Response (D) is obtained by incorrectly finding the product of $^3/_4$ and $^1/_{10}$ to be the unknown part. Response (B) is obtained by dividing $^3/_4$ by $^1/_{10}$.

2.   **(C)**   Based on the information given in the first sentence of the problem one needs to first represent the unknown numbers. So let x be a number. Then, the other number is given by $3x + 2$, which is two more than 3 times the first number. So the two numbers are:

x and $3x + 2$.

   Next, form an equation by adding the two numbers and setting the sum equal to 22 and then solve the equation for the two numbers.

$$\begin{aligned} x + 3x + 2 &= 22 \\ 4x + 2 &= 22 \\ 4x &= 20 \\ x &= 5, \end{aligned}$$

one of the numbers. The other number is given by

$$3x + 2 = 3(5) + 2 = 15 + 2 = 17,$$

the other number. Hence, answer choice (C) is correct. The other answer choices fail to satisfy the equation $x + 3x + 2 = 22$.

3.   **(D)**   The median is defined as the middle score or value when a se-
quence of numbers is arranged in either ascending or descending order. Thus,
when this is done the middle score is 27. The answer choice (B) is the mode, the
most frequent score. The other answer choices do not represent the median according to its definition.

4.   **(B)**   In order to find what percent of 260 is 13 one needs only to form
the following equation:

$$x\%(260) = 13$$

$$\frac{x(260)}{100} = 13$$

$$260x = 13(100)$$

$$x = 1300/260 = 5 \text{ percent} = 5\%.$$

The other answer choices are incorrect, however. Response (A) is obtained by
dividing 13 by 260 and attaching the percent symbol. Response (D) is obtained
by again dividing 13 by 260, moving the decimal point one place to the right and
attaching the percent symbol. Response (E) is obtained by dividing 260 by 13
and attaching the percent sign. Finally, response (C) is absurd because 50% of
260 is half of 260 which is 130 or 10 times 13.

5.   **(B)**

$$4\frac{1}{3} - 1\frac{5}{6} = 4\frac{2}{6} - 1\frac{5}{6}$$

$$= 3\frac{2+6}{6} - 1\frac{5}{6}$$

$$= 3\frac{8}{6} - 1\frac{5}{6}$$

$$= 2\frac{3}{6} = 2\frac{1}{2}.$$

6.   **(C)**   Observe that to find the product the following multiplications
should be done.

$$(\sqrt{3} + 6)(\sqrt{3} - 2) = \sqrt{3}(\sqrt{3} - 2) + 6(\sqrt{3} - 2)$$

$$= 3 - 2\sqrt{3} + 6\sqrt{3} - 12$$

$$= -9 + 4\sqrt{3}.$$

7.   **(C)**   The difference between the first two numbers is 4 (6 − 2); the
difference between the second and third numbers is 6 (12 − 6) which is two more
than the first difference; the difference between the third and fourth numbers is

8 (20 – 12) which is two more than the second difference; the difference between the fourth and fifth numbers is 10 ($x - 20$). Thus, the value of x is given by $x - 20 = 10$. Solving for x yields $x = 30$. So, the correct answer choice is (C). Similar analysis of each of the other choices will fail to satisfy the missing value of x such that it is a consistant distance in relation to the other numbers in the series.

8. **(B)**

$$\frac{1}{1+\dfrac{1}{1+\dfrac{1}{1+\dfrac{1}{4}}}} = \frac{1}{1+\dfrac{1}{4+1}} = \frac{1}{1+\dfrac{4}{5}} = \frac{5}{5+4} = \frac{5}{9}.$$

9. **(B)**   Note that $\dfrac{.1}{2} = \dfrac{.1 \times 10}{2 \times 10} = \dfrac{1}{20}$ for response (B).

For Choice (A), $\dfrac{1}{.2} = \dfrac{1 \times 10}{.2 \times 10} = \dfrac{10}{2} = 5$ which is larger than $1/20$.

For Choice (C), $\dfrac{.2}{1} = \dfrac{.2 \times 10}{1 \times 10} = \dfrac{2}{10} = \dfrac{1}{5}$ which is larger than $1/20$.

For Choice (D), $\dfrac{.2}{.1} = \dfrac{.2 \times 10}{.1 \times 10} = \dfrac{2}{1} = 2$ which is larger than $1/20$.

For Choice (E), $\dfrac{2}{.1} = \dfrac{2 \times 10}{.1 \times 10} = \dfrac{20}{1} = 20$ which is larger than $1/20$.

10. **(D)**   To find the smallest number we will calculate each one

(A) $\dfrac{5 \cdot 10^{-3}}{3 \cdot 10^{-3}} = \dfrac{5 \cdot 10^{-3}}{3 \cdot 10^{-3}} = \dfrac{5}{3} = 1.6$

(B) $\dfrac{.3}{.2} = \dfrac{.3}{.2} = 1.5$

(C) $\dfrac{.3}{3} \cdot 10^{-3} = \dfrac{.3}{3 \cdot 10^{-3}} = \dfrac{.3 \cdot 10^3}{3} = \dfrac{3 \cdot 10^2}{3} = 100$

(D) $5 \cdot \dfrac{10^{-2}}{.1} = \dfrac{5 \cdot 10^{-2}}{.1} = \dfrac{5 \cdot 10^{-2}}{10^{-1}} = 5 \cdot 10^{-1} = .5$

(E) $\dfrac{.3}{3} \cdot 10^{-1} = \dfrac{.3}{3 \cdot 10^{-1}} = \dfrac{.3 \cdot 10}{3} = \dfrac{3}{3} = 1$

The correct answer is (D).

11.   **(E)** $10^3 + 10^5 = 10^3 \cdot 1 + 10^3 \cdot 10^2$

$= 10^3 (1 + 10^2)$

$= 10^3 (101)$ or $10^3 = 1,000$ and $10^5 = 100,000$

$= 1,000 \cdot 101$ and thus $10^3 + 10^5 = 101,000$

$= 101,000.$

12.   **(B)** $2^{31} \cdot 5^{27} = 2^4 \cdot 2^{27} \cdot 5^{27}$

$= 2^4 (2 \cdot 5)^{27}$

$= 2^4 \cdot 10^{27}$

Since $2^4 = 16$, the standard numeral for $2^4 \cdot 10^{27}$ is 16 followed by 27 zeros. Hence $2^{31} \cdot 5^{27}$ has 29 digits.

13.   **(D)**   Using the distributive property,

$475,826 \cdot 521,653 + 524,174 \cdot 521,653$

$= (475,826 + 524,174)521,653$

$= 1,000,000(521,653)$

$= 521,653,000,000.$

14.   **(D)**   The table below indicates the ways that change for a quarter can be made.

Dimes	Nickels	Pennies
2	1	0
2	0	5
1	3	0
1	2	5
1	1	10
1	0	15
0	5	0
0	4	5
0	3	10
0	2	15
0	1	20
0	0	25

15.   **(E)**   The decimal representation of $^1/_7$ is

.142857142857142857...,

and the digit in the 6th, 12th, 18th, ... 60th place is 7.

16.   **(B)**   Since 7^9 and 11^{25} are both odd numbers, their sum is even. Thus, 2 is a divisor of $7^9 + 11^{25}$. Also 2 is the smallest (least) prime.

17.   **(A)**   Remember the order of operation rules are PEMDAS, meaning parentheses, exponents, multiplication, division, addition, and subtraction. The correct solution is

$$10 - 5[8 + 9 - 2)(-2)] \Rightarrow 10 - 5(21) \Rightarrow 10 - 105 = -95.$$

Choice (B) comes from subtracting 10 and 5 before multiplying. $10 - 5 = 5$ and $5(21) = 105$.

Choice (C) comes from $17 - 4$ instead of $17 + 4$ inside the parentheses and also the mistake of subtracting $10 - 5$ first. This gives $5(13) = 65$.

Choice (D) comes from the mistake of $17 - 4$ without the additional mistake of subtracting $10 - 5$ first. This gives $10 - 5(13) = 10 - 65 = -55$.

Choice (E) comes from making $2^3 = 6$ instead of 8. This gives $10 - 5(19) = 10 - 95 = -85$.

18.   **(E)**   If X is the number, then $.15X = 60$. Therefore,

$$X = {}^{60}/_{.15} = 400.$$

19.   **(E)**   Since $^1/_5 = {}^2/_{10}$, $^2/_9$ is larger than either $^1/_5$ or $^2/_{11}$. Also $^4/_{17}$ is larger than $^4/_{19}$. Now $^2/_9 = {}^4/_{18}$ so that $^4/_{17}$ is larger than the two.

20.   **(C)**   The arithmetic mean of scores is

$$(10 + 20 + 30 + 35 + 55)/5 = 150/5 = 30.$$

Since only two scores, namely, 35 and 55 are larger than 30, the answer is (C).

21.   **(E)**

$$(1 - \sqrt{3})(1 + \sqrt{3}) = 1 - 3 = -2.$$

And $2^{-2} = \dfrac{1}{2^2} = \dfrac{1}{4}.$

Choice (A) comes from adding the exponents $1 - \sqrt{3} + 1 + \sqrt{3} = 2$, and $2^2 = 4$.

Choice (B) comes from incorrectly letting $2^{-2} = -4$.

Choice (C) comes from $2^{1+3} = 2^4 = 16$.

22.   **(E)**
$$\frac{2^{100} + 2^{98}}{2^{100} - 2^{98}} = \frac{2^{98}(2^2 + 1)}{2^{98}(2^2 - 1)}$$
$$= \frac{2^2 + 1}{2^2 - 1} = \frac{5}{3}.$$

23.   **(E)**   Notice the product below. Starting from the left, it is obvious that 2 and 3 are needed as factors. For the product to be a multiple of 4, two 2 factors are needed and that is the reason for the second 2 factor. Obviously, a factor of 5 is needed; but since 2 and 3 are already listed, the product is already a multiple of 6. A factor of 7 is needed, but only new factors of 2 and 3 are required to make the product a multiple of 8 and 9. Since 2 and 5 are already listed as factors, the product is already a multiple of 10.

$$2 \cdot 3 \cdot 2 \cdot 5 \cdot 7 \cdot 2 \cdot 3 = 2{,}520$$

24.   **(C)**   Since $AB = BC$, angle C has measure 46°. However, the sum of the measures of the angles of a tringle is 180° and $180 - (46 + 46) = 88$ so the measure of angle B is 88°.

25.   **(B)**   The last digit in the successive powers of 3 repeat at intervals of 4:

$$3^1 = 3,\ 3^5 = 243$$
$$3^2 = 9,\ 3^6 = 729$$
$$3^3 = 27,\ 3^7 = 2{,}187$$
$$3^4 = 81,\ 3^8 = 6{,}561.$$

The pattern is 3, 9, 7, 1, 3, 9, 7, 1, ... and since $2000 = 4(500)$, 3^{2000} has a last digit of 1.

Choice (A) comes from $3(2000) = 6000$.

Choices (C), (D), and (E), which are 3, 7, and 9, respectively are the other ending digits in the power of 3.

26.   **(E)**   For a 4-digit number, there are $9 \cdot 10 \cdot 10 \cdot 10$ possibilities because 0 may not be used for the thousands place but if the digit 5 is not allowed, then there are $8 \cdot 9 \cdot 9 \cdot 9 = 5{,}832$ possibilities.

Choice (A) is $9 \cdot 9 \cdot 9 \cdot 9$.

Choice (C) is $9 \cdot 10 \cdot 10 \cdot 10$.

27.   **(B)**   When $c \neq 0$

$$a + c + b + c = (a + b) + c.$$

Thus

$$15{,}561 + 25 + 9{,}439 + 25 = (15{,}561 + (9{,}439) + 25$$
$$= 25{,}000 + 25$$
$$= 1{,}000.$$

28.   **(A)**   When n is odd, the units digit for 4^n is 4, and when n is even, the units digit for $4n$ is 6.

29.   **(D)**

$$\frac{1}{1\cdot2}+\frac{1}{2\cdot3}=\frac{1}{2}+\frac{1}{6} \qquad \frac{1}{1\cdot2}+\frac{1}{2\cdot3}+\frac{1}{3\cdot4}=\frac{1}{2}+\frac{1}{6}+\frac{1}{12}$$

$$=\frac{2}{3} \qquad\qquad\qquad =\frac{3}{4}$$

$$\frac{1}{1\cdot2}+\frac{1}{2\cdot3}+\frac{1}{3\cdot4}+\frac{1}{4\cdot5}=\frac{1}{2}+\frac{1}{6}+\frac{1}{12}+\frac{1}{20}$$

$$=\frac{4}{5}$$

and $$\frac{1}{1\cdot2}+\frac{1}{2\cdot3}+\frac{1}{3\cdot4}+\ldots+\frac{1}{99\cdot100}=\frac{99}{100}$$

30.   **(E)**

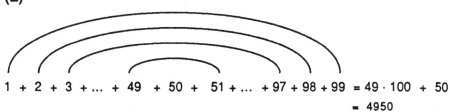

$$1 + 2 + 3 + \ldots + 49 + 50 + 51 + \ldots + 97 + 98 + 99 = 49\cdot100 + 50$$
$$= 4950$$

31.   **(A)**   Let $.24\overline{24}=X$. Then,

$$100X = 100(.24\overline{24}) = 24.\overline{24} = 24.24\overline{24}.$$

It follows that

$$100X - X = 24.2424 - .24\overline{24} = 24,$$

so that $X = {}^{24}/_{99} = {}^{8}/_{33}.$

32.   **(E)**

$$\frac{2^{-4}+2^{-1}}{2^{-3}} = \frac{\dfrac{1}{2^4}+\dfrac{1}{2}}{\dfrac{1}{2^3}} = \frac{2^4\left(\dfrac{1}{2^4}+\dfrac{1}{2}\right)}{2^4\dfrac{1}{2^3}} = \frac{1+2^3}{2} = \frac{9}{2}.$$

33.   **(C)**   First find the least common multiple (LCM) of 3, 4, and 5, which is simply

$$3 \times 4 \times 5 = 60.$$

Since 3 divides 60, 4 divides 60, and 5 divides 60, then one needs only to add 2 to 60 in order to guarantee that the remainder in each case will be 2 when 3, 4, and 5, respectively, are divided into 62.

34.   **(C)**   First, observe that three eights is $3/8$ and one tenth is $1/10$. Let x be the unknown part which must be found. Then, one can write from the statement of the problem that the x part of three eighths is given by:

$$\frac{3}{8}x.$$

The equation for the problem is given by

$$\frac{3}{8}x = \frac{1}{10}.$$

Multiplying both sides of the equation by the reciprocal of $3/8$ one obtains the following:

$$\frac{8}{3}\frac{3}{8}x = \frac{8}{3}\frac{1}{10} \quad \text{or} \quad x = \frac{8}{30} \quad \text{or} \quad x = \frac{4}{15}$$

which is choice (C).

Response (D) is obtained by incorrectly finding the product of $3/4$ and $1/10$ to be the unknown part. Response (B) is obtained by dividing $3/4$ by $1/10$.

35.   **(B)**   A common denominator is needed to add fractions. The least common denominator in this problem is 9 since the smallest number that both 3 and 9 will divide into is 9. If the denominator of $2/3$ is multiplied by 3 then the numerator must also be multiplied by 3. Thus

$$(2 \times 3) / (3 \times 3) = 6/9.$$

Adding the numerators and using the common denominator,

$$(6/9) + (5/9) = (6 + 5)/9 = 11/9.$$

36.   **(B)**   To add fractions with a common denominator, add the numerators.

$$3 + 2 = 5$$

Write the sum over the common denominator. The correct answer is $5/6$.

37.   **(A)**   To change percent to a decimal, drop the percent sign and move the decimal point two place values to the left. The correct answer is 1.25937.

38.   **(C)**   Units of measurement must be the same to create a ratio. Multiply 8

* 12 to find the number of inches in 8 feet which is 96. The ratio of 96 to 28 is 96/28. Find a common factor of 96 and 28, which is 4. Divide 96 by 4, which is 24, and 28 by 4, which is 7. The correct answer is 24/7.

39.   **(D)**   In order of operations, do all multiplication and division from left to right first. Next, do all addition and subtraction from left to right.

$3 * 6 - 12/2$ multiply 3 times 6, divide 12 by 2

$18 - 6$ subtract 6 from 18

12.

40.   **(B)**   This problem can be solved as follows:

1.   Divide each price by the number of ounces in each price to obtain the following prices per ounce for the given prices in answer choices (A) through (E):

$$(A)\frac{16}{10}\text{¢, } (B)\frac{3}{2}\text{¢, } (C)\frac{7}{4}\text{¢, } (D)\frac{34}{20}\text{¢, } (E)\frac{13}{8}\text{¢}$$

2.   Change each of the prices per ounce obtained in step (1) above to an equivalent fraction having a denominator equal to the least common denominator, 40, we obtain,

$$(A)\frac{16}{10} = \frac{64}{40}; (B)\frac{3}{2} = \frac{60}{40}; (C)\frac{7}{4} = \frac{70}{40}; (D)\frac{34}{20} = \frac{68}{40}; \text{ and } (E)\frac{13}{8} = \frac{65}{40}.$$

Since the smallest of the resulting fractions in step (2) is $^{60}/_{40}$, it follows that the most economical price among the given prices is 2 oz. for 3¢.

41.   **(C)**   To change a mixed number to an improper fraction, multiply the whole number (4) by the denominator (6) of the fraction (4 times 6 is 24). Add the numerator (5) to the product (24). Write the sum (29) over the denominator of the fraction, $^{29}/_6$.

42.   **(A)**   If the smallest number is X, then

$$X + (X + 1) + (X + 2) + (X + 3) = 226,$$

giving

$$4X + 6 = 226$$

Therefore

$$4X = 220, \text{ or, } X = 55.$$

43.   **(B)**   The meter shows that $^3/_{10}$ of the total time on the meter is left. However, this is a $^1/_2$-hour meter. Since

$$^3/_{10} \cdot ^1/_2 = ^3/_{20},$$

this means that there is $^3/_{20}$ of an hour left on the meter, and $^3/_{20}$ of an hour is 9 minutes.

44.   **(B)**   When $c \neq 0$

$$a + c - b + c = (a - b) + c.$$

Thus,

$$15{,}561 + 25 - 9{,}561 + 25 = (15{,}561 - 9{,}561) + 25$$
$$= 6{,}000 + 25$$
$$= 240.$$

45.   **(B)**

$$4\% \cdot 4\% = .04 \cdot .04$$
$$= .0016$$
$$= .16\%$$

46.   **(A)**   Since $.\overline{85} = .858585 \ldots$ and

$.\overline{851} = .851851851 \ldots ,$

$.\overline{851} < .\overline{85} < .\overline{86}$

47.   **(D)**   To change a fraction to a decimal, divide the numerator (7) by the denominator (8)

$8 + 7.$

Add a decimal point after the 7 and necessary zeros.

48.   **(C)**   Certainly, the easiest and the most direct way to solve this problem is to perform the indicated operations.
    Performing the indicated operations yields,

$$\sqrt{75} - 3\sqrt{48} + \sqrt{147} = \sqrt{(25)(3)} - 3\sqrt{(16)(3)} + \sqrt{(49)(3)}$$
$$= 5\sqrt{3} - 3(4)\sqrt{3} + 7\sqrt{3}$$
$$= 5\sqrt{3} - 12\sqrt{3} + 7\sqrt{3}$$
$$= (5 - 12 + 7)\sqrt{3}$$
$$= (12 - 12)\sqrt{3}$$
$$= 0.\sqrt{3}$$
$$= 0$$

49.   **(A)**   Since 40 seconds is $^2/_3$ minute and $^1/_6$ hour is ten minutes, the ratio is

$^2/_3 : 1.5 : 10.$

Multiplying by 6 yields

$6(^2/_3) : 6(3/2) : 6(10)$ or $4 : 9 : 60.$

Thus the correct choice is (A).

50.   **(B)**   To combine radicals, the radicands (the value under the radical sign) must be equal. The distributive property allows you to add and subtract radicals.

$$\left(6\sqrt{7} + 4\sqrt{7}\right) - \sqrt{5} + 5\sqrt{7}$$
$$(6+4)\sqrt{7} - \sqrt{5} + 5\sqrt{7}$$
$$10\sqrt{7} - \sqrt{5} + 5\sqrt{7}$$
$$(10+5)\sqrt{7} - \sqrt{5}$$
$$15\sqrt{7} - \sqrt{5}$$

ARITHMETIC REVIEW

1. Integers and Real Numbers

Most of the numbers used in algebra belong to a set called the **real numbers** or **reals**. This set can be represented graphically by the real number line.

Given the number line below, we arbitrarily fix a point and label it with the number 0. In a similar manner, we can label any point on the line with one of the real numbers, depending on its position relative to 0. Numbers to the right of zero are positive, while those to the left are negative. Value increases from left to right, so that if *a* is to the right of *b*, it is said to be greater than *b*.

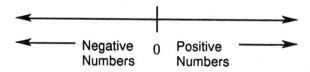

If we now divide the number line into equal segments, we can label the points on this line with real numbers. For example, the point 2 lengths to the left of zero is − 2, while the point 3 lengths to the right of zero is + 3 (the + sign is usually assumed, so + 3 is written simply as 3). The number line now looks like this:

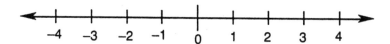

These boundary points represent the subset of the reals known as the **integers**. The set of integers is made up of both the positive and negative whole numbers: {... − 4, − 3, − 2, − 1, 0, 1, 2, 3, 4, ...}. Some subsets of integers are:

Natural Numbers or Positive Numbers—the set of integers starting with 1 and increasing: $\mathcal{N} = \{1, 2, 3, 4, ...\}$.

Whole Numbers—the set of integers starting with 0 and increasing: $\mathcal{W} = \{0, 1, 2, 3, ...\}$.

Negative Numbers—the set of integers starting with − 1 and decreasing: $\mathcal{Z} = \{− 1, − 2, − 3 ...\}$.

Prime Numbers—the set of positive integers greater than 1 that are divisible only by 1 and themselves: {2, 3, 5, 7, 11, ...}.

Even Integers—the set of integers divisible by 2: {..., − 4, − 2, 0, 2, 4, 6, ...}.

Odd Integers—the set of integers not divisible by 2: { ..., − 3, − 1, 1, 3, 5, 7, ...}.

PROBLEM

> Classify each of the following numbers into as many different sets as possible. Example: real, integer ...
>
> (1)   0   (2)   9   (3) $\sqrt{6}$
>
> (4) $\frac{1}{2}$ (5) $\frac{2}{3}$ (6)   1.5

SOLUTION

(1)   Zero is a real number and an integer.

(2)   9 is a real, natural number, and an integer.

(3) $\sqrt{6}$ is a real number.

(4) $\frac{1}{2}$ is a real number.

(5) $\frac{2}{3}$ is a real number.

(6)   1.5 is a real number.

ABSOLUTE VALUE

The **absolute value** of a number is represented by two vertical lines around the number, and is equal to the given number, regardless of sign.

The absolute value of a real number A is defined as follows:

$$|A| = \begin{cases} A \text{ if } A \geq 0 \\ -A \text{ if } A < 0 \end{cases}$$

EXAMPLE

$|5| = 5, |-8| = -(-8) = 8.$

Absolute values follow the given rules:

(A) $|-A| = |A|$

(B) $|A| \geq 0$, equality holding only if $A = 0$

(C) $\left|\dfrac{A}{B}\right| = \dfrac{|A|}{|B|}, B \neq 0$

(D) $|AB| = |A| \times |B|$

(E) $|A|^2 = A^2$

Absolute value can also be expressed on the real number line as the distance of the point represented by the real number from the point labeled 0.

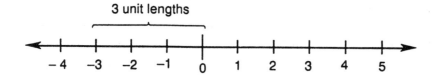

So $|-3| = 3$ because -3 is 3 units to the left of 0.

PROBLEM

Classify each of the following statements as true or false. If it is false, explain why.

(1) $|-120| > 1$

(2) $|4-12| = |4| - |12|$

(3) $|4 - 9| = 9 - 4$

(4) $|12-3| = 12 - 3$

(5) $|-12a| = 12|a|$

SOLUTION

(1) True

(2) False, $|4 - 12| = |4| - |12|$

$\qquad |-8| = 4 - 12$

$\qquad 8 \neq -8$

In general, $|a + b| \neq |a| + |b|$

(3) True

(4) True

(5) True

PROBLEM

Calculate the value of each of the following expressions:

(1) $||2-5| + 6 - 14|$

(2) $|-5| \cdot |4| + \dfrac{|-12|}{4}$

SOLUTION

Before solving this problem, one must remember the order of operations: parenthesis, multiplication and division, addition and subtraction.

(1) $||-3| + 6 - 14| = |3 + 6 - 14| = |9 - 14| = |-5| = 5$

(2) $(5 \times 4) + {}^{12}/_4 = 20 + 3 = 23$

PROBLEM

Find the absolute value for each of the following:

(1)   zero   (3) $-\pi$

(2)   4   (4) a, where a is a real number

SOLUTION

(1) $|0| = 0$

(2) $|4| = 4$

(3) $|-\pi| = \pi$

(4)   for $a > 0 \; |a| = a$

  for $a = 0 \; |a| = 0$

  for $a < 0 \; |a| = -a$

$$\text{i.e., } |a| = \begin{cases} a \text{ if } a > 0 \\ 0 \text{ if } a = 0 \\ -a \text{ if } a < 0 \end{cases}$$

POSITIVE AND NEGATIVE NUMBERS

A)   **To add two numbers with like signs,** add their absolute values and write the sum with the common sign. So,

$$6 + 2 = 8, (-6) + (-2) = -8$$

B)   **To add two numbers with unlike signs,** find the difference between their absolute values, and write the result with the sign of the number with the greater absolute value. So,

$$(-4) + 6 = 2, 15 + (-19) = -4$$

C)   **To subtract a number b from another number a,** change the sign of b and add to a. Examples:

$$10 - (3) = 10 + (-3) = 7 \tag{1}$$

$$2 - (-6) = 2 + 6 = 8 \tag{2}$$

$$(-5) - (-2) = -5 + (+2) = -3 \tag{3}$$

D)   **To multiply (or divide) two numbers having like signs,** multiply (or divide) their absolute values and write the result with a positive sign. Examples:

$$(5)(3) = 15 \tag{1}$$

$$-6/-3 = 2 \tag{2}$$

E)   **To multiply (or divide) two numbers having unlike signs,** multiply (or divide) their absolute values and write the result with a negative sign. Examples:

$$(-2)(8) = -16 \tag{1}$$

$$9/-3 = -3 \tag{2}$$

According to the law of signs for real numbers, the square of a positive or negative number is always positive. This means that it is impossible to take the square root of a negative number in the real number system.

Drill 1: Integers and Real Numbers

Addition

1.   Simplify $4 + (-7) + 2 + (-5)$.

(A) -6 (B) -4 (C)   0   (D)   6   (E)   18

2.   Simplify $144 + (-317) + 213$.

(A) -357 (B) -40 (C)   40   (D)   357   (E)   674

3.   Simplify $|4 + (-3)| + |-2|$.

(A) -2 (B) -1 (C)   1   (D)   3   (E)   9

4.   What integer makes the equation $-13 + 12 + 7 + ? = 10$ a true statement?

(A) -22 (B) -10 (C)   4   (D)   6   (E)   10

5.   Simplify $4 + 17 + (-29) + 13 + (-22) + (-3)$.

(A) -44 (B) -20 (C)   23   (D)   34   (E)   78

Subtraction

6.   Simplify $319 - 428$.

(A) -111 (B) -109 (C) -99 (D)   109   (E)   747

7.   Simplify $91,203 - 37,904 + 1,073$.

(A)   54,372   (B)   64,701   (C)   128,034   (D)   129,107   (E)   130,180

8. Simplify $| 43 - 62 | - | - 17 - 3 |$.

(A) $- 39$ (B) $- 19$ (C) $- 1$ (D) 1   (E) 39

9. Simplify $- (- 4 - 7) + (- 2)$.

(A) $- 22$ (B) $- 13$ (C) $- 9$ (D) 7   (E) 9

10. In the Great Smoky Mountains National Park, Mt. Le Conte rises from 1,292 feet above sea level to 6,593 feet above sea level. How tall is Mt. Le Conte?

(A) 4,009 ft   (B) 5,301 ft   (C) 5,699 ft   (D) 6,464 ft   (E) 7,885 ft

Multiplication

11. Simplify $- 3 (- 18) (- 1)$.

(A) $- 108$ (B) $- 54$ (C) $- 48$ (D) 48   (E) 54

12. Simplify $| - 42 | * | 7 |$.

(A) $- 294$ (B) $- 49$ (C) $- 35$ (D) 284   (E) 294

13. Simplify $- 6 * 5 (- 10) (- 4) 0 * 2$.

(A) $- 2,400$ (B) $- 240$ (C) 0   (D) 280   (E) 2,700

14. Simplify $- | - 6 * 8 |$.

(A) $- 48$ (B) $- 42$ (C) 2   (D) 42   (E) 48

15. A city in Georgia had a record low temparature of –3°F one winter. During the same year, a city in Michigan experienced a record low that was nine times the record low set in Georgia. What was the record low in Michigan that year?

(A) $- 31°F$ (B) $- 27°F$ (C) $- 21°F$ (D) $- 12°F$ (E) $- 6°F$

Division

16. Simplify $- 24 + 8$.

(A) $- 4$ (B) $- 3$ (C) $- 2$ (D) 3   (E) 4

17. Simplify $(- 180) + (- 12)$.

(A) $- 30$ (B) $- 15$ (C) 1.5   (D) 15   (E) 216

18. Simplify $| - 76 | + | - 4 |$.

(A) $- 21$ (B) $- 19$ (C) 13   (D) 19   (E) 21.5

19.   Simplify $|216 \div (-6)|$.

(A) -36 (B) -12 (C) 36 (D) 38 (E) 43

20.   At the end of the year, a small firm has $2,996 in its account for bonuses. If the entire amount is equally divided among the 14 employees, how much does each one receive?

(A) $107   (B) $114   (C) $170   (D) $210   (E) $214

Order of Operations

21.   Simplify $\dfrac{4 + 8 * 2}{5 - 1}$

(A) 4   (B) 5   (C) 6   (D) 8   (E) 12

22. $96 \div 3 \div 4 + 2 =$

(A) 65   (B) 64   (C) 16   (D) 8   (E) 4

23. $3 + 4 * 2 - 6 \div 3 =$

(A) -1 (B) 5/3   (C) 8/3   (D) 9   (E) 12

24. $[(4 + 8) * 3] \div 9 =$

(A) 4   (B) 8   (C) 12   (D) 24   (E) 36

25. $18 \div 3 * 4 + 3 =$

(A) 3   (B) 5   (C) 10   (D) 22   (E) 28

26. $(29 - 17 + 4) \div 4 + |-2| =$

(A) $2^2/_3$ (B) 4   (C) $4^2/_3$ (D) 6   (E) 15

27. $(-3) * 5 - 20 \div 4 =$

(A) -75 (B) -20 (C) -10 (D) $-8^3/_4$ (E) 20

28. $\dfrac{11 * 2 + 2}{16 - 2 * 2} =$

(A) 11/16   (B) 1   (C) 2   (D) 3 2/3   (E) 4

29. $|-8 - 4| + 3 * 6 \div (-4) =$

(A) 20   (B) 26   (C) 32   (D) 62   (E) 212

30. $32 \div 2 + 4 - 15 \div 3 =$

(A) 0   (B) 7   (C) 15   (D) 23   (E) 63

2. Fractions

The fraction, *a/b*, where the **numerator** is *a* and the **denominator** is *b*, implies that *a* is being divided by *b*. The denominator of a fraction can never be zero since a number divided by zero is not defined. If the numerator is greater than the denominator, the fraction is called an **improper fraction**. A **mixed number** is the sum of a whole number and a fraction, i.e., $4^3/_8 = 4 + {}^3/_8$.

Operations with Fractions

A) **To change a mixed number to an improper fraction,** simply multiply the whole number by the denominator of the fraction and add the numerator. This product becomes the numerator of the result and the denominator remains the same. E.g.,

$$5\frac{2}{3} = \frac{(5 \cdot 3) + 2}{3} = \frac{15 + 2}{3} = \frac{17}{3}$$

To change an improper fraction to a mixed number, simply divide the numerator by the denominator. The remainder becomes the numerator of the fractional part of the mixed number, and the denominator remains the same. E.g.,

$$\frac{35}{4} = 35 \div 4 = 8\frac{3}{4}$$

To check your work, change your result back to an improper fraction to see if it matches the original fraction.

B) **To find the sum of two fractions having a common denominator,** simply add together the numerators of the given fractions and put this sum over the common denominator.

$$\frac{11}{3} + \frac{5}{3} = \frac{11 + 5}{3} = \frac{16}{3}$$

Similarly for subtraction,

$$\frac{11}{3} - \frac{5}{3} = \frac{11 - 5}{3} = \frac{6}{3} = 2$$

C) **To find the sum of the two fractions having different denominators,** it is necessary to find the **lowest common denominator,** (LCD) of the different denominators using a process called **factoring.**

To **factor** a number means to find two numbers that when multiplied together have a product equal to the original number. These two numbers are then said to be **factors** of the original number. E.g., the factors of 6 are

(1) 1 and 6 since $1 \times 6 = 6$.

(2) 2 and 3 since $2 \times 3 = 6$.

Every number is the product of itself and 1. A **prime factor** is a number that does not have any factors besides itself and 1. This is important when finding the LCD of two fractions having different denominators.

To find the LCD of $^{11}/_6$ and $^5/_{16}$, we must first find the prime factors of each of the two denominators.

$6 = 2 \times 3$

$16 = 2 \times 2 \times 2 \times 2$

$LCD = 2 \times 2 \times 2 \times 2 \times 3 = 48$

Note that we do not need to repeat the 2 that appears in both the factors of 6 and 16.

Once we have determined the LCD of the denominators, each of the fractions must be converted into equivalent fractions having the LCD as a denominator.

Rewrite 11/6 and 5/16 to have 48 as their denominators.

$6 \times ? = 48$ $\qquad\qquad$ $16 \times ? = 48$

$6 \times 8 = 48$ $\qquad\qquad$ $16 \times 3 = 48$

If the numerator and denominator of each fraction is multiplied (or divided) by the same number, the value of the fraction will not change. This is because a fraction b/b, b being any number, is equal to the multiplicative identity, 1.

Therefore,

$$\frac{11}{6} \cdot \frac{8}{8} = \frac{88}{48} \qquad\qquad \frac{5}{16} \cdot \frac{3}{3} = \frac{15}{48}$$

We may now find

$$\frac{11}{6} + \frac{5}{16} = \frac{88}{48} + \frac{15}{48} = \frac{103}{48}$$

Similarly for subtraction,

$$\frac{11}{6} - \frac{5}{16} = \frac{88}{48} - \frac{15}{48} = \frac{73}{48}$$

D)   **To find the product of two or more fractions,** simply multiply the numerators of the given fractions to find the numerator of the product and multiply the denominators of the given fractions to find the denominator of the product. E.g.,

$$\frac{2}{3} \cdot \frac{1}{5} \cdot \frac{4}{7} = \frac{2 \times 1 \times 4}{3 \times 5 \times 7} = \frac{8}{105}$$

E)   To find the quotient of two fractions, simply invert the divisor and multiply. E.g.,

$$\frac{8}{9} \div \frac{1}{3} = \frac{8}{9} \times \frac{3}{1} = \frac{24}{9} = \frac{8}{3}$$

F)   **To simplify a fraction** is to convert it into a form in which the numerator and denominator have no common factor other than 1, E.g.,

$$\frac{12}{18} = \frac{12 \div 6}{18 \div 6} = \frac{2}{3}$$

G)   A **complex fraction** is a fraction whose numerator and/or denominator is made up of fractions. To simplify the fraction, find the LCD of all the fractions. Multiply both the numerator and denominator by this number and simplify.

PROBLEM

> If $a = 4$ and $b = 7$, find the value of $\dfrac{a + \frac{a}{b}}{a - \frac{a}{b}}$

SOLUTION

By substitution,

$$\frac{a + \frac{a}{b}}{a - \frac{a}{b}} = \frac{4 + \frac{4}{7}}{4 - \frac{4}{7}}$$

In order to combine the terms, we must find the LCD of 1 and 7. Since both are prime factors, the LCD = 1 × 7 = 7.

Multiplying both numerator and denominator by 7, we get:

$$\frac{7(4 + \frac{4}{7})}{7(4 - \frac{4}{7})} = \frac{28 + 4}{28 - 4} = \frac{32}{24}$$

By dividing both numerator and denominator by 8, 32/24 can be reduced to 4/3.

Drill 2: Fractions

Fractions

<u>DIRECTIONS</u>: Add and write the answer in simplest form.

1.   5/12 + 3/12 =

(A) 5/24   (B)   1/3   (C)   8/12   (D)   2/3   (E)   1 1/3

2.   5/8 + 7/8 + 3/8 =

(A) 15/24   (B)   3/4   (C)   5/6   (D)   7/8   (E)   1 7/8

3.   131 2/15 + 28 3/15 =

(A) 159 1/6   (B)   159 1/5   (C)   159 1/3   (D)   159 1/2   (E)   159 3/5

4.   3 5/18 + 2 1/18 + 8 7/18 =

(A) 13 13/18 (B)   13 3/4   (C)   13 7/9   (D)   14 1/6   (E)   14 2/9

5.   17 9/20 + 4 3/20 + 8 11/20 =

(A) 29 23/60   (B)   29 23/20   (C)   30 3/20

(D) 30 1/5   (E)   30 3/5

Subtract Fractions with the Same Denominator

<u>DIRECTIONS</u>: Subtract and write the answer in simplest form.

6.   4 7/8 – 3 1/8 =

(A) 1 1/4   (B)   1 3/4   (C)   1 12/16 (D)   1 7/8   (E)   2

7.   132 5/12 – 37 3/12 =

(A) 94 1/6   (B)   95 1/12   (C)   95 1/6   (D)   105 1/6 (E)   169 2/3

8.   19 1/3 – 2 2/3 =

(A) 16 2/3   (B)   16 5/6   (C)   17 1/3   (D)   17 2/3   (E)   17 5/6

9.   8/21 – 5/21 =

(A) 1/21   (B)   1/7   (C)   3/21   (D)   2/7   (E)   3/7

10.   82 7/10 – 38 9/10 =

(A) 43 4/5   (B)   44 1/5   (C)   44 2/5   (D)   45 1/5   (E)   45 2/10

Finding the LCD

DIRECTIONS: Find the lowest common denominator of each group of fractions.

11. 2/3, 5/9, and 1/6.

(A) 9   (B) 18   (C) 27   (D) 54   (E) 162

12. 1/2, 5/6, and 3/4.

(A) 2   (B) 4   (C) 6   (D) 12   (E) 48

13. 7/16, 5/6, and 2/3.

(A) 3   (B) 6   (C) 12   (D) 24   (E) 48

14. 8/15, 2/5, and 12/25.

(A) 5   (B) 15   (C) 25   (D) 75   (E) 375

15. 2/3, 1/5, and 5/6.

(A) 15   (B) 30   (C) 48   (D) 90   (E) 120

16. 1/3, 9/42, and 4/21.

(A) 21   (B) 42   (C) 126   (D) 378   (E) 4,000

17. 4/9, 2/5, and 1/3.

(A) 15   (B) 17   (C) 27   (D) 45   (E) 135

18. 7/12, 11/36, and 1/9.

(A) 12   (B) 36   (C) 108   (D) 324   (E) 432

19. 3/7, 5/21, and 2/3.

(A) 21   (B) 42   (C) 31   (D) 63   (E) 441

20. 13/16, 5/8, and 1/4.

(A) 4   (B) 8   (C) 16   (D) 32   (E) 64

Adding Fractions with Different Denominators

DIRECTIONS: Add and write the answer in simplest form.

21. 1/3 + 5/12 =

(A) 2/5   (B) 1/2   (C) 9/12   (D) 3/4   (E) 1 1/3

22. 3 5/9 + 2 1/3 =

(A) 5 1/2   (B) 5 2/3   (C) 5 8/9   (D) 6 1/9   (E) 6 2/3

23. 12 9/16 + 17 3/4 + 8 1/8 =

(A) 37 7/16   (B) 38 7/16   (C) 38 1/2   (D) 38 2/3   (E) 39 3/16

24. 28 4/5 + 11 16/25 =

(A) 39 2/3   (B) 39 4/5   (C) 40 9/25   (D) 40 2/5   (E) 40 11/25

25. 2 1/8 + 1 3/16 + 5/12 =

(A) 3 35/48   (B) 3 3/4   (C) 3 19/24   (D) 3 13/16   (E) 4 1/12

Subtraction with Different Denominators

DIRECTIONS: Subtract and write the answer in simplest form.

26. 8 9/12 – 2 2/3 =

(A) 6 1/12   (B) 6 1/6   (C) 6 1/3   (D) 6 7/12   (E) 6 2/3

27. 185 11/15 – 107 2/5 =

(A) 77 2/15   (B) 78 1/5   (C) 78 3/10   (D) 78 1/3   (E) 78 9/15

28. 34 2/3 – 16 5/6 =

(A) 16   (B) 16 1/3   (C) 17 1/2   (D) 17   (E) 17 5/6

29. 3 11/48 – 2 3/16 =

(A) 47/48   (B) 1 1/48   (C) 1 1/24   (D) 1 8/48   (E) 1 7/24

30. 81 4/21 – 31 1/3 =

(A) 47 3/7   (B) 49 6/7   (C) 49 1/6   (D) 49 5/7   (E) 49 13/21

Multiplication

DIRECTIONS: Multiply and reduce the answer.

31. 2/3 * 4/5 =

(A) 6/8   (B) 3/4   (C) 8/15   (D) 10/12   (E) 6/5

32. 7/10 * 4/21 =

(A) 2/15   (B) 11/31   (C) 28/210   (D) 1/6   (E) 4/15

33. 5 1/3 * 3/8 =

(A) 4/11   (B) 2   (C) 8/5   (D) 5 1/8   (E) 5 17/24

34. 6 1/2 * 3 =

(A) 9 1/2   (B) 18 1/2   (C) 19 1/2   (D) 20   (E) 12 1/2

35. 3 1/4 * 2 1/3 =

(A) 5 7/12   (B) 6 2/7   (C) 6 5/7   (D) 7 7/12   (E) 7 11/12

Division

DIRECTIONS: Divide and reduce the answer.

36. 3/16 ÷ 3/4 =

(A) 9/64   (B) 1/4   (C) 6/16   (D) 9/16   (E) 3/4

37. 4/9 ÷ 2/3 =

(A) 1/3   (B) 1/2   (C) 2/3   (D) 7/11   (E) 8/9

38. 5 1/4 ÷ 7/10 =

(A) 2 4/7   (B) 3 27/40   (C) 5 19/20   (D) 7 1/2   (E) 8 1/4

39. 4 2/3 ÷ 7/9 =

(A) 2 24/27   (B) 3 2/9   (C) 4 14/27   (D) 5 12/27   (E) 6

40. 3 2/5 ÷ 1 7/10 =

(A) 2   (B) 3 4/7   (C) 4 7/25   (D) 5 1/10   (E) 5 2/7

Changing an Improper Fraction to a Mixed Number

DIRECTIONS: Write each improper fraction as a mixed number in simplest form.

41. 50/4

(A) 10 1/4   (B) 11 1/2   (C) 12 1/4   (D) 12 1/2   (E) 25

42. 17/5

(A) 3 2/5   (B) 3 3/5   (C) 3 4/5   (D) 4 1/5   (E) 4 2/5

43. 42/3

(A) 10 2/3   (B) 12   (C) 13 1/3   (D) 14   (E) 21 1/3

44.   85/6

(A) 9 1/6   (B) 10 5/6   (C) 11 1/2   (D) 12   (E) 14 1/6

45.   151/7

(A) 19 6/7   (B) 20 1/7   (C) 21 4/7   (D) 31 2/7   (E) 31 4/7

Changing a Mixed Number to an Improper Fraction

<u>DIRECTIONS</u>: Change each mixed number to an improper fraction in simplest form.

46.   2 3/5

(A) 4/5   (B) 6/5   (C) 11/5   (D) 13/5   (E) 17/5

47.   4 3/4

(A) 7/4   (B) 13/4   (C) 16/3   (D) 19/4   (E) 21/4

48.   6 7/6

(A) 13/6   (B) 43/6   (C) 19/36   (D) 42/36   (E) 48/6

49.   12 3/7

(A) 87/7   (B) 164/14   (C) 34/3   (D) 187/21   (E) 252/7

50.   21 1/2

(A) 11/2   (B) 22/2   (C) 24/2   (D) 42/2   (E) 43/2

3. Decimals

When we divide the denominator of a fraction into its numerator, the result is a **decimal**. The decimal is based upon a fraction with a denominator of 10, 100, 1,000, ... and is written with a **decimal point**. Whole numbers are placed to the left of the decimal point where the first place to the left is the units place; the second to the left is the tens; the third to the left is the hundreds, etc. The fractions are placed on the right where the first place to the right is the tenths; the second to the right is the hundredths, etc.

EXAMPLE

$$12\frac{3}{10} = 12.3 \qquad 4\frac{17}{100} = 4.17 \qquad \frac{3}{100} = .03$$

Since a **rational number** is of the form a/b, $b \neq 0$, then all rational numbers can be expressed as decimals by dividing b into a. The result is either a **terminat-**

ing decimal, meaning that b divides a with a remainder of 0 after a certain point; or **repeating decimal,** meaning that b continues to divide a so that the decimal has a repeating pattern of integers.

EXAMPLE

(A) $\quad {}^1/_2 = .5$

(B) $\quad {}^1/_3 = .333...$

(C) $\quad {}^{11}/_{16} = .6875$

(D) $\quad {}^2/_7 = .285714285714...$

(A) and (C) are terminating decimals; (B) and (D) are repeating decimals. This explanation allows us to define **irrational numbers** as numbers whose decimal form is non-terminating and non-repeating, e.g.,

$$\sqrt{2} = 1.414...$$
$$\sqrt{3} = 1.732...$$

PROBLEM

Express $- {}^{10}/_{20}$ as a decimal.

SOLUTION

$- {}^{10}/_{20} = - {}^{50}/_{100} = - .5$

PROBLEM

Write ${}^2/_7$ as a repeating decimal.

SOLUTION

To write a fraction as a repeating decimal divide the numerator by the denominator until a pattern of repeated digits appears.

$2 \div 7 = .285714285714...$

Identify the entire portion of the decimal which is repeated. The repeating decimal can then be written in the shortened form:

$\frac{2}{7} = .\overline{285714}$

Operations with Decimals

A)   **To add numbers containing decimals,** write the numbers in a column making sure the decimal points are lined up, one beneath the other. Add the numbers as usual, placing the decimal point in the sum so that it is still in line with the others. It is important not to mix the digits in the tenths place with the digits in the hundredths place, and so on.

EXAMPLES

2.558 + 6.391   57.51 + 6.2

```
  2.558            57.51
+ 6.391          +  6.20
  8.949            63.71
```

Similarly with subtraction,

78.54 – 21.33   7.11 – 4.2

```
  78.54             7.11
– 21.33           – 4.20
  57.21             2.91
```

Note that if two numbers differ according to the amount of digits to the right of the decimal point, zeros must be added.

.63 – .214   15.224 – 3.6891

```
  .630           15.2240
– .214          – 3.6891
  .416           11.5349
```

B)   **To multiply numbers with decimals,** simply multiply as usual. Then, to figure out the number of decimal places that belong in the product, find the total number of decimal places in the numbers being multiplied.

EXAMPLES

```
   6.555  (3 decimal places)        5.32  (2 decimal places)
×    4.5  (1 decimal place)       ×  .04  (2 decimal places)
  32775                            2128
  26220                            000
  294975                           2128
  29.4975 (4 decimal places)      .2128  (4 decimal places)
```

C)   **To divide numbers with decimals,** you must first make the divisor a whole number by moving the decimal point the appropriate number of places to the right. The decimal point of the dividend should also be moved the same number of places. Place a decimal point in the quotient, directly in line with the decimal point in the dividend.

EXAMPLES

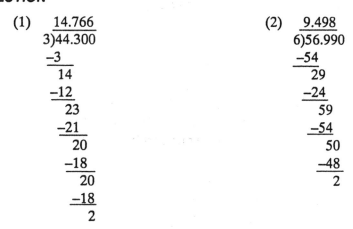

If the question asks to find the correct answer to two decimal places, simply divide until you have three decimal places and then round off. If the third decimal place is a 5 or larger, the number in the second decimal place is increased by 1. If the third decimal place is less than 5, that number is simply dropped.

PROBLEM

Find the answer to the following to 2 decimal places:

(1)   44.3 ÷ 3   (2)   56.99 ÷ 6

SOLUTION

(1)   14.766
    3)44.300
     −3
     ───
      14
     −12
     ───
       23
      −21
      ───
       20
      −18
      ───
        20
       −18
       ───
         2

(2)   9.498
    6)56.990
     −54
     ───
      29
     −24
     ───
      59
     −54
     ───
       50
      −48
      ───
        2

14.766 can be rounded off to 14.77

9.498 can be rounded off to 9.50

D)   When comparing two numbers with decimals to see which is the larger, first look at the tenths place. The larger digit in this place represents the larger number. If the two digits are the same, however, take a look at the digits in the hundredths place, and so on.

EXAMPLES

.518 and .216   .723 and .726

5 is larger than 2, therefore   6 is larger than 3, therefore

.518 is larger than .216   .726 is larger than .723

Drill 3: Decimals

Addition

1.   1.032 + 0.987 + 3.07 =

(A)   4.089   (B)   5.089   (C)   5.189   (D)   6.189   (E)   13.972

2.   132.03 + 97.1483 =

(A)   98.4686   (B)   110.3513   (C)   209.1783

(D)   229.1486   (E)   229.1783

3.   7.1 + 0.62 + 4.03827 + 5.183 =

(A)   0.2315127   (B)   16.94127   (C)   17.57127

(D)   18.561   (E)   40.4543

4.   8 + 17.43 + 9.2 =

(A)   34.63   (B)   34.86   (C)   35.63   (D)   176.63   (E)   189.43

5.   1036.173 + 289.04 =

(A)   382.6573   (B)   392.6573   (C)   1065.077

(D)   1325.213   (E)   3926.573

Subtraction

6.   3.972 − 2.04 =

(A)   1.932   (B)   1.942   (C)   1.976   (D)   2.013   (E)   2.113

7.   16.047 − 13.06 =

(A)   2.887   (B)   2.987   (C)   3.041   (D)   3.141   (E)   4.741

8.   87.4 − 56.27 =

(A)   30.27   (B)   30.67   (C)   31.1   (D)   31.13   (E)   31.27

9.   1046.8 − 639.14 =

(A)   303.84   (B)   313.74   (C)   407.66   (D)   489.74   (E)   535.54

10.   10,000 − 842.91 =

(A)   157.09   (B)   942.91   (C)   5236.09   (D)   9057.91   (E)   9157.09

Multiplication

11.   1.03 * 2.6 =
(A) 2.18   (B) 2.678   (C) 2.78   (D) 3.38   (E) 3.63

12.   93 * 4.2 =
(A) 39.06   (B) 97.2   (C) 223.2   (D) 390.6   (E) 3906

13.   0.04 * 0.23 =
(A) 0.0092   (B) 0.092   (C) 0.27   (D) 0.87   (E) 0.920

14.   0.0186 * 0.03 =
(A) 0.000348 (B) 0.000558 (C) 0.0548   (D) 0.0848   (E) 0.558

15.   51.2 * 0.17 =
(A) 5.29   (B) 8.534   (C) 8.704   (D) 36.352   (E) 36.991

Division

16.   123.39 ÷ 3 =
(A) 31.12   (B) 41.13   (C) 401.13   (D) 411.3   (E) 4,113

17.   1428.6 ÷ 6 =
(A) 0.2381   (B) 2.381   (C) 23.81   (D) 238.1   (E) 2,381

18.   25.2 ÷ 0.3 =
(A) 0.84   (B) 8.04   (C) 8.4   (D) 84   (E) 840

19.   14.95 ÷ 6.5 =
(A) 2.3   (B) 20.3   (C) 23   (D) 230   (E) 2,300

20.   46.33 ÷ 1.13 =
(A) 0.41   (B) 4.1   (C) 41   (D) 410   (E) 4,100

Comparing

21.   Which is the **largest** number in this set — {0.8, 0.823, 0.089, 0.807, 0.852}?
(A) 0.8   (B) 0.823   (C) 0.089   (D) 0.807   (E) 0.852

22. Which is the **smallest** number in this set – {32.98, 32.099, 32.047, 32.5, 32.304}?

(A)   32.98   (B)   32.099   (C)   32.047   (D)   32.5   (E)   32.304

23. In which set below are the numbers arranged correctly from smallest to largest?

(A)   {0.98, 0.9, 0.993}   (D)   {0.006, 0.061, 0.06}

(B)   {0.113, 0.3, 0.31}   (E)   {12.84, 12.801, 12.6}

(C)   {7.04, 7.26, 7.2}

24. In which set below are the numbers arranged correctly from largest to smallest?

(A)   {1.018, 1.63, 1.368}   (D)   {16.34, 16.304, 16.3}

(B)   {4.219, 4.29, 4.9}   (E)   {12.98, 12.601, 12.86}

(C)   {0.62, 0.6043, 0.643}

25. Which is the **largest** number in this set — {0.87, 0.89, 0.889, 0.8, 0.987}?

(A)   0.87   (B)   0.89   (C)   0.889   (D)   0.8   (E)   0.987

Changing a Fraction to a Decimal

26. What is 1/4 written as a decimal?

(A)   1.4   (B)   0.14   (C)   0.2   (D)   0.25   (E)   0.3

27. What is 3/5 written as a decimal?

(A)   0.3   (B)   0.35   (C)   0.6   (D)   0.65   (E)   0.8

28. What is 7/20 written as a decimal?

(A)   0.35   (B)   0.4   (C)   0.72   (D)   0.75   (E)   0.9

29. What is 2/3 written as a decimal?

(A)   0.23   (B)   0.33   (C)   0.5   (D)   0.6   (E) $0.\overline{6}$

30. What is 11/25 written as a fraction?

(A)   0.1125   (B)   0.25   (C)   0.4   (D)   0.44   (E)   0.5

4. Percentages

A **percent** is a way of expressing the relationship between part and whole, where whole is defined as 100%. A percent can be defined by a fraction with a denominator of 100. Decimals can also represent a percent. For instance,

$$56\% = 0.56 = 56/100$$

PROBLEM

Compute the value of

(1)   90% of 400   (3)   50% of 500

(2)   180% of 400   (4)   200% of 4

SOLUTION

The symbol % means per hundred, therefore $5\% = 5/100$

(1) 90% of $400 = 90/100 \times 400 = 90 \times 4 = 360$

(2) 180% of $400 = 180/100 \times 400 = 180 \times 4 = 720$

(3) 50% of $500 = 50/100 \times 500 = 50 \times 5 = 250$

(4) 200% of $4 = 200/100 \times 4 = 2 \times 4 = 8$

PROBLEM

What percent of

(1)   100 is 99.5   (2)   200 is 4

SOLUTION

(1) $99.5 = x \times 100$

$99.5 = 100x$

$.995 = x;$ but this is the value of x per hundred. Therefore,

$x = 99.5\%$

(2) $4 = x \times 200$

$4 = 200x$

$.02 = x.$ Again this must be changed to percent, so

$x = 2\%$

Equivalent Forms of a Number

Some problems may call for converting numbers into an equivalent or simplified form in order to make the solution more convenient.

1.   Converting a fraction to a decimal:

$^1/_2 = 0.50$

Divide the numerator by the denominator:

$$\begin{array}{r} .50 \\ \overline{2)1.00} \\ \underline{-10} \\ 00 \end{array}$$

2.   Converting a number to a percent:

0.50 = 50%

Multiply by 100:

0.50 = (0.50 × 100)% = 50%

3.   Converting a percent to a decimal:

30% = 0.30

Divide by 100:

30% = 30/100 = 0.30

4.   Converting a decimal to a fraction:

$0.500 = {}^1/_2$

Convert .500 to 500/1000 and then simplify the fraction by dividing the numerator and denominator by common factors:

$$\frac{2 \times 2 \times 5 \times 5 \times 5}{2 \times 2 \times 2 \times 5 \times 5 \times 5}$$

and then cancel out the common numbers to get $^1/_2$.

PROBLEM

Express

(1)   1.65 as a percentage of 100

(2)   0.7 as a fraction

(3) $- {}^{10}/_{20}$ as a decimal

(4) $^4/_2$ as an integer

SOLUTION

(1)   (1.65/100) × 100 = 1.65%

(2)　$0.7 = {}^7/_{10}$

(3)　$-{}^{10}/_{20} = -0.5$

(4)　${}^4/_2 = 2$

Drill 4: Percentages

Finding Percents

1.　Find 3% of 80.

(A) 0.24　(B) 2.4　(C) 24　(D) 240　(E) 2,400

2.　Find 50% of 182.

(A) 9　(B) 90　(C) 91　(D) 910　(E) 9,100

3.　Find 83% of 166.

(A) 0.137　(B) 1.377　(C) 13.778　(D) 137　(E) 137.78

4.　Find 125% of 400.

(A) 425　(B) 500　(C) 525　(D) 600　(E) 825

5.　Find 300% of 4.

(A) 12　(B) 120　(C) 1200　(D) 12,000　(E) 120,000

6.　Forty-eight percent of the 1,200 students at Central High are males. How many male students are there at Central High?

(A) 57　(B) 576　(C) 580　(D) 600　(E) 648

7.　For 35% of the last 40 days, there has been measurable rainfall. How many days out of the last 40 days have had measurable rainfall?

(A) 14　(B) 20　(C) 25　(D) 35　(E) 40

8.　Of every 1,000 people who take a certain medicine, 0.2% develop severe side effects. How many people out of every 1,000 who take the medicine develop the side effects?

(A) 0.2　(B) 2　(C) 20　(D) 22　(E) 200

9.　Of 220 applicants for a job, 75% were offered an initial interview. How many people were offered an initial interview?

(A) 75　(B) 110　(C) 120　(D) 155　(E) 165

10.   Find 0.05% of 4,000.

(A)   0.05   (B)   0.5   (C)   2   (D)   20   (E)   400

Changing Percents to Fractions

11.   What is 25% written as a fraction?

(A)   1/25   (B)   1/5   (C)   1/4   (D)   1/3   (E)   1/2

12.   What is 33 1/3% written as a fraction?

(A)   1/4   (B)   1/3   (C)   1/2   (D)   2/3   (E)   5/9

13.   What is 200% written as a fraction?

(A)   1/2   (B)   2/1   (C)   20/1   (D)   200/1   (E)   2000/1

14.   What is 84% written as a fraction?

(A)   1/84   (B)   4/8   (C)   17/25   (D)   21/25   (E)   44/50

15.   What is 2% written as a fraction?

(A)   1/50   (B)   1/25   (C)   1/10   (D)   1/4   (E)   1/2

Changing Fractions to Percents

16.   What is 2/3 written as a percent?

(A)   23%   (B)   32%   (C)   33 1/3%   (D)   57 1/3%   (E)   66 2/3%

17.   What is 3/5 written as a percent?

(A)   30%   (B)   35%   (C)   53%   (D)   60%   (E)   65%

18.   What is 17/20 written as a percent?

(A)   17%   (B)   70%   (C)   75%   (D)   80%   (E)   85%

19.   What is 45/50 written as a percent?

(A)   45%   (B)   50%   (C)   90%   (D)   95%   (E)   97%

20.   What is 1 1/4 written as a percent?

(A)   114%   (B)   120%   (C)   125%   (D)   127%   (E)   133%

Changing Percents to Decimals

21.   What is 42% written as a decimal?

(A)   0.42   (B)   4.2   (C)   42   (D)   420   (E)   422

22.   What is 0.3% written as a decimal?

(A)   0.0003   (B)   0.003   (C)   0.03   (D)   0.3   (E)   3

23.   What is 8% written as a decimal?

(A)   0.0008   (B)   0.008   (C)   0.08   (D)   0.80   (E)   8

24.   What is 175% written as a decimal?

(A)   0.175   (B)   1.75   (C)   17.5   (D)   175   (E)   17,500

25.   What is 34% written as a decimal?

(A)   0.00034   (B)   0.0034   (C)   0.034   (D)   0.34   (E)   3.4

Changing Decimals to Percents

26.   What is 0.43 written as a percent?

(A)   0.0043%   (B)   0.043%   (C)   4.3%   (D)   43%   (E)   430%

27.   What is 1 written as a percent?

(A)   1%   (B)   10%   (C)   100%   (D)   111%   (E)   150%

28.   What is 0.08 written as a percent?

(A)   0.08%   (B)   8%   (C)   8.8%   (D)   80%   (E)   800%

29.   What is 3.4 written as a percent?

(A)   0.0034%   (B)   3.4%   (C)   34%   (D)   304%   (E)   340%

30.   What is 0.645 written as a percent?

(A)   64.5%   (B)   65%   (C)   69%   (D)   70%   (E)   645%

5. Radicals

The **square root** of a number is a number that when multiplied by itself results in the original number. So, the square root of 81 is 9 since $9 \times 9 = 81$. However, -9 is also a root of 81 since $(-9)(-9) = 81$. Every positive number will have two roots. Yet, the principal root is the positive one. Zero has only one square root, while negative numbers do not have real numbers as their roots.

A **radical sign** indicates that the root of a number or expression will be taken. The **radicand** is the number of which the root will be taken. The **index** tells how many times the root needs to be multiplied by itself to equal the radicand. E.g.,

$$\underset{\text{radical sign}}{\text{index}}\ \sqrt{\quad}\ \text{radicand}$$

(1) $\sqrt[3]{64}$;

3 is the index and 64 is the radicand. Since $4 \cdot 4 \cdot 4 = 64$, $\sqrt[3]{64} = 4$

(2) $\sqrt[5]{32}$;

5 is the index and 32 is the radicand. Since $2 \cdot 2 \cdot 2 \cdot 2 \cdot 2 = 32$, $\sqrt[5]{32} = 2$

Operations with Radicals

A) **To multiply two or more radicals**, we utilize the law that states,

$$\sqrt{a} \cdot \sqrt{b} = \sqrt{ab}.$$

Simply multiply the whole numbers as usual. Then, multiply the radicands and put the product under the radical sign and simplify. E.g.,

(1) $\sqrt{12} \cdot \sqrt{5} = \sqrt{60} = 2\sqrt{15}$

(2) $3\sqrt{2} \cdot 4\sqrt{8} = 12\sqrt{16} = 48$

(3) $2\sqrt{10} \cdot 6\sqrt{5} = 12\sqrt{50} = 60\sqrt{2}$

B) **To divide radicals**, simplify both the numerator and the denominator. By multiplying the radical in the denominator by itself, you can make the denominator a rational number. The numerator, however, must also be multiplied by this radical so that the value of the expression does not change. You must choose as many factors as necessary to rationalize the denominator. E.g.,

(1) $\dfrac{\sqrt{128}}{\sqrt{2}} = \dfrac{\sqrt{64} \cdot \sqrt{2}}{\sqrt{2}} = \dfrac{8\sqrt{2}}{\sqrt{2}} = 8$

(2) $\dfrac{\sqrt{10}}{\sqrt{3}} = \dfrac{\sqrt{10} \cdot \sqrt{3}}{\sqrt{3} \cdot \sqrt{3}} = \dfrac{\sqrt{30}}{3}$

(3) $\dfrac{\sqrt{8}}{2\sqrt{3}} = \dfrac{\sqrt{8} \cdot \sqrt{3}}{2\sqrt{3} \cdot \sqrt{3}} = \dfrac{\sqrt{24}}{2 \cdot 3} = \dfrac{2\sqrt{6}}{6} = \dfrac{\sqrt{6}}{3}$

C) **To add two or more radicals**, the radicals must have the same index and the same radicand. Only where the radicals are simplified can these similarities be determined.

EXAMPLE

(1) $6\sqrt{2} + 2\sqrt{2} = (6+2)\sqrt{2} = 8\sqrt{2}$

(2) $\sqrt{27} + 5\sqrt{3} = \sqrt{9}\sqrt{3} + 5\sqrt{3} = 3\sqrt{3} + 5\sqrt{3} = 8\sqrt{3}$

(3) $7\sqrt{3} + 8\sqrt{2} + 5\sqrt{3} = 12\sqrt{3} + 8\sqrt{2}$

Similarly to subtract,

(1) $12\sqrt{3} - 7\sqrt{3} = (12-7)\sqrt{3} = 5\sqrt{3}$

(2) $\sqrt{80} - \sqrt{20} = \sqrt{16}\sqrt{5} - \sqrt{4}\sqrt{5} = 4\sqrt{5} - 2\sqrt{5} = 2\sqrt{5}$

(3) $\sqrt{50} - \sqrt{3} = 5\sqrt{2} - \sqrt{3}$

DRILL 5: Radicals

Multiplication

DIRECTIONS: Multiply and simplify each answer.

1. $\sqrt{6} * \sqrt{5} =$
(A) $\sqrt{11}$ (B) $\sqrt{30}$ (C) $2\sqrt{5}$ (D) $3\sqrt{10}$ (E) $2\sqrt{3}$

2. $\sqrt{3} * \sqrt{12} =$
(A) 3   (B) $\sqrt{15}$ (C) $\sqrt{36}$ (D) 6   (E) 8

3. $\sqrt{7} * \sqrt{7} =$
(A) 7   (B) 49   (C) $\sqrt{14}$ (D) $2\sqrt{7}$ (E) $2\sqrt{14}$

4. $3\sqrt{5} * 2\sqrt{5} =$
(A) $5\sqrt{5}$ (B) 25   (C) 30   (D) $5\sqrt{25}$ (E) $6\sqrt{5}$

5. $4\sqrt{6} * \sqrt{2} =$
(A) $4\sqrt{8}$ (B) $8\sqrt{2}$ (C) $5\sqrt{8}$ (D) $4\sqrt{12}$ (E) $8\sqrt{3}$

Division

DIRECTIONS: Divide and simplify the answer.

6. $\sqrt{10} \div \sqrt{2} =$

(A) $\sqrt{8}$ (B) $2\sqrt{2}$ (C) $\sqrt{5}$ (D) $2\sqrt{5}$ (E) $2\sqrt{3}$

7. $\sqrt{30} \div \sqrt{15} =$

(A) $\sqrt{2}$ (B) $\sqrt{45}$ (C) $3\sqrt{5}$ (D) $\sqrt{15}$ (E) $5\sqrt{3}$

8. $\sqrt{100} \div \sqrt{25} =$

(A) $\sqrt{4}$ (B) $5\sqrt{5}$ (C) $5\sqrt{3}$ (D) 2 (E) 4

9. $\sqrt{48} \div \sqrt{8} =$

(A) $4\sqrt{3}$ (B) $3\sqrt{2}$ (C) $\sqrt{6}$ (D) 6 (E) 12

10. $3\sqrt{12} \div \sqrt{3} =$

(A) $3\sqrt{15}$ (B) 6 (C) 9 (D) 12 (E) $3\sqrt{36}$

Addition

DIRECTIONS: Simplify each radical and add.

11. $\sqrt{7} + 3\sqrt{7} =$

(A) $3\sqrt{7}$ (B) $4\sqrt{7}$ (C) $3\sqrt{14}$ (D) $4\sqrt{14}$ (E) $3\sqrt{21}$

12. $\sqrt{5} + 6\sqrt{5} + 3\sqrt{5} =$

(A) $9\sqrt{5}$ (B) $9\sqrt{15}$ (C) $5\sqrt{10}$ (D) $10\sqrt{5}$ (E) $18\sqrt{15}$

13. $3\sqrt{32} + 2\sqrt{2} =$

(A) $5\sqrt{2}$ (B) $\sqrt{34}$ (C) $14\sqrt{2}$ (D) $5\sqrt{34}$ (E) $6\sqrt{64}$

14. $6\sqrt{15} + 8\sqrt{15} + 16\sqrt{15} =$

(A) $15\sqrt{30}$ (B) $30\sqrt{45}$ (C) $30\sqrt{30}$ (D) $15\sqrt{45}$ (E) $30\sqrt{15}$

15. $6\sqrt{5} + 2\sqrt{45} =$

(A) $12\sqrt{5}$ (B) $8\sqrt{50}$ (C) $40\sqrt{2}$ (D) $12\sqrt{50}$ (E) $8\sqrt{5}$

Subtraction

<u>DIRECTIONS</u>: Simplify each radical and subtract.

16. $8\sqrt{5} - 6\sqrt{5} =$

(A) $2\sqrt{5}$ (B) $3\sqrt{5}$ (C) $4\sqrt{5}$ (D) $14\sqrt{5}$ (E) $48\sqrt{5}$

17. $16\sqrt{33} - 5\sqrt{33} =$

(A) $3\sqrt{33}$ (B) $33\sqrt{11}$ (C) $11\sqrt{33}$ (D) $11\sqrt{0}$ (E) $\sqrt{33}$

18. $14\sqrt{2} - 19\sqrt{2} =$

(A) $5\sqrt{2}$ (B) $-5\sqrt{2}$ (C) $-33\sqrt{2}$ (D) $33\sqrt{2}$ (E) $-4\sqrt{2}$

19. $10\sqrt{2} - 3\sqrt{8} =$

(A) $6\sqrt{6}$ (B) $-2\sqrt{2}$ (C) $7\sqrt{6}$ (D) $4\sqrt{2}$ (E) $-6\sqrt{6}$

20. $4\sqrt{3} - 2\sqrt{12} =$

(A) $-2\sqrt{9}$ (B) $-6\sqrt{15}$ (C) 0 (D) $6\sqrt{15}$ (E) $2\sqrt{12}$

6. Exponents

When a number is multiplied by itself a specific number of times, it is said to be **raised to a power**. The way this is written is $a^n = b$ where a is the number or **base**, n is the **exponent** or **power** that indicates the number of times the base is to be multiplied by itself, and b is the product of this multiplication.

In the expression 3^2, 3 is the base and 2 is the exponent. This means that 3 is multiplied by itself 2 times and the product is 9.

An exponent can be either positive or negative. A negative exponent implies a fraction. Such that, if n is a positive integer

$$a^{-n} = \frac{1}{a^n}, a \neq 0. \text{ So, } 2^{-4} = \frac{1}{2^4} = \frac{1}{16}.$$

An exponent that is zero gives a result of 1, assuming that the base is not equal to zero.

$$a^0 = 1, a \neq 0.$$

An exponent can also be a fraction. If m and n are positive integers,

$$a^{\frac{m}{n}} = \sqrt[n]{a^m}$$

The numerator remains the exponent of *a*, but the denominator tells what root to take. For example,

(1) $4^{\frac{3}{2}} = \sqrt[2]{4^3} = \sqrt{64} = 8$ (2) $3^{\frac{4}{2}} = \sqrt[2]{3^4} = \sqrt{81} = 9$

If a fractional exponent were negative, the same operation would take place, but the result would be a fraction. For example,

(1) $27^{-\frac{2}{3}} = \dfrac{1}{27^{2/3}} = \dfrac{1}{\sqrt[3]{27^2}} = \dfrac{1}{\sqrt[3]{729}} = \dfrac{1}{9}$

PROBLEM

Simplify the following expressions:

(1) -3^{-2} (3) $\dfrac{-3}{4^{-1}}$

(2) $(-3)^{-2}$

SOLUTION

(1)   Here the exponent applies only to 3. Since

$$x^{-y} = \frac{1}{x^y}, -3^{-2} = -(3)^{-2} = -\frac{1}{3^2} = -\frac{1}{9}$$

(2)   In this case the exponent applies to the negative base. Thus,

$$(-3)^{-2} = \frac{1}{(-3)^2} = \frac{1}{(-3)(-3)} = \frac{1}{9}$$

(3) $\dfrac{-3}{4^{-1}} = \dfrac{-3}{(\frac{1}{4})^1} = \dfrac{-3}{\frac{1^1}{4^1}} = \dfrac{-3}{\frac{1}{4}}$

Division by a fraction is equivalent to multiplication by that fraction's reciprocal, thus

$$\frac{-3}{\frac{1}{4}} = -3 \cdot \frac{4}{1} = -12 \text{ and } \frac{-3}{4^{-1}} = -12$$

General Laws of Exponents

A) $a^p a^q = a^{p+q}$

$4^2 4^3 = 4^{2+3} = 1{,}024$

B) $(a^p)^q = a^{pq}$

$(2^3)^2 = 2^6 = 64$

C) $\dfrac{a^p}{a^q} = a^{p-q}$

$\dfrac{3^6}{3^2} = 3^4 = 81$

D) $(ab)^p = a^p b^p$

$(3 \cdot 2)^2 = 3^2 \cdot 2^2 = (9)\,(4) = 36$

E) $\left(\dfrac{a}{b}\right)^p = \dfrac{a^p}{b^p}$, $b \neq 0$

$\left(\dfrac{4}{5}\right)^2 = \dfrac{4^2}{5^2} = \dfrac{16}{25}$

Drill 6: Exponents

Multiplication

Simplify

1. $4^6 \cdot 4^2 =$

(A) 4^4 (B) 4^8 (C) 4^{12} (D) 16^8 (E) 16^{12}

2. $2^2 \cdot 2^5 \cdot 2^3 =$

(A) 2^{10} (B) 4^{10} (C) 8^{10} (D) 2^{30} (E) 8^{30}

3. $6^6 \cdot 6^2 \cdot 6^4 =$

(A) 18^8 (B) 18^{12} (C) 6^{12} (D) 6^{48} (E) 18^{48}

4. $a^4 b^2 \cdot a^3 b =$

(A) ab (B) $2a^7 b^2$ (C) $2a^{12} b$ (D) $a^7 b^3$ (E) $a^7 b^2$

5. $m^8 n^3 \cdot m^2 n \cdot m^4 n^2 =$

(A) $3m^{16} n^6$ (B) $m^{14} n^6$ (C) $3m^{14} n^6$ (D) $3m^{14} n^5$ (E) m^2

Division

Simplify

6. $6^5 + 6^3 =$

(A) 0   (B) 1   (C) 6   (D) 12   (E) 6^2

7. $11^8 + 11^5 =$

(A) 1^3 (B) 11^3 (C) 11^{13} (D) 11^{40} (E) 88^5

8. $x^{10}y^8 + x^7y^3 =$

(A) x^2y^5 (B) x^3y^4 (C) x^3y^5 (D) x^2y^4 (E) x^5y^3

9. $a^{14} + a^9 =$

(A) 1^5 (B) a^5 (C) $2a^5$ (D) a^{23} (E) $2a^{23}$

10. $c^{17}d^{12}e^4 + c^{12}d^8e =$

(A) $c^4d^5e^3$ (B) $c^4d^4e^3$ (C) $c^5d^8e^4$ (D) $c^5d^4e^3$ (E) $c^5d^4e^4$

Power to a Power

Simplify

11. $(3^6)^2 =$

(A) 3^4 (B) 3^8 (C) 3^{12} (D) 9^6 (E) 9^8

12. $(4^3)^5 =$

(A) 4^2 (B) 2^{15} (C) 4^8 (D) 20^3 (E) 4^{15}

13. $(a^4b^3)^2 =$

(A) $(ab)^9$ (B) a^8b^6 (C) $(ab)^{24}$ (D) a^6b^5 (E) $2a^4b^3$

14. $(r^3p^6)^3 =$

(A) r^9p^{18} (B) $(rp)^{12}$ (C) r^6p^9 (D) $3r^3p^6$ (E) $3r^9p^{18}$

15. $(m^6n^5q^3)^2 =$

(A) $2m^6n^5q^3$ (B) m^4n^3q (C) $m^8n^7q^5$

(D) $m^{12}n^{10}q^6$ (E) $2m^{12}n^{10}q^6$

7. Averages

Mean

The mean is the arithmetic average. It is the sum of the values divided by the total number of variables. For example:

$$\frac{4+3+8}{3} = 5$$

PROBLEM

Find the mean salary for four company employees who make $5/hr., $8/hr., $12/hr., and $15/hr.

SOLUTION

The mean salary is the average.

$$\frac{\$5 + \$8 + \$12 + \$15}{4} = \frac{\$40}{4} = \$10 / hr$$

PROBLEM

Find the mean length of five fish with lengths of 7.5 in, 7.75 in, 8.5 in, 8.5 in., 8.25 in.

SOLUTION

The mean length is the average length.

$$\frac{7.5 + 7.75 + 8.5 + 8.5 + 8.25}{5} = \frac{40.5}{5} = 8.1\text{in}$$

Median

The median is the middle value in a set when there is an odd number of values. There is an equal number of values larger and smaller than the median. When the set is an even number of values, the average of the two middle values is the median. For example:

The median of (2, 3, 5, 8, 9) is 5.

The median of (2, 3, 5, 9, 10, 11) is $\frac{5+9}{2} = 7$.

Mode

The mode is the most frequently occurring value in the set of values. For example the mode of 4, 5, 8, 3, 8, 2 would be 8, since it occurs twice while the other values occur only once.

PROBLEM

For this series of observations find the mean, median, and mode.

500, 600, 800, 800, 900, 900, 900, 900, 900, 1000, 1100

SOLUTION

The mean is the value obtained by adding all the measurements and dividing by the number of measurements.

$$\frac{500 + 600 + 800 + 800 + 900 + 900 + 900 + 900 + 900 + 1000 + 1100}{11}$$

$$= \frac{9300}{11} = 845.45.$$

The median is the observation in the middle. We have 11 observations, so here the sixth, 900, is the median.

The mode is the observation that appears most frequently. That is also 900, since it has 5 appearances.

All three of these numbers are measures of central tendency. They describe the "middle" or "center" of the data.

PROBLEM

Nine rats run through a maze. The time each rat took to traverse the maze is recorded and these times are listed below.

1 min, 2.5 min, 3 min, 1.5 min, 2 min, 1.25 min, 1 min, .9 min, 30 min

Which of the three measures of central tendency would be the most appropriate in this case?

SOLUTION

We will calculate the three measures of central tendency and then compare them to determine which would be the most appropriate in describing these data.

The mean is the sum of observations divided by the number of observations. In this case

$$\frac{1 + 2.5 + 3 + 1.5 + 2 + 1.25 + 1 + .9 + 30}{9} = \frac{43.15}{9} = 4.79.$$

The median is the "middle number" in an array of the observations from the lowest to the highest.

0.9, 1.0, 1.0, 1.25, 1.5, 2.0, 2.5, 3.0, 30.0

The median is the fifth observation in this array or 1.5. There are four observations larger than 1.5 and four observations smaller than 1.5.

The mode is the most frequently occurring observation in the sample. In this data set the mode is 1.0.

mean = 4.79

median = 1.5

mode = 1.0

The mean is not appropriate here. Only one rat took more than 4.79 minutes to run the maze and this rat took 30 minutes. We see that the mean has been distorted by this one large observation.

The median or mode seems to describe this data set better and would be more appropriate to use.

Drill 7: Averages

Mean

DIRECTIONS: Find the mean of each set of numbers:

1. 18, 25, and 32.

(A) 3   (B) 25   (C) 50   (D) 75   (E) 150

2. 4/9, 2/3, and 5/6.

(A) 11/18   (B) 35/54   (C) 41/54   (D) 35/18   (E) 54/18

3. 97, 102, 116, and 137.

(A) 40   (B) 102   (C) 109   (D) 113   (E) 116

4. 12, 15, 18, 24, and 31.

(A) 18   (B) 19.3   (C) 20   (D) 25   (E) 100

5. 7, 4, 6, 3, 11, and 14.

(A) 5   (B) 6.5   (C) 7   (D) 7.5   (E) 8

Median

DIRECTIONS: Find the median value of each set of numbers.

6.   3, 8, and 6.

(A)   3   (B)   6   (C)   8   (D)   17   (E)   20

7.   19, 15, 21, 27, and 12.

(A)   19   (B)   15   (C)   21   (D)   27   (E)   94

8.   1 2/3, 1 7/8, 1 3/4, and 1 5/6.

(A)   1 30/48 (B)   1 2/3   (C)   1 3/4   (D)   1 19/24   (E)   1 21/24

9.   29, 18, 21, and 35.

(A)   29   (B)   18   (C)   21   (D)   35   (E)   25

10.   8, 15, 7, 12, 31, 3, and 28.

(A)   7   (B)   11.6   (C)   12   (D)   14.9   (E)   104

Mode

DIRECTIONS: Find the mode(s) of each set of numbers.

11.   1, 3, 7, 4, 3, and 8.

(A)   1   (B)   3   (C)   7   (D)   4   (E)   None

12.   12, 19, 25, and 42

(A)   12   (B)   19   (C)   25   (D)   42   (E)   None

13.   16, 14, 12, 16, 30, and 28.

(A)   6   (B)   14   (C)   16   (D)   19.3   (E)   None

14.   4, 3, 9, 2, 4, 5, and 2.

(A)   3 and 9   (B)   5 and 9   (C)   4 and 5   (D)   2 and 4   (E)   None

15.   87, 42, 111, 116, 39, 111, 140, 116, 97, and 111.

(A)   111   (B)   116   (C)   39   (D)   140   (E)   None

ARITHMETIC DRILLS

ANSWER KEY

Drill 1—Integers and Real Numbers

1.	(A)	9.	(E)	17.	(D)	25.	(D)
2.	(C)	10.	(B)	18.	(D)	26.	(D)
3.	(D)	11.	(B)	19.	(C)	27.	(B)
4.	(C)	12.	(E)	20.	(E)	28.	(C)
5.	(B)	13.	(C)	21.	(B)	29.	(A)
6.	(B)	14.	(A)	22.	(E)	30.	(C)
7.	(A)	15.	(B)	23.	(D)		
8.	(C)	16.	(B)	24.	(A)		

Drill 2—Fractions

1.	(D)	14.	(D)	27.	(D)	40.	(A)
2.	(E)	15.	(B)	28.	(E)	41.	(D)
3.	(C)	16.	(B)	29.	(C)	42.	(A)
4.	(A)	17.	(D)	30.	(B)	43.	(D)
5.	(C)	18.	(B)	31.	(C)	44.	(E)
6.	(B)	19.	(A)	32.	(A)	45.	(C)
7.	(C)	20.	(C)	33.	(B)	46.	(D)
8.	(A)	21.	(D)	34.	(C)	47.	(D)
9.	(B)	22.	(C)	35.	(D)	48.	(B)
10.	(A)	23.	(B)	36.	(B)	49.	(A)
11.	(B)	24.	(E)	37.	(C)	50.	(E)
12.	(D)	25.	(A)	38.	(D)		
13.	(E)	26.	(A)	39.	(E)		

Drill 3—Decimals

1.	(B)	9.	(C)	17.	(D)	25.	(E)
2.	(E)	10.	(E)	18.	(D)	26.	(D)
3.	(B)	11.	(B)	19.	(A)	27.	(C)
4.	(A)	12.	(D)	20.	(C)	28.	(A)
5.	(D)	13.	(A)	21.	(E)	29.	(E)
6.	(A)	14.	(B)	22.	(C)	30.	(D)
7.	(B)	15.	(C)	23.	(B)		
8.	(D)	16.	(B)	24.	(D)		

Drill 4—Percentages

1.	(B)	9.	(E)	17.	(D)	25.	(D)
2.	(C)	10.	(C)	18.	(E)	26.	(D)
3.	(E)	11.	(C)	19.	(C)	27.	(C)
4.	(B)	12.	(B)	20.	(C)	28.	(B)
5.	(A)	13.	(B)	21.	(A)	29.	(E)
6.	(B)	14.	(D)	22.	(B)	30.	(A)
7.	(A)	15.	(A)	23.	(C)		
8.	(B)	16.	(E)	24.	(B)		

Drill 5—Radicals

1.	(B)	6.	(C)	11.	(B)	16.	(A)
2.	(D)	7.	(A)	12.	(D)	17.	(C)
3.	(A)	8.	(D)	13.	(C)	18.	(B)
4.	(C)	9.	(C)	14.	(E)	19.	(D)
5.	(E)	10.	(B)	15.	(A)	20.	(C)

Drill 6—Exponents

1.	(B)	9.	(B)
2.	(A)	10.	(D)
3.	(C)	11.	(C)
4.	(D)	12.	(E)
5.	(B)	13.	(B)
6.	(E)	14.	(A)
7.	(B)	15.	(D)
8.	(C)		

Drill 7—Averages

1.	(B)	9.	(E)
2.	(B)	10.	(C)
3.	(D)	11.	(B)
4.	(C)	12.	(E)
5.	(D)	13.	(C)
6.	(B)	14.	(D)
7.	(A)	15.	(A)
8.	(D)		

GLOSSARY: ARITHMETIC

Absolute Value

The value of a number without regard to sign (i.e., it is always nonnegative).

Additive Identity

The number that, when added to another, results in that number. Thus the additive identity is 0.

Additive Inverse

The number that, when added to the original number, results in the additive identity, 0. The additive inverse of a number is the negative of that number.

Associative Property

The property that states (for addition) that $a + (b + c) = (a + b) + c$. This also holds for multiplication but not for subtraction or division.

Base

A number to be raised to a power.

Commutative Property

The property that states (for addition) that $a + b = b + a$. This is also true for multiplication, but not subtraction or division.

Complex Fraction

A fraction in which either the numerator, the denominator, or both are a fraction.

Composite Number

An integer that is not prime, i.e., a number that has factors besides itself and 1.

Cube Root

A number that, when multiplied by itself twice (i.e., number × number × number), results in the original number.

Decimal

A number expressed as a whole number (to the left of the decimal point) and a remainder (to the right of the decimal point). When there is no whole number to the left of the decimal point, that number is considered 0.

Decimal Point

The point that separates the whole number in a decimal from the remainder.

Denominator

The number dividing the numerator in a fraction.

Difference

The result of subtracting one number from another.

Distributive Property

The property that states (for addition and multiplication) that $a * (b + c) = a*b + a*c$. This also holds for subtraction and multiplication (i.e., $a*(b - c) = a*b - a*c$) but not for division and addition or division and subtraction. It is *not* true that $a/(b+c) = (a/b) + (a/c)$. It is true, however, that $(a+b)/c = (a/c) + (b/c)$.

Even Integer

An integer that, when divided by 2, results in an integer.

Exponent

The number of times the base is to be multiplied by itself.

Factors of a number

A set of numbers that, when multiplied together, results in the original number.

Fraction

A number expressed in the form of one number (the numerator) divided by another (the denominator).

Improper Fraction

A fraction in which the numerator exceeds the denominator.

Integer

The set of numbers $\{..., -3, -2, -1, 0, 1, 2, 3, ...\}$.

Irrational Number

A number that is not rational, i.e., cannot be expressed as a ratio of integers.

Least Common Denominator

The smallest whole number that results in a whole number when divided by each of the numbers in a set.

Mean

The sum of a set of numbers divided by how many numbers there are in the set.

Median

The number such that half of the numbers in the given set exceed this number, and half are smaller than it (i.e., if the numbers are ordered, then the median is in the middle).

Mixed Number

The sum of a whole number and a proper fraction.

Mode

> The number that occurs most often in a set of numbers.

Multiplicative Identity

> The number that, when multiplied by another number, results in that number. Hence the multiplicative identity is 1.

Multiplicative Inverse

> The number that, when multiplied by the original number, results in the multiplicative identity, or 1. Hence the multiplicative inverse of a number is 1 divided by that number, or the reciprocal of the number.

Natural Number

> A positive integer, i.e., {1, 2, 3, ...}

Negative Number

> A number that is less than 0 or that falls to the left of 0 on the number line.

Number Line

> A line of infinite length with a 0 and positive numbers to the right of 0 and negative numbers to the left. The numbers are ordered, so each is to the left of numbers larger than it, and to the right of smaller numbers. The distances between numbers is preserved, e.g., the distance between 1 and 2 is the same as that between 6 and 7.

Numerator

> The number being divided in a fraction.

Odd Integer

> An integer that is not even, i.e., when divided by 2, the quotient is not an integer. An integer is odd if, and only if, the preceding integer is even.

Order of Operations

> The law that requires dealing first with parentheses, then powers of exponents, then multiplication or division, and finally addition or subtraction.

Percent

> A number expressed as a part of a whole (i.e., 100% = 1).

Positive Number

> A number that exceeds 0 or that falls to the right of 0 on the number line.

Power

> The exponent.

Prime Factor

> A factor of a number that is prime. That is, it has no factor besides itself and 1.

Prime Number

> An integer whose only factors are itself and 1.

Product

> The result of multiplying two or more numbers together.

Proper Fraction

> A fraction in which the denominator exceeds the numerator.

Quotient

> The result of division.

Radical Sign

> The symbol that indicates to find a root of a number.

Radicand

> The number whose root (possibly square or cube) is to be found.

Range

> The largest of a set of numbers minus the smallest of the set.

Rational Number

> A number that can be expressed as the ratio of two integers.

Real Number

> Any single number (in one dimension).

Reciprocal

> The multiplicative inverse.

Repeating Decimal

> A decimal with a repeating pattern after the decimal point.

Square Root

> A number that, when multiplied by itself, results in the original number.

Sum

> The result of adding two or more numbers together.

Terminating Decimal

> A decimal with a finite number of places after the decimal point.

Weighted Mean

> The sum of (the original numbers multiplied by the weights) divided by (the sum of the weights).

Whole Number

> A nonnegative integer, i.e., {0, 1, 2, 3, ...}.

CHAPTER 7

Practicing to take Standardized Tests in Geometry

- ➤ *Answer Sheet*
- ➤ *Geometry Diagnostic Test*
- ➤ *Answer Key*
- ➤ *Detailed Explanations of Answers*
- ➤ *Geometry Review and Drills*
- ➤ *Answer Key to Drills*
- ➤ *Geometry Glossary*

GEOMETRY DIAGNOSTIC TEST

1. Ⓐ Ⓑ Ⓒ Ⓓ Ⓔ	26. Ⓐ Ⓑ Ⓒ Ⓓ Ⓔ
2. Ⓐ Ⓑ Ⓒ Ⓓ Ⓔ	27. Ⓐ Ⓑ Ⓒ Ⓓ Ⓔ
3. Ⓐ Ⓑ Ⓒ Ⓓ Ⓔ	28. Ⓐ Ⓑ Ⓒ Ⓓ Ⓔ
4. Ⓐ Ⓑ Ⓒ Ⓓ Ⓔ	29. Ⓐ Ⓑ Ⓒ Ⓓ Ⓔ
5. Ⓐ Ⓑ Ⓒ Ⓓ Ⓔ	30. Ⓐ Ⓑ Ⓒ Ⓓ Ⓔ
6. Ⓐ Ⓑ Ⓒ Ⓓ Ⓔ	31. Ⓐ Ⓑ Ⓒ Ⓓ Ⓔ
7. Ⓐ Ⓑ Ⓒ Ⓓ Ⓔ	32. Ⓐ Ⓑ Ⓒ Ⓓ Ⓔ
8. Ⓐ Ⓑ Ⓒ Ⓓ Ⓔ	33. Ⓐ Ⓑ Ⓒ Ⓓ Ⓔ
9. Ⓐ Ⓑ Ⓒ Ⓓ Ⓔ	34. Ⓐ Ⓑ Ⓒ Ⓓ Ⓔ
10. Ⓐ Ⓑ Ⓒ Ⓓ Ⓔ	35. Ⓐ Ⓑ Ⓒ Ⓓ Ⓔ
11. Ⓐ Ⓑ Ⓒ Ⓓ Ⓔ	36. Ⓐ Ⓑ Ⓒ Ⓓ Ⓔ
12. Ⓐ Ⓑ Ⓒ Ⓓ Ⓔ	37. Ⓐ Ⓑ Ⓒ Ⓓ Ⓔ
13. Ⓐ Ⓑ Ⓒ Ⓓ Ⓔ	38. Ⓐ Ⓑ Ⓒ Ⓓ Ⓔ
14. Ⓐ Ⓑ Ⓒ Ⓓ Ⓔ	39. Ⓐ Ⓑ Ⓒ Ⓓ Ⓔ
15. Ⓐ Ⓑ Ⓒ Ⓓ Ⓔ	40. Ⓐ Ⓑ Ⓒ Ⓓ Ⓔ
16. Ⓐ Ⓑ Ⓒ Ⓓ Ⓔ	41. Ⓐ Ⓑ Ⓒ Ⓓ Ⓔ
17. Ⓐ Ⓑ Ⓒ Ⓓ Ⓔ	42. Ⓐ Ⓑ Ⓒ Ⓓ Ⓔ
18. Ⓐ Ⓑ Ⓒ Ⓓ Ⓔ	43. Ⓐ Ⓑ Ⓒ Ⓓ Ⓔ
19. Ⓐ Ⓑ Ⓒ Ⓓ Ⓔ	44. Ⓐ Ⓑ Ⓒ Ⓓ Ⓔ
20. Ⓐ Ⓑ Ⓒ Ⓓ Ⓔ	45. Ⓐ Ⓑ Ⓒ Ⓓ Ⓔ
21. Ⓐ Ⓑ Ⓒ Ⓓ Ⓔ	46. Ⓐ Ⓑ Ⓒ Ⓓ Ⓔ
22. Ⓐ Ⓑ Ⓒ Ⓓ Ⓔ	47. Ⓐ Ⓑ Ⓒ Ⓓ Ⓔ
23. Ⓐ Ⓑ Ⓒ Ⓓ Ⓔ	48. Ⓐ Ⓑ Ⓒ Ⓓ Ⓔ
24. Ⓐ Ⓑ Ⓒ Ⓓ Ⓔ	49. Ⓐ Ⓑ Ⓒ Ⓓ Ⓔ
25. Ⓐ Ⓑ Ⓒ Ⓓ Ⓔ	50. Ⓐ Ⓑ Ⓒ Ⓓ Ⓔ

GEOMETRY DIAGNOSTIC TEST

This diagnostic test is designed to help you determine your strengths and your weaknesses in geometry. Follow the directions for each part and check your answers.

50 Questions

DIRECTIONS: Choose the correct answer for each of the following problems. Fill in each answer on the answer sheet.

1.   An old picture has dimensions 33 inches by 24 inches. What one length must be cut from each dimension so that the ratio of the shorter side to the longer side is $2/3$?

   (A) $4^{1}/_{2}$ inches   (B)   9 inches   (C)   6 inches

   (D) $10^{1}/_{2}$ inches   (E)   3 inches

2.   The greatest area that a rectangle whose perimeter is 52 m can have is

   (A) $12 \, m^2$ (B) $169 \, m^2$ (C) $172 \, m^2$

   (D) $168 \, m^2$ (E) $52 \, m^2$

3.   If the triangle ABC has angle $A = 35°$ and angle $B = 85°$, then the measure of the angle x in degrees is:

   (A)   85

   (B)   90

   (C)   100

   (D)   120

   (E)   180

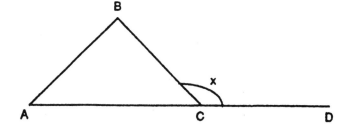

4. In the following figure, O is the center of the circle. If arc *ABC* has length 2π, what is the area of the circle?

    (A) 3 π

    (B) 6 π

    (C) 9 π

    (D) 12 π

    (E) 15 π

    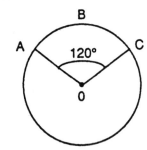

5. If the area of a rectangle is 120 and the perimeter is 44, then the length is

    (A) 30   (B) 20   (C) 15

    (D   12   (E) 10

6. What is the measure of the angle made by the minute and hour hand of a clock at 3:30?

    (A) 60°   (B) 75°   (C) 90°

    (D) 115°   (E) 120°

7. A rectangular piece of metal has an area of 35m^2 and a perimeter of 24 m. Which of the following are possible dimensions of the piece?

    (A) $^{35}/_2$ m × 2 m   (B) 5 m × 7 m   (C) 35 m × 1 m

    (D) 6 m × 6 m   (E) 8 m × 4 m

8. The area of ∆*ADE* is 12 square units. If *B* is the midpoint of $\overline{AD}$ and *C* is the midpoint of $\overline{AE}$, what is the area of ∆*ABC*?

    (A) 2 square units

    (B) 3 square units

    (C) 3$^1/_2$ square units

    (D) 4 square units

    (E) 6 square units

    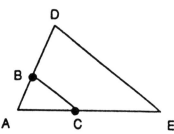

9. If the quadrilateral *ABCD* has angle *A* = 35°, angle *B* = 85°, and angle *C* = 120°, then the measure of the angle *D* in degrees is:

    (A) 85   (B) 90   (C) 100

    (D) 120   (E) 180

10. In the figure shown, two chords of the circle intersect, making the angles shown. What is the value of $x + y$?

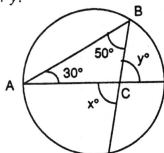

(A) 40°

(B) 50°

(C) 80°

(D) 160°

(E) 320°

11. In the figure shown, three chords of the circle intersect making the angles shown. What is the value of θ?

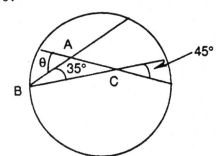

(A) 35°

(B) 45°

(C) 60°

(D) 75°

(E) 80°

12. If a triangle of base 6 units has the same area as a circle of radius 6 units, what is the altitude of the triangle?

(A) π   (B) 3π   (C) 6π

(D) 12π   (E) 36π

13. A cube consists of 96 square feet. What is the volume of the cube in cubic feet?

(A) 16   (B) 36   (C) 64

(D) 96   (E) 216

14. If the angles of a triangle ABC are in the ratio of 3 : 5 : 7, then the triangle is:

(A) acute   (B) right   (C) isosceles

(D) obtuse   (E) equilateral

15. If the measures of the three angles of a triangle are $(3x + 15)°$, $(5x - 15)°$, and $(2x + 30)°$, what is the measure of each angle?

(A) 75°   (B) 60°   (C) 45°

(D) 25°   (E) 15°

16. In the figure shown below, line *l* is parallel to line *m*. If the area of triangle *ABC* is 40 cm³, what is the area of triangle *ABD*?

(A) Less than 40 cm³

(B) More than 40 cm³

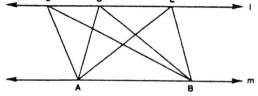

(C) The length of segment $\overline{AD}$ times 40 cm²

(D) Exactly 40 cm³

(E) Cannot be determined from the information given

17. If the length of segment $\overline{EB}$, base of triangle *EBC*, is equal to ¹/₄ the length of segment $\overline{AB}$ ($\overline{AB}$ is the length of rectangle *ABCD*), and the area of triangle *EBC* is 12 square units, find the area of the shaded region.

(A) 24 square units

(B) 96 square units

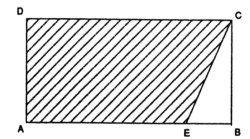

(C) 84 square units

(D) 72 square units

(E) 120 square units

18. What is the perimeter of triangle *ABC*?

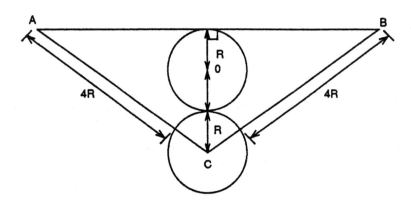

(A) 12*R*   (B) 18*R*²   (C) 12*R*²

(D) 18*R*   (E) 16*R*

19. Which of the following alternatives is correct?

   (A) $\alpha + \beta + \gamma = 180°$

   (B) $\gamma - \alpha + 180° = \beta$

   (C) $\alpha = \beta + \gamma$

   (D) $\gamma = \alpha + \beta$

   (E) $\alpha = 180° - \beta - \alpha$

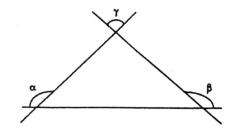

20. In the figure shown, all segments meet at right angles. Find the figure's perimeter in terms of r and s.

   (A) $r + s$

   (B) $2r + s$

   (C) $2s + r$

   (D) $r^2 + s^2$

   (E) $2r + 2s$

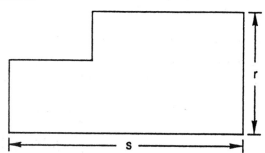

21. If lines l, m, and n intersect at point P, express $x + y$ in terms of a.

   (A) $180 - {}^a/_2$

   (B) ${}^a/_2 - 180$

   (C) $90 - {}^a/_2$

   (D) $a - 180$

   (E) $180 - a$

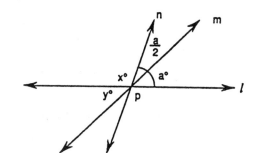

22. The measure of an inscribed angle is equal to one-half the measure of its inscribed arc. In the figure shown, triangle ABC is inscribed in circle O, and line $\overline{BD}$ is tangent to the circle at point B. If the measure of angle CBD is 70°, what is the measure of angle BAC?

   (A) 110°

   (B) 70°

   (C) 140°

   (D) 35°

   (E) 40°

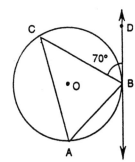

23. What is the value of *x*?

    (A) 20°

    (B) 40°

    (C) 60°

    (D) 90°

    (E) 30°

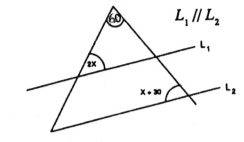

24. If the triangle *ABC* has angle *A* = 35° and angle *B* = 85°, then the measure of the angle *x* in degrees is:

    (A) 85

    (B) 90

    (C) 100

    (D) 120

    (E) 180

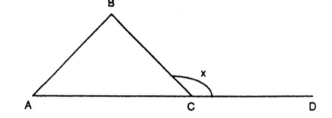

25. In the figure shown, line *r* is parallel to line *l*. Find the measure of angle *RBC*.

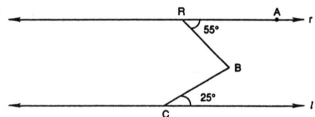

    (A) 30°   (B) 80°   (C) 90°

    (D) 100°   (E) 110°

26. In the five-pointed star shown, what is the sum of the measures of angles *A*, *B*, *C*, *D*, and *E*?

    (A) 108°

    (B) 72°

    (C) 36°

    (D) 150°

    (E) 180°

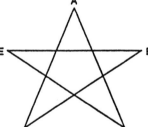

27. A room measures 13 feet by 26 feet. A rug which measures 12 feet by 18 feet is placed on the floor. What is the area of the uncovered portion of the floor?

   (A) 554 sq. ft.   (B) 216 sq. ft.   (C) 100 sq. ft.

   (D) 122 sq. ft.   (E) 338 sq. ft.

28. The area of $\triangle ADE$ is 12 square units. If B is the midpoint of $\overline{AD}$ and C is the midpoint of $\overline{AE}$, what is the area of $\triangle ABC$?

   (A) 2 square units

   (B) 3 square units

   (C) $3\frac{1}{2}$ square units

   (D) 4 square units

   (E) 6 square units

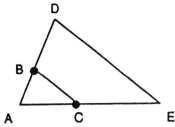

29. In $\triangle ABC$, $AB = 6$, $BC = 4$ and $AC = 3$. What kind of a triangle is it?

   (A) right and scalene   (B) obtuse and scalene

   (C) acute and scalene   (D) right and isosceles

   (E) obtuse and isosceles

30. What is the area of the shaded portion of the rectangle? The heavy dot represents the center of the semicircle.

   (A) $200 - 100\pi$ (B) $200 - 25\pi$

   (C) $30 - \dfrac{25\pi}{2}$ (D) $\dfrac{200 - 25\pi}{2}$

   (E) $\dfrac{400 - 25\pi}{2}$

31. Find the area of the isosceles trapezoid.

   (A) $250\sqrt{3}$

   (B) 150

   (C) 250

   (D) $125\sqrt{3}$

   (E) Area cannot be found.

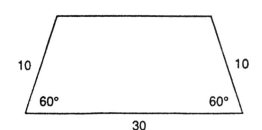

32. If the radius of a sphere is increased by a factor of 3, then the volume of the sphere is increased by a factor of

(A) 3   (B) 6   (C) 9

(D) 18   (E) 27

33. In the diagram shown, *ABC* is an isosceles triangle. Sides *AC* and *BC* are extended through *C* to *E* and *D* to form triangle *CDE*. The sum of the measures of angles *D* and *E* is

(A) 150°

(B) 105°

(C) 90°

(D) 60°

(E) 30°

34. The box pictured has a square base with side *x* and a closed top. The surface area of the box is

(A) $4x + h$

(B) $4x + 4h$

(C) hx^2

(D) $x^2 + 4xh$

(E) $2x^2 + 4xh$

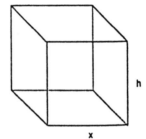

35. Quadrilaterals *ABCD* and *AFED* are squares with sides of length 10 cm. Arc *BD* and arc *DF* are quarter circles. What is the area of the shaded region?

(A) 50 sq. cm

(B) 100 sq. cm

(C) 80 sq. cm

(D) 40 sq. cm

(E) 10 sq. cm

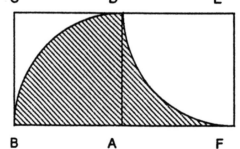

36. If the distance between two adjacent vertical or horizontal dots is 1, what is the perimeter of Δ*ABC*? (See figure following)

(A) 5

(B) $\sqrt{3} + \sqrt{10} + \sqrt{11}$

(C) 8

(D) 9

(E) $\sqrt{2} + \sqrt{13} + \sqrt{17}$

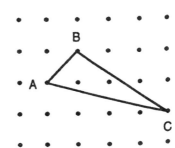

37. If the hypotenuse of a right triangle is $x + 1$ and one of the legs is x, then the other leg is

(A) $\sqrt{2x+1}$ (B) $\sqrt{2x}+1$ (C) $\sqrt{x^2+(x+1)^2}$

(D) 1   (E) $2x + 1$

38. The measures of the lengths of two sides of an isosceles triangle are x and $2x + 1$. Then, the perimeter of the triangle is

(A) $4x$ (B) $4x + 1$ (C) $5x + 1$

(D) $5x + 2$ (E) None of the above

39. Find the length of the diagonal of the rectangular solid shown in the following figure.

(A) 7

(B) $2\sqrt{10}$

(C) $3\sqrt{5}$

(D) 11

(E) None of the above.

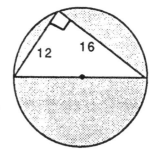

40. Find the area of the shaded portion in the following figure. The heavy dot represents the center of the circle.

(A) $100\pi - 96$

(B) $400\pi - 96$

(C) $400\pi - 192$

(D) $100\pi - 192$

(E) $256\pi - 192$

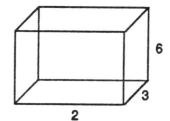

41. $m(\angle A) + m(\angle C) =$

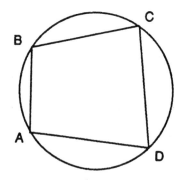

(A) 160°

(B) 180°

(C) 190°

(D) 195°

(E) 200°

42. The area of the shaded region is:

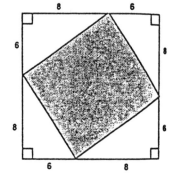

(A) 25 sq. units

(B) 36 sq. units

(C) 49 sq. units

(D) 100 sq. units

(E) None of the above

43. In the figure shown, $\triangle ABC$ is an equilateral triangle. Also, $AC = 3$ and $DB = BE = 1$. Find the perimeter of quadrilateral $ACED$.

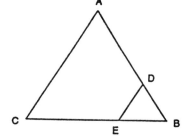

(A) 6

(B) $6^{1}/_{2}$

(C) 7

(D) $7^{1}/_{2}$

(E) 8

44. The sum of the exterior angles of the hexagon shown, one angle at each vertex is

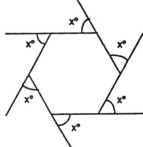

(A) 120°

(B) 270°

(C) 360°

(D) 450°

(E) None of the above

45. Find the area of the shaded region in the figure on the following page, given that $\overline{AB} = \overline{CD} = 4$ and $\overline{BC} = 8$.

(A) 40π

(B) 32π

(C) 68π

(D) 76π

(E) 36π

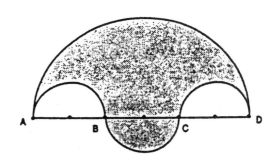

46. In the figure shown, the area of the inscribed circle is A. What is the length of a side of the square?

(A) $\sqrt{A/\pi}$

(B) $\sqrt{2A/\pi}$

(C) A/π

(D) $2\sqrt{A/\pi}$

(E) $2A/\pi$

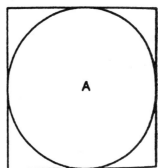

47. In the cube $ABCDEFGH$ with side $AB = 2$, what is the length of diagonal AF?

(A) 2

(B) $2\sqrt{2}$

(C) $2\sqrt{3}$

(D) 4

(E) $2\sqrt{5}$

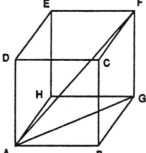

48. Find the area of the shaded region. O is the center of the given circle, whose radius is 6. The distance $\overline{AB} = 6\sqrt{2}$.

(A) 9π

(B) 72π

(C) 18π

(D) $18\pi - 36$

(E) 36

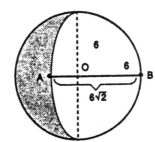

49. In the given figure, the area of the triangle *ABC* is

    (A) 65

    (B) 40

    (C) 28

    (D) 16

    (E) 14

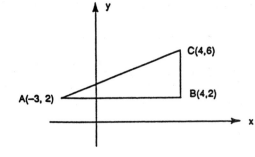

50. In the figure shown the right-angled figure is a square of length *r*, and the circular region on top of the square has radius *r*. The perimeter of the figure is

    (A) $4r + 2\pi r$

    (B) $2r + \pi r/3$

    (C) $3r + 2\pi r$

    (D) $3r + \pi r/3$

    (E) $3r + 5\pi r/3$

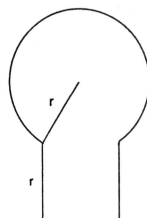

GEOMETRY DIAGNOSTIC TEST

ANSWER KEY

1. (C)	11. (E)	21. (A)	31. (D)	41. (B)
2. (B)	12. (D)	22. (B)	32. (E)	42. (D)
3. (D)	13. (C)	23. (E)	33. (A)	43. (E)
4. (C)	14. (A)	24. (D)	34. (E)	44. (C)
5. (D)	15. (B)	25. (B)	35. (B)	45. (E)
6. (B)	16. (D)	26. (E)	36. (E)	46. (D)
7. (B)	17. (C)	27. (D)	37. (A)	47. (C)
8. (B)	18. (D)	28. (B)	38. (D)	48. (E)
9. (D)	19. (B)	29. (B)	39. (A)	49. (E)
10. (D)	20. (E)	30. (E)	40. (A)	50. (E)

DETAILED EXPLANATIONS
OF ANSWERS

1.   **(C)** Let x = the number of inches that must be cut from each dimension so that the ratio of the shorter side to the longer side is $2/3$.

Cutting off x inches from the shorter side, which is 24 inches, its length will be

$(24 - x)$ inches.

Cutting off x inches from the larger side, which is 33 inches, its length will be

$(33 - x)$ inches.

Since the ratio of the shorter side to the larger side is $2/3$, it follows that,

$$\frac{24 - x}{33 - x} = \frac{2}{3}$$

Solving this equation for x yields the required one length. Thus,

$$\frac{24 - x}{33 - x} = \frac{2}{3}$$

Cross-multiplication yields,

$$3(24 - x) = 2(33 - x)$$
$$72 - 3x = 66 - 2x$$
$$-3x + 2x = 66 - 72$$
$$-x = -6$$
$$x = 6.$$

2.   **(B)**   In order for a rectangle to encompass the greatest area all of its sides must be equal. If this is the case, its perimeter $p = 4S$; and its area $A = S^2$. We were given that its perimeter $p = 52$ m. Substituting, we get $4S = 52$ m or $S = 13$ m. Substituting into the area formula we get $A = (13 \text{ m})^2 = 169 \text{ m}^2$.

3.   **(D)**   The measure of the exterior angle x of triangle ABC is equal to the sum of the measures of the two remote interior angles, A and B, respectively. Thus,

angle $x = 35° + 85° = 120°$.

Another approach is to remember that the sum of the angles in triangle ABC is 35 + 85 + angle C = 180 degrees. Hence, angle C = 60 degrees. Then, since angle C

and angle x are supplementary angles it follows that angle x must be 120 degrees since angle C is 60 degrees.

4.   **(C)**

$$\frac{2\pi}{120°} = \frac{2\pi r}{360°}$$

$$r = 3$$

Area $= \pi r^2 = 9\pi$.

5.   **(D)**   If l is the length and w the width, then $lw = 120$ and $2(l + w) = 44$ so that $l + w = 22$. Now

$$(l - w)^2 = (l + w)^2 - 4lw = (22)^2 - 4(120) = 4,$$

or, $l - w = 2$. Adding $l + w = 22$ and $l - w = 2$, we get $2l = 24$, or, $l = 12$.

6.   **(B)**   At 3:30 the hands of the clock will be shown below. The angle has measure 75°.

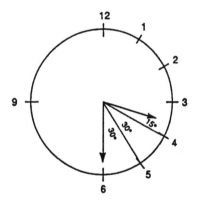

7.   **(B)**   The shape given is a rectangle. Its area is equal to the length multiplied by the width.
The perimeter is twice the length plus twice the width.
Let $x =$ length, $y =$ width. The relevant equations are:

$$xy = 35\text{m}^2. \tag{1}$$

$$2x + 2y = 24 \text{ m}. \tag{2}$$

Rewriting equation (1):

$$y = \frac{35\text{m}^2}{x}.$$

Substituting for y in equation (2):

$$2x + 2\left(\frac{35\ m^2}{x}\right) = 24\ m.$$

Multiplying by x:

$2x^2 + 70m^2 = 24xm.$

Subtracting $24xm$ from both sides:

$2x^2 - 24xm + 70m^2 = 0.$

Dividing all terms by 2:

$x^2 - 12xm + 35m^2 = 0.$

This can be factored into:

$(x - 7m)(x - 5m) = 0.$

From this we get:

$x - 5m = 0 \quad \text{or} \quad x - 7m = 0.$

Two possible lengths: $x = 5m$, $x = 7m$.
   Substituting back into equation (1):

$(5m)y = 35m^2 \Rightarrow y = 7m$

$(7m)y = 35m^2 \Rightarrow y = 5m$

Thus the possible dimensions are:

$5m \times 7m \quad \text{and} \quad 7m \times 5m.$

$5m \times 7m$ are the only dimensions that correspond to the choices.

8.   **(B)**   Let F be the midpoint of $\overline{DE}$. Then the four small triangles are congruent and have the same area. Thus, each small triangle (including $\triangle ABC$) has $1/4$ the area of the large triangle and $1/4$ of 12 is 3.

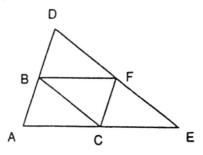

9.   **(D)**   The measure of the angle D is equal to 360° minus the sum of the measures of the other three angles, or

angle $D = 360° - 35° - 85° - 120° = 120°.$

10. **(D)**

$$x = \angle CBA + \angle CAB$$

$$= 50° + 30°$$

$$= 80°$$

$$x = y \text{ (vertically opposite angles)}$$

Therefore, $x + y = 2(80°) = 160°$.

11. **(E)**

$$\angle ACB = 45° \text{ (vertically opposite angles)}$$

$$\theta = \angle ABC + \angle ACB$$

$$= 35° + 45°$$

$$= 80°.$$

12. **(D)**   To find the altitude of the triangle one must recall that the area of a triangle is given by

$$A = (1/2)bh,$$

where b denotes the base and h denotes the altitude. Also, one must recall that the area of a circle is given by

$$A = \pi r^2,$$

where r denotes the radius of the circle.

Since $b = 6$ units then

$$(1/2)(6)h = 3h = A,$$

the area of the triangle. In addition, since $r = 6$ units, then

$$A = \pi r^2 = \pi(6)^2 = 36\pi,$$

the area of the circle. But the area is the same for both figures. Thus,

$$3h = 36\pi$$

$$h = 12\pi$$

is the altitude of the triangle.

The other answer choices are incorrect and are obtained by inappropriately applying the formulas or committing errors in the calculations.

13. **(C)**   One needs to first recall that a cube has 6 equal sized faces. Thus, the area of each face is found by dividing 6 into 96 to obtain 16 square feet. Since each face contains 16 square feet, then one can conclude that each edge of a face is 4 feet long. So, the volume of the cube, given by the formula,

V = (length of edge)^3

is found to be

$V = (4 \text{ feet})^3 = 64$ cubic feet.

Response (A) is found by incorrectly choosing the area of a face as the volume; response (B) is found by incorrectly squaring the 6 faces as the volume; response (E) is found by incorrectly cubing 6 as the volume; and, response (D) is found by incorrectly taking 96 as the volume of the cube.

14.   **(A)**   Note that the ratio (3:5:7) of the angles in the triangle *ABC* can be represented as three distinct angles, $3x$, $5x$, and $7x$. Since the total number of degrees in a triangle is 180 degrees, one can write and solve the equation

$$3x + 5x + 7x = 180$$
$$15x = 180$$
$$x = 12.$$

Thus, the measures of the angles in triangle *ABC* are:

$$3x = 3(12) = 36°, 5x = 5(12) = 60°, \text{ and } 7x = 7(12) = 84°,$$

respectively. Since each of the three angles is less than 90°, then triangle *ABC* is an acute triangle.

15.   **(B)**   This problem can be solved easily by simply using the fact that the sum of the measures of the three interior angles of a triangle is 180°. Thus,

$$(3x + 15) + (5x - 15) + (2x + 30) = 180$$
$$3x + 5x + 2x + 30 = 180$$
$$10x = 180 - 30$$
$$10x = 150$$
$$x = 15.$$

This gives us the measure of the

first angle $= (3x + 15)°$ $= (3 \times 15 + 15)° = 60°$

second angle $= (5x - 15)°$ $= (5 \times 15 - 15)° = 60°$

third angle $= (2x + 30)°$ $= (2 \times 15 + 30)° = 60°.$

16.   **(D)**   Area of a triangle is equal to the product of the length of its base (any one of its sides) and the length of its altitude (the perpendicular segment drawn from the opposite vertex to the base of the triangle or to the line containing the base of the triangle).

In this problem, side $\overline{AB}$ can be taken as the base of triangle *ABC*, and segment $\overline{CE}$ as its altitude. Hence area of triangle ABC is equal to the

(length of $\overline{AB}$) × (length of $\overline{CE}$) = 40 cm².

In triangle ABD, side $\overline{AB}$ can be considered the base of the triangle and segment $\overline{DF}$ can be considered as its altitude. Hence,

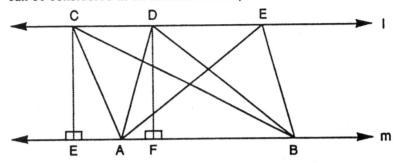

17.   **(C)**   Let (AB) represent the measure (length) of segment $\overline{AB}$, then the length of rectangle $ABCD$ is equal to (AB) and the length of its width is (BC).

Obviously, the shaded region is equal to the area of rectangle $ABCD$ minus the area of triangle EBC.

Recall that the area of a rectangle is equal to the product of the measure of its length and the measure of its width. Thus,

Area of rectangle $ABCD = (AB)\,(BC)$

The area of any triangle is equal to $1/2$ times the measure of its base, (any side of the triangle), times the measure of its altitude (the length of the perpendicular segment drawn from the vertex opposite the base to that base or to the line containing the base). That is, the area of a triangle is equal to $1/2bh$.

Thus,

Area of triangle $EBC = 1/2\,(EB)\,(BC)$.

But $(EB) = 1/4(AB)$, hence,

Area of triangle EBC = $1/2(1/4(AB))(BC)$

= $1/8\,(AB)\,(BC)$

Since the area of triangle ABC is equal to 12 square units, we have

$1/8\,(AB)\,(BC) = 12$

or $(AB)\,(BC) = 96$.

But, $(AB)\,(BC)$ is the area of rectangle $ABCD$. Hence, area of rectangle $ABCD =$ 96 square units.

Thus, area of shaded region = $96 - 12 = 84$ square units.

18.   **(D)**   Redraw the figure. It is easy to see that

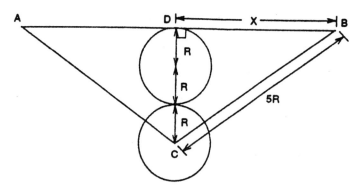

$AC = BC = 5R.$

Let $X = BD$, then $AB = 2X$. Using the Pythagorean theorem in triangle BCD

$$(3R)^2 + x^2 = (5R)^2$$

$$9R^2 + x^2 = 25R^2$$

$$x^2 = 16R^2$$

$$x = 4R$$

and the perimeter of triangle ABC will be:

$$5R + 5R + 2(4R) = 18R.$$

19.   **(B)**   Redraw the figure and put the interior angles in the triangle. The sum of the interior angles is 180°.

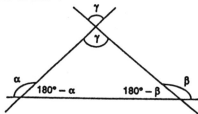

$$180° - \alpha + 180° - \beta + \gamma = 180°$$

rearranging and simplifying

$$180° - \alpha + \gamma = \beta, \quad \text{or} \quad \gamma - \alpha + 180° = \beta.$$

20.   **(E)**   Label the vertices of the given figure A, B, C, D, E, F and the segment $\overline{DE}$ to meet $\overline{AB}$ at G, and let $m\overline{AB}$ denote the length of segment $\overline{AB}$.

    Since all the segments in the figure meet at right angles, it follows that each of the quadrilaterals $AGEF$ and $GBCD$ is a rectangle. This implies that

$$m\overline{DE} + m\overline{EG} = m\overline{CB} = r$$

But, the $m\overline{EG} = m\overline{AF}$ (since $AGEF$ is a rectangle). Hence,

$$m\overline{AF} + m\overline{ED} = r.$$

Also, $m\overline{DC} = m\overline{GB}$ (since *GBCD* is a rectangle), and the $m\overline{FE} = m\overline{AG}$ (since *AGEF* is a rectangle). Thus,

$$m\overline{DC} + m\overline{EF} = m\overline{GB} + m\overline{AG}$$
$$= m\overline{AB}$$
$$= S$$

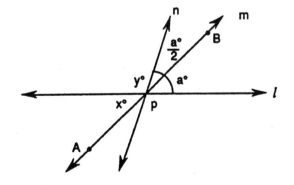

Recall that the perimeter of a closed polygon such as the figure given is equal to the sum of the measures of its segments.

Thus, the perimeter of the given figure is equal to

$$m\overline{AB} + m\overline{BC} + m\overline{CD} + m\overline{DE} + m\overline{EF} =$$
$$= m\overline{AB} + m\overline{CB} + (m\overline{DC} + m\overline{EF}) + (m\overline{ED} + m\overline{AF})$$
$$= s + r + s + r$$
$$= 2s + 2r.$$

21.   **(A)**   Let $m \angle A$ represent the measure of angle *A*. Since *l*, *m*, and *n* are lines intersecting at point *P*, angle *APB* is a straight angle. Recall that the measure of a straight angle is equal to 180°. That is,

$$m \angle APB = 180°.$$

Thus

$$x + y + \frac{a}{2} = 180$$
$$x + y = 180 - \frac{a}{2}$$

Now, we would like to check if any of the quantities given in the answer choices (B), (C), (D), and (E) can be equal to $x + y$. To do so, note that,

$$x + y = 180 - \frac{a}{2}$$
$$= \frac{360 - a}{2}$$

Thus, if any of the quantities given in the answer choices (B), (C), (D), and (E) are correct, that quantity must be equivalent to $\frac{360-a}{2}$. Thus,

(B) $\frac{a}{2} - 180 = \frac{a-360}{2}$

(C) $90 - \frac{a}{2} = \frac{180-a}{2}$

(D) $a - 180$

(E) $180 - a$

Obviously, none of these quantities are equivalent to the quantity $\frac{360-a}{2}$.

22.   **(B)**   Let

$m \angle A$ = the measure of angle A,

$m(\overset{\frown}{ABC})$ = the measure of arc $\overset{\frown}{ABC}$.

Since angle DBC is formed by a tangent to circle O, $\overline{BD}$ and a chord, $\overline{CB}$, intersecting at the point of tangency B, it follows that,

$m\angle DBC = \frac{1}{2}m(\overset{\frown}{BEC})$
$\qquad 70 = \frac{1}{2}m(\overset{\frown}{BEC})$
$m(\overset{\frown}{BEC}) = (70)(2)$
$m(\overset{\frown}{BEC}) = 140$

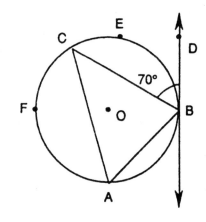

Since $\angle BAC$ is an inscribed angle in the arc $\overset{\frown}{BAC}$, and since arc $\overset{\frown}{BEC}$ is intercepted by angle BAC, it follows that

$m\angle BAC = \frac{1}{2}m(\overset{\frown}{BEC})$
$\qquad\qquad = \frac{1}{2}(140)$
$\qquad\qquad = 70°.$

23.   **(E)**   Redraw the figure as below since $L_1 \parallel L_2$.

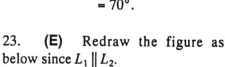

$2x + x + 30° + 60° = 180°$

$3x + 90° = 180°$

$3x = 90°$

$x = 30°.$

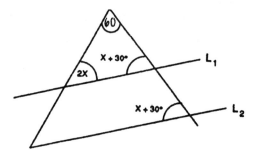

24. **(D)** The measure of the exterior angle x of triangle ABC is equal to the sum of the measures of the two remote interior angles, A and B, respectively. Thus,

angle $x = 35° + 85° = 120°$.

Another approach is to remember that the sum of the angles in triangle ABC *is* *35 + 85 + angle* C = 180 degrees. Hence, angle C = 60 degrees. Then, since angle C and angle x are supplementary angles it follows that angle x must be 120 degrees since angle C is 60 degrees.

25. **(B)** Extend $\overline{RB}$ to meet line l at point E, then angle ARB and angle CER are alternate interior angles. Since r is parallel to l, it follows that the measure of angle ARB is equal to the measure of angle CER. Thus, the measure of angle $CER = 55°$.

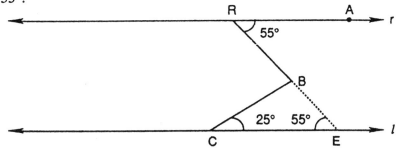

Since angle RBC is an exterior angle of triangle BEC, and the measure of an exterior angle of a triangle is equal to the sum of the measures of the two non-adjacent interior angles of the triangles, it follows that the measure of angle RBC is equal to the sum of the measures of angle BEC and angle BCE. Thus

measure of angle RBC = $55° + 25°$

= $80°$.

26. **(E)** Let $m \angle A$ represent the measure of angle A. Though there are several ways to attack this question, one way is to recall that the sum of the measures of the three interior angles of a triangle is equal to $180°$, and the measure of an exterior angle of a triangle is equal to the sum of the measures of the two non-adjacent interior angles of the triangle.

We can now start by considering triangle ACL. Of course,

$$m \angle A + m \angle C + m \angle 1 = 180°, ... \tag{1}$$

But $\angle 1$ is an exterior angle to triangle LEF, thus,

$$m \angle 1 = m \angle E + m \angle 2.$$

Substituting this in equation (1) yields,

$$m \angle A + m \angle C + m \angle E + m \angle 2 = 180°, ... \tag{2}$$

However, ∠ 2 is an exterior angle to triangle *FBD*, thus,

$$m \angle 2 = m \angle B + m \angle D$$

Substituting this result in equation (2) yields,

$$m \angle A + m \angle C + m \angle E + m \angle B + m \angle D = 180°$$

Thus, the sum of the measures of angles *A, B, C, D*, and *E* is equal to 180°.

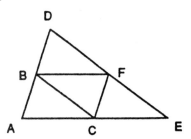

27. **(D)**   Since

$$26 \cdot 13 = 338,$$

the room area is 338 square feet and since

$$18 \cdot 12 = 216,$$

the rug area is 216 square feet, but

$$338 - 216 = 122,$$

so the area of the uncovered portion of the room is 122 square feet.

28. **(B)**   Let *F* be the midpoint of $\overline{DE}$. Then the four small triangles are congruent and have the same area. Thus, each small triangle (including △*ABC*) has ¹/₄ the area of the large triangle and ¹/₄ of 12 is 3.

29. **(B)**   Since all the sides are of different length, the triangle is scalene. A triangle with sides of lengths 3, 4, and 5 is a right triangle. Thus, a triangle with sides of length 3, 4, and 6 is an obtuse triangle.

30. **(E)**

$$A = LW.$$

$$A = 20(10) = 200$$

is the area of the rectangle. The area of the semicircle is half of πr^2 where *r* = 5 or $25\pi/2$. Therefore, the shaded area is

$$200 - \frac{25\pi}{2} = \frac{400 - 25\pi}{2}.$$

Choice (D) comes from forgetting to multiply the 200 by 2 before putting both terms over the common denominator 2. Choice (A) uses 10 for the radius of the circle and does not divide the area of the circle by 2. Choice (B) does use 5 for the radius of the circle but then does not divide the area of the circle by 2.

31.   **(D)**   The height of the trapezoid must be drawn inside the figure in order to use the formula for the area of a trapezoid

$$= \frac{1}{2}h(a + b)$$

where a and b are the bases. When h is drawn, a $30° - 60° - 90°$ triangle is formed with hypotenuse given as 10 (the side of the trapezoid). The side opposite the $30°$ is 5, making the height (the side opposite the $60°$) = $5\sqrt{3}$. Base $b = 30$ as given and base $a = 30 - 10 = 20$.

$$\text{Area} = \frac{1}{2}5\sqrt{3}(20 + 20) = 25(5\sqrt{3}) = 125\sqrt{3}.$$

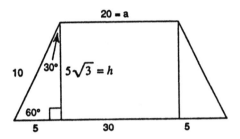

32.   **(E)**   If r is the radius of the sphere, then its volume is πr^3. If r is increased by a factor of 3, then the radius becomes $3r$ and the volume is increased to $\pi(3r)^3 = 27\pi r^3$. Thus the volume is increased by a factor of 27.

33.   **(A)**   Since the sum of measures of the interior angles of a triangle is $180°$, the measure of $\angle ACB$ is $180 - (75 + 75) = 30°$. This is also the measure of $\angle DCE$. Therefore, the sum of measures of angles D and E is $180 - 30 = 150°$.

34.   **(E)**   The surface area of the box equals the area of the base, plus area of the top, plus sum of areas of the four faces. Hence surface area of the box

$$= 2x^2 + 4xh.$$

35.   **(B)**   The shaded portion of square $ABCD$ together with the shaded portion of square $ADEF$ would cover a 10 cm by 10 cm square.

36.   **(E)**   Applying the Pythagorean theorem

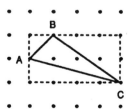

$$AB = \sqrt{1^2 + 1^2} \quad BC = \sqrt{3^2 + 2^2} \quad AC = \sqrt{1^2 + 4^2}$$
$$= \sqrt{2} \qquad\qquad = \sqrt{13} \qquad\qquad = \sqrt{17}$$

37.   **(A)**   By Pythagoras' theorem the square of the length of the hypotenuse is equal to the sum of the squares of the lengths of the legs. Therefore, if Y is the length of the other leg then

$$(X + 1)^2 = X^2 + Y^2,$$

or, $Y^2 = (X + 1)^2 - X^2 = 2X + 1.$

Hence, $Y = \sqrt{2X + 1}.$

38.   **(D)**   The sum of measures of lengths of any two sides of a triangle must be greater than the measure of length of the third side. Since the triangle is isosceles, the only possibility is a triangle with length of sides x, $2x + 1$, $2x + 1$ which has perimeter

$$x + (2x + 1) + (2x + 1) = 5x + 2.$$

39.   **(A)**

$$\text{Diagonal} = \sqrt{4 + 9 + 36} = \sqrt{49} = 7.$$

Choice (B) comes from finding the diagonal of the face with 2 and 6,

$$\sqrt{4 + 36} = \sqrt{40} = 2\sqrt{10}.$$

Choice (C) comes from finding the diagonal of the other face

$$\sqrt{9 + 36} = \sqrt{45} = 3\sqrt{5}.$$

40.   **(A)**   The triangle is a right triangle because from geometry, an angle inscribed in a semicircle is a right angle. The hypotenuse of the triangle, which is also the diameter of the circle, is 20 (3, 4, 5 is a pythagorean triple and this triangle is 4 times 3, 4, 5). The radius of the circle is 10 and the area of the circle is $\pi r^2 = 100\pi$. The area of the triangle is

$$\tfrac{1}{2} bh = \tfrac{1}{2} \, 12(16) = 96$$

so shaded area is $100\pi - 96$. Choice (B) comes from using the diameter, 20 of the circle, instead of the radius. Choice (C) comes from using 20 for the circle radius and forgetting to take half of 12(16). Choice (D) comes from not taking half of 12(16).

41.   **(B)**   Since $\angle A$ and $\angle C$ are inscribed angles, the measure of each of these angles is half the measure of the intercepted arc. Since the two arcs comprise the entire circle, the sum of the measures of these angles is $1/2 \cdot 360°$.

42.   **(D)**   The four right triangles each have legs of length 6 and 8. Thus, the hypotenuse of each of those triangles is length 10 and the required area is 100 square units.

43.   **(E)**   In this case

$$AC = 3, AD = CE = 2 \text{ and } DE = 1.$$

Thus the perimeter is 8.

44.   **(C)**   Each interior angle of a regular polygon is found by

$$\frac{(n-2)180°}{n}$$

where n = number of sides. For this hexagon, $n = 6$, each angle is

$$\frac{(6-2)180°}{6} = \frac{720°}{6} = 120°$$

∴ each exterior angle is 60°, and the sum of the exterior angles

$$= 60° \times 6 = 360°.$$

45.   **(E)**   Diameter $\overline{AD}$ of large circle is 16, therefore, area of semicircle is

$$\frac{\pi r^2}{2} = \frac{\pi 8^2}{2} = 32\pi.$$

Area of "cut-out" small circles is

$$2(\tfrac{1}{2}\pi \cdot 2^2) = 2(2\pi) = 4\pi.$$

Area of semicircle located below the diameter of large semicircle is

$$\tfrac{1}{2}\pi \cdot 4^2 = 8\pi.$$

Therefore, area of shaded region is

$$32\pi + 8\pi - 4\pi = 36\pi.$$

Choice (A) comes from not deleting 2 small circles, i.e., $32\pi + 8\pi$. Choice (B) comes from not taking half of area of small semicircles, i.e., $32\pi + 8\pi - 8\pi$. Choice (C) comes from not taking half of large semicircle, i.e., $64\pi + 8\pi - 4\pi$. Choice (D) comes from not taking half of both of the larger semicircles, i.e., $64\pi + 16\pi - 4\pi$.

46.   **(D)**   If r is the radius of a circle, then the length of a side of the square is $2r$. Since

$$A = \pi r^2, \; r = \sqrt{A/\pi} \text{ and } 2r = 2\sqrt{A/\pi}.$$

47.   **(C)**   In order to find AF, we consider the right triangle AGF. By Pythagoras' theorem

$$(AF)^2 = (FG)^2 + (AG)^2 = (2)^2 + (AG)^2.$$

Also by Pythagoras' theorem

$$(AG)^2 = (AB)^2 + (BG)^2 = 2^2 = 8.$$

Hence,

$$(AF)^2 = 4 + 8 = 12 = (2\sqrt{3})^2 \text{ so that } AF = 2\sqrt{3}.$$

48.   **(E)**   Use the accompanying figure for the solution.

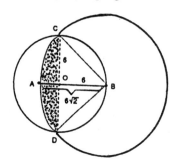

Find the area of the segment bounded by arc $\overparen{CAD}$ and subtract it from the area of the semicircle of the circle O with radius 6. In order to do this, an auxiliary circle, centered at B, is needed. Its radius is $6\sqrt{2}$. Draw

$$\overline{BC} = \overline{BD} = 6\sqrt{2}$$

as radii. Then the area of the segment = area of sector outlined by points B, C, A, D – area of triangle BCD.

$$\text{A (sector)} = {}^1\!/_2 r^2 \cdot \theta$$

where $\theta = 90° = {}^\pi\!/_2$.

$$\text{Area (triangle)} = {}^1\!/_2\, bh.$$

Area segment = area sector – area triangle

$$\frac{1}{2}(6\sqrt{2})^2 \cdot \frac{\pi}{2} - \frac{1}{2} \cdot 12 \cdot 6$$
$$18\pi - 36.$$

Area of original semicircle

$$\frac{\pi r^2}{2} = \frac{\pi \cdot 36}{2} = 18\pi$$

so that shaded area asked for is

$18\pi \, (18\pi - 36) = 36.$

Choice (A) comes from $\frac{1}{4}$ of $\pi r^2 = \frac{1}{4} \cdot 36\pi = 9\pi.$

Choice (B) comes from $(6\sqrt{2})^2 \pi = 72\pi.$

Choice (C) is the area of semicircle $18\pi.$

Choice (D) is area of segment $= 18\pi - 36.$

49.   **(E)**   Since BC is parallel to the vertical axis and AB is parallel to the horizontal axis, CB is perpendicular to AB. Hence, length of BC = height of triangle

$$ABC = 6 - 2 = 4$$

and base = length of $AB = 4 - (-3) = 7.$

Therefore, area of triangle $ABC = (\frac{1}{2})(4)(7) = 14.$

50.   **(E)**   Since the radius of the circular region is r, the angle subtended by the top side of the square at the center of the circle is 60°. Therefore, only 60/360 = 1/6 of the circumference of the circle is excluded from the perimeter of the figure. The perimeter is equal to

$$3r + \frac{5}{6}(2\pi r) = 3r + 5\pi r/3.$$

GEOMETRY REVIEW

1. Points, Lines, and Angles

Geometry is built upon a series of undefined terms. These terms are those which we accept as known in order to define other undefined terms.

A) **Point:** Although we represent points on paper with small dots, a point has no size, thickness, or width.

B) **Line:** A line is a series of adjacent points which extends indefinitely. A line can be either curved or straight; however, unless otherwise stated, the term "line" refers to a straight line.

C) **Plane:** A plane is a collection of points lying on a flat surface, which extends indefinitely in all directions.

If A and B are two points on a line, then the **line segment** AB is the set of points on that line between A and B and including A and B, which are endpoints. The line segment is referred to as AB.

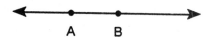

A **ray** is a series of points that lie to one side of a single endpoint.

PROBLEM

How many lines can be found that contain (a) one given point (b) two given points (c) three given points?

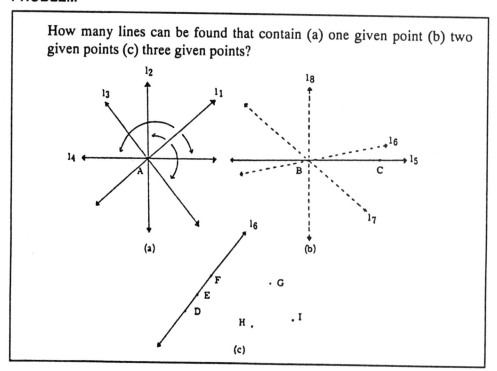

SOLUTION

(a)   *Given one point A*, there are an infinite number of distinct lines that contain the given point. To see this, consider line l_1 passing through point A. By rotating l_1 around A like the hands of a clock, we obtain different lines l_2, l_3, etc. Since we can rotate l_1 in infinitely many ways, there are infinitely many lines containing A.

(b)   *Given two distinct points B and C*, there is one and only one distinct line. To see this, consider all the lines containing point B; l_5, l_6, l_7 and l_8. Only l_5 contains both points B and C. Thus, there is only one line containing both points B and C. Since there is always at least one line containing two distinct points and never more than one, the line passing through the two points is said to be determined by the two points.

(c)   *Given three distinct points*, there may be one line or none. If a line exists that contains the three points, such as D, E, and F, then the points are said to be **colinear**. If no such line exists — as in the case of points G, H, and I, then the points are said to be **noncolinear**.

Intersection Lines and Angles

An **angle** is a collection of points which is the union of two rays having the same endpoint. An angle such as the one illustrated below can be referred to in any of the following ways:

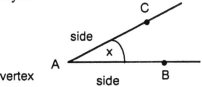

A)   by a capital letter which names its vertex, i.e., $\angle A$;

B)   by a lower-case letter or number placed inside the angle, i.e., $\angle x$;

C)   by three capital letters, where the middle letter is the vertex and the other two letters are not on the same ray, i.e., $\angle CAB$ or $\angle BAC$, both of which represent the angle illustrated in the figure.

Types of Angles

A)   **Vertical angles** are formed when two lines intersect. These angles are equal.

$\angle a = \angle b$

B)   **Adjacent angles** are two angles with a common vertex and a common side, but no common interior points. In the following figure, $\angle DAC$ and $\angle BAC$ are adjacent angles. $\angle DAB$ and $\angle BAC$ are not.

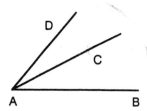

C)   A **right angle** is an angle whose measure is 90°.

D)   An **acute angle** is an angle whose measure is larger than 0° but less than 90°.

E)   An **obtuse angle** is an angle whose measure is larger than 90° but less than 180°.

F)   A **straight angle** is an angle whose measure is 180°. Such an angle is, in fact, a straight line.

G)   A **reflex angle** is an angle whose measure is greater than 180° but less than 360°.

H)   **Complementary angles** are two angles, the sum of the measures of which equals 90°.

I)   **Supplementary angles** are two angles, the sum of the measures of which equals 180°.

J)   **Congruent angles** are angles of equal measure.

PROBLEM

In the figure, we are given $\overline{AB}$ and triangle *ABC*. We are told that the measure of ∠ 1 is five times the measure of ∠ 2. Determine the measures of ∠ 1 and ∠ 2.

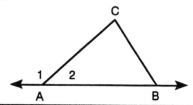

SOLUTION

Since ∠ 1 and ∠ 2 are adjacent angles whose non-common sides lie on a straight line, they are, by definition, supplementary. As supplements, their measures must sum to 180°.

If we let x = the measure of ∠2, then, $5x$ = the measure of ∠ 1.

To determine the respective angle measures, set $x + 5x = 180$ and solve for x. $6x = 180$. Therefore, $x = 30$ and $5x = 150$.

Therefore, the measure of ∠ 1 = 150 and the measure of ∠ 2 = 30.

Perpendicular Lines

Two lines are said to be **perpendicular** if they intersect and form right angles. The symbol for perpendicular (or, is therefore perpendicular to) is ⊥; $\overline{AB}$ is perpendicular to $\overline{CD}$ is written $\overline{AB} \perp \overline{CD}$.

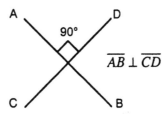

$$\overline{AB} \perp \overline{CD}$$

PROBLEM

We are given straight lines $\overline{AB}$ and $\overline{CD}$ intersecting at point P. $\overline{PR} \perp \overline{AB}$ and the measure of $\angle APD$ is 170°. Find the measures of $\angle 1$, $\angle 2$, $\angle 3$, and $\angle 4$. (See figure below.)

SOLUTION

This problem will involve making use of several of the properties of supplementary and vertical angles, as well as perpendicular lines.

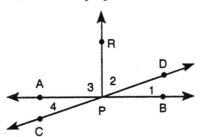

$\angle APD$ and $\angle 1$ are adjacent angles whose non-common sides lie on a straight line, $\overline{AB}$. Therefore, they are supplements and their measures sum to 180°.

$$m \angle APD + m \angle 1 = 180°.$$

We know $m \angle APD = 170°$. Therefore, by substitution, $170° + m \angle 1 = 180°$. This implies $m \angle 1 = 10°$.

$\angle 1$ and $\angle 4$ are vertical angles because they are formed by the intersection of two straight lines, $\overline{CD}$ and $\overline{AB}$, and their sides form two pairs of opposite rays. As vertical angles, they are, by theorem, of equal measure. Since $m \angle 1 = 10°$, then $m \angle 4 = 10°$.

Since $\overline{PR} \perp \overline{AB}$, at their intersection the angles formed must be right angles. Therefore, $\angle 3$ is a right angle and its measure is 90°. $m \angle 3 = 90°$.

The figure shows us that $\angle APD$ is composed of $\angle 3$ and $\angle 2$. Since the measure of the whole must be equal to the sum of the measures of its parts, $m \angle APD = m \angle 3 + m \angle 2$. We know the $m \angle APD = 170°$ and $m \angle 3 = 90°$, therefore, by substitution, we can solve for $m \angle 2$, our last unknown.

$$170° = 90° + m \angle 2$$

$$80° = m \angle 2$$

Therefore, $m \angle 1 = 10°$, $m \angle 2 = 80°$

$\qquad\qquad m \angle 3 = 90°$, $m \angle 4 = 10°$.

PROBLEM

In the accompanying figure $\overline{SM}$ is the perpendicular bisector of $\overline{QR}$, and $\overline{SN}$ is the perpendicular bisector of $\overline{QP}$. Prove that $SR = SP$.

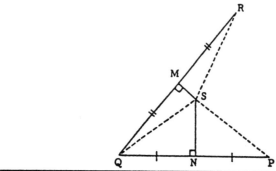

SOLUTION

Every point on the perpendicular bisector of a segment is equidistant from the endpoints of the segment.

Since point S is on the perpendicular bisector of $\overline{QR}$,

$$SR = SQ \qquad\qquad (1)$$

Also, since point S is on the perpendicular bisector of $\overline{QP}$,

$$SQ = SP \qquad\qquad (2)$$

By the transitive property (quantities equal to the same quantity are equal), we have:

$$SR = SP. \qquad\qquad (3)$$

Parallel Lines

Two lines are called **parallel lines** if, and only if, they are in the same plane (coplanar) and do not intersect. The symbol for parallel, or is parallel to, is $||$; $\overline{AB}$ is parallel to $\overline{CD}$ is written $\overline{AB} \, || \, \overline{CD}$.

The distance between two parallel lines is the length of the perpendicular segment from any point on one line to the other line.

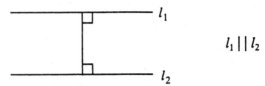

$l_1 \,||\, l_2$

Given a line l and a point P not on line l, there is one and only one line through point P that is parallel to line l.

Two coplanar lines are either intersecting lines or parallel lines.

If two (or more) lines are perpendicular to the same line, then they are parallel to each other.

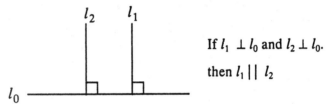

If $l_1 \perp l_0$ and $l_2 \perp l_0$.

then $l_1 \,||\, l_2$

If two lines are cut by a transversal so that alternate interior angles are equal, the lines are parallel.

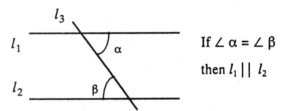

If $\angle \alpha = \angle \beta$

then $l_1 \,||\, l_2$

If two lines are parallel to the same line, then they are parallel to each other.

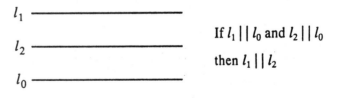

If $l_1 \,||\, l_0$ and $l_2 \,||\, l_0$

then $l_1 \,||\, l_2$

If a line is perpendicular to one of two parallel lines, then it is perpendicular to the other line, too.

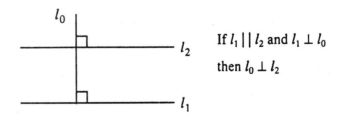

If $l_1 \,||\, l_2$ and $l_1 \perp l_0$

then $l_0 \perp l_2$

If two lines being cut by a transversal form congruent corresponding angles, then the two lines are parallel.

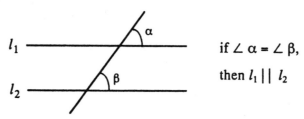

if $\angle \alpha = \angle \beta$,

then $l_1 \parallel l_2$

If two lines being cut by a transversal form interior angles on the same side of the transversal that are supplementary, then the two lines are parallel.

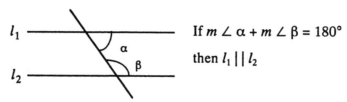

If $m \angle \alpha + m \angle \beta = 180°$

then $l_1 \parallel l_2$

If a line is parallel to one of two parallel lines, it is also parallel to the other line.

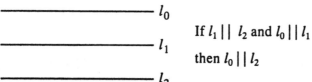

If $l_1 \parallel l_2$ and $l_0 \parallel l_1$

then $l_0 \parallel l_2$

If two parallel lines are cut by a transversal, then:

A)   The alternate interior angles are congruent.

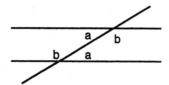

B)   The corresponding angles are congruent.

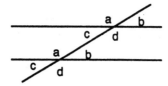

C)   The consecutive interior angles are supplementary.

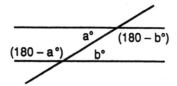

D) The alternate exterior angles are congruent.

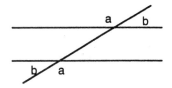

PROBLEM

Given: ∠ 2 is supplementary to ∠ 3.

Prove: $l_1 \parallel l_2$.

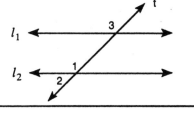

SOLUTION

Given two lines intercepted by a transversal, if a pair of corresponding angles are congruent, then the two lines are parallel. In this problem, we will show that since ∠ 1 and ∠ 2 are supplementary and ∠ 2 and ∠ 3 are supplementary, ∠ 1 and ∠ 3 are congruent. Since corresponding angles ∠ 1 and ∠ 3 are congruent, it follows $l_1 \parallel l_2$.

	Statement		**Reason**
1.	∠ 2 is supplementary to ∠ 3.	1.	Given.
2.	∠ 1 is supplementary to ∠ 2.	2.	Two angles that form a linear pair are supplementary.
3.	∠ 1 ≅ ∠ 3	3.	Angles supplementary to the same angle are congruent.
4.	$l_1 \parallel l_2$.	4.	Given two lines intercepted by a transversal, if a pair of corresponding angles are congruent, then the two lines are parallel.

PROBLEM

If line $\overline{AB}$ is parallel to line $\overline{CD}$ and line $\overline{EF}$ is parallel to line $\overline{GH}$, prove that $m \angle 1 = m \angle 2$.

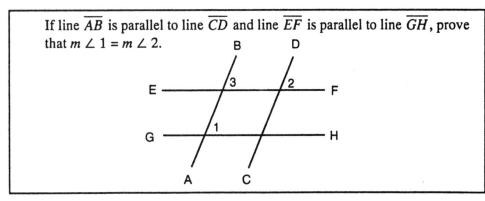

SOLUTION

To show ∠ 1 ≅ ∠ 2, we relate both to ∠ 3. Because $\overline{EF} \parallel \overline{GH}$, corresponding angles 1 and 3 are congruent. Since $\overline{AB} \parallel \overline{CD}$, corresponding angles 3 and 2 are congruent. Because both ∠ 1 and ∠ 2 are congruent to the same angle, it follows that ∠ 1 ≅ ∠ 2.

	Statement		**Reason**
1.	$\overline{EF} \cong \overline{GH}$	1.	Given.
2.	$m \angle 1 = m \angle 3$	2.	If two parallel lines are cut by a transversal, corresponding angles are of equal measure.
3.	$\overline{AB} \parallel \overline{CD}$	3.	Given.
4.	$m \angle 2 = m \angle 3$	4.	If two parallel lines are cut by a transversal, corresponding angles are equal in measure.
5.	$m \angle 1 = m \angle 2$	5.	If two quantities are equal to the same quantity, they are equal to each other.

Drill 1: Lines and Angles

Intersection Lines

1. Find *a*.

(A) 38°   (B) 68°   (C) 78°

(D) 90°   (E) 112°

2. Find *c*.

(A) 32°   (B) 48°   (C) 58°

(D) 82°   (E) 148°

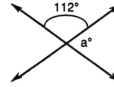
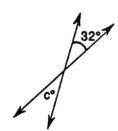

3. Determine *x*.

(A) 21°   (B) 23°   (C) 51°

(D) 102°   (E) 153°

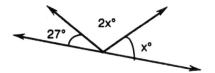

4.   Find *x*.

(A)   8   (B)   11.75   (C)   21

(D)   23   (E)   32

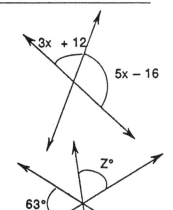

5.   Find *z*.

(A)   29°   (B)   54°   (C)   61°

(D)   88°   (E)   92°

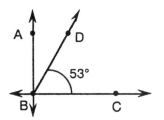

Perpendicular Lines

6. $\overline{BA} \perp \overline{BC}$ and $m \angle DBC = 53$. Find $m \angle ABD$.

(A)   27°   (B)   33°   (C)   37°

(D)   53°   (E)   90°

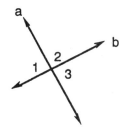

7. $m \angle 1 = 90°$. Find $m \angle 2$.

(A)   80°   (B)   90°   (C)   100°

(D)   135°   (E)   180°

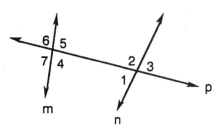

8.   If $n \perp p$, which of the following statements is true?

(A) $\angle 1 \cong \angle 2$

(B) $\angle 4 \cong \angle 5$

(C) $m\angle 4 + m \angle 5 > m \angle 1 + m \angle 2$

(D) $m \angle 3 > m \angle 2$

(E) $m \angle 4 = 90°$

9. $\overline{CD} \perp \overline{EF}$. If $m \angle 1 = 2x$, $m \angle 2 = 30°$, and $m \angle 3 = x$, find *x*.

(A)   5°   (B)   10°   (C)   12°

(D)   20°   (E)   25°

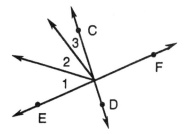

10.   In the figure, $p \perp t$ and $q \perp t$. Which of the following statements is false?

(A) $\angle 1 \cong \angle 4$

(B) $\angle 2 \cong \angle 3$

(C) $m\angle 2 + m\angle 3 = m\angle 4 + m\angle 6$

(D) $m\angle 5 + m\angle 6 = 180°$

(E) $m\angle 2 > m\angle 5$

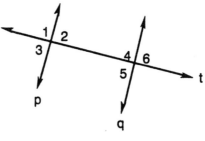

Parallel Lines

11.   If $a \parallel b$, find z.

(A)   26°   (B)   32°   (C)   64°

(D)   86°   (E)   116°

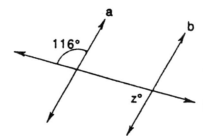

12.   In the figure, $p \parallel q \parallel r$. Find $m\angle 7$.

(A)   27°   (B)   33°   (C)   47°

(D)   57°   (E)   64°

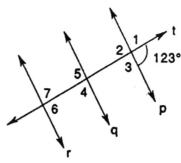

13.   If $m \parallel n$, which of the following statements is false?

(A) $\angle 2 \cong \angle 5$

(B) $\angle 3 \cong \angle 6$

(C) $m\angle 4 + m\angle 5 = 180°$

(D) $\angle 2 \cong \angle 8$

(E) $m\angle 7 + m\angle 3 = 180°$

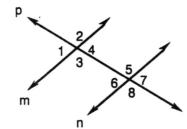

14.   If $r \parallel s$, find $m\angle 2$.

(A)   17°   (B)   27°   (C)   43°

(D)   67°   (E)   73°

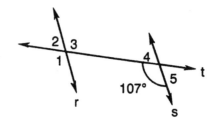

15.   If $a \,||\, b$ and $c \,||\, d$, find $m \angle 5$.

(A)   55°   (B)   65°   (C)   75°

(D)   95°   (E)   125°

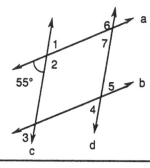

2. Polygons (Convex)

A **polygon** is a figure with the same number of sides as angles.

An **equilateral polygon** is a polygon all of whose sides are of equal measure.

An **equiangular polygon** is a polygon all of whose angles are of equal measure.

A **regular polygon** is a polygon that is both equilateral and equiangular.

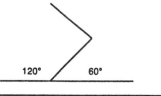

PROBLEM

Each interior angle of a regular polygon contains 120°. How many sides does the polygon have?

SOLUTION

At each vertex of a polygon, the exterior angle is supplementary to the interior angle, as shown in the diagram.

Since we are told that the interior angles measure 120 degrees, we can deduce that the exterior angle measures 60°.

Each exterior angle of a regular polygon of *n* sides measure $360°/_n$ degrees. We know that each exterior angle measures 60°, and, therefore, by setting $360°/_n$ equal to 60°, we can determine the number of sides in the polygon. The calculation is as follows:

$$360°/_n = 60°$$

$$60°n = 360°$$

$$n = 6.$$

Therefore, the regular polygon, with interior angles of 120°, has 6 sides and is called a hexagon.

The area of a regular polygon can be determined by using the **apothem** and **radius** of the polygon. The apothem (*a*) of a regular polygon is the segment from the center of the polygon perpendicular to a side of the polygon. The radius (*r*) of a regular polygon is the segment joining any vertex of a regular polygon with the center of that polygon.

(1)   All radii of a regular polygon are congruent.

(2)   The radius of a regular polygon is congruent to a side.

(3)   All apothems of a regular polygon are congruent.

The **area** of a regular polygon equals one-half the product of the length of the apothem and the perimeter.

Area = $^1/_2\, a \cdot p$

PROBLEM

Find area of the regular polygon whose radius is 8 and whose apothem is 6.

SOLUTION

If the radius is 8, the length of a side is also 8. Therefore, the perimeter of the polygon is 40.

$$A = {}^1/_2\, a \cdot p$$

$$A = {}^1/_2\,(6)\,(40)$$

$$A = 120.$$

PROBLEM

Find the area of a regular hexagon if one side has length 6.

SOLUTION

Since the length of a side equals 6, the radius also equals 6 and the perimeter equals 36. The base of the right triangle, formed by the radius and apothem, is half the length of a side, or 3. Using the Pythagorean theorem, you can find the length of the apothem.

$$a^2 + b^2 = c^2$$

$$a^2 + (3)^2 = (6)^2$$

$$a^2 = 36 - 9$$

$$a^2 = 27$$

$$a = 3\sqrt{3}$$

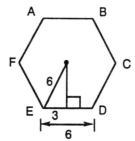

The apothem equals $3\sqrt{3}$. Therefore, the area of the hexagon

$$= \frac{1}{2} a \cdot p$$

$$= \frac{1}{2}(3\sqrt{3})(36)$$

$$= 54\sqrt{3}$$

Drill 2: Regular Polygons

1. Find the measure of an interior angle of a regular pentagon.

(A) 55   (B) 72   (C) 90   (D) 108   (E) 540

2. Find the measure of an exterior angle of a regular octagon.

(A) 40   (B) 45   (C) 135   (D) 540   (E) 1080

3. Find the sum of the measures of the exterior angles of a regular triangle.

(A) 90   (B) 115   (C) 180   (D) 250   (E) 360

4. Find the area of a square with a perimeter of 12 cm.

(A) 9 cm²   (B) 12 cm²   (C) 48 cm²   (D) 96 cm²   (E) 144 cm²

5. A regular triangle has sides of 24 mm. If the apothem is $4\sqrt{3}$ mm, find the area of the triangle.

(A) 72 mm²   (B) $96\sqrt{3}$ mm²   (C) 144 mm²

(D) $144\sqrt{3}$ mm²   (E) 576 mm²

6.   Find the area of a regular hexagon with sides of 4 cm.

(A) $12\sqrt{3}$ cm²   (B) 24 cm²   (C) $24\sqrt{3}$ cm²

(D) 48 cm²   (E) $48\sqrt{3}$ cm²

7.   Find the area of a regular decagon with sides of length 6 cm and an apothem of length 9.2 cm.

(A) 55.2 cm²   (B) 60 cm²   (C) 138 cm²

(D) 138.3 cm²   (E) 276 cm²

8.   The perimeter of a regular heptagon (7-gon) is 36.4 cm. Find the length of each side.

(A) 4.8 cm   (B) 5.2 cm   (C) 6.7 cm   (D) 7 cm   (E) 10.4 cm

9.   The apothem of a regular quadrilateral is 4 in. Find the perimeter.

(A) 12 in   (B) 16 in   (C) 24 in   (D) 32 in   (E) 64 in

10.   A regular triangle has a perimeter of 18 cm; a regular pentagon has a perimeter of 30 cm; a regular hexagon has a perimeter of 33 cm. Which figure (or figures) have sides with the longest measure?

(A)   regular triangle

(B)   regular triangle and regular pentagon

(C)   regular pentagon

(D)   regular pentagon and regular hexagon

(E)   regular hexagon

3. Triangles

A closed three-sided geometric figure is called a **triangle**. The points of the intersection of the sides of a triangle are called the **vertices** of the triangle.

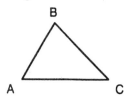

The **perimeter** of a triangle is the sum of the measures of the sides of the triangle.

A triangle with no equal sides is called a **scalene** triangle.

A triangle having at least two equal sides is called an **isosceles** triangle. The third side is called the **base** of the triangle.

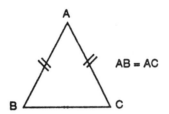

A side of a triangle is a line segment whose endpoints are the vertices of two angles of the triangle.

An interior angle of a triangle is an angle formed by two sides and includes the third side within its collection of points.

An equilateral triangle is a triangle having three equal sides. $AB = AC = BC$

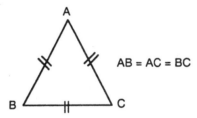

A triangle with an obtuse angle (greater than 90°) is called an **obtuse triangle**.

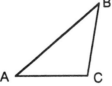

An **acute triangle** is a triangle with three acute angles (less than 90°).

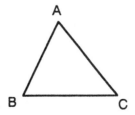

A triangle with a right angle is called a **right triangle**. The side opposite the right angle in a right triangle is called the hypotenuse of the right triangle. The other two sides are called arms or legs of the right triangle.

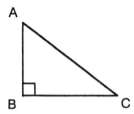

An **altitude** of a triangle is a line segment from a vertex of the triangle perpendicular to the opposite side.

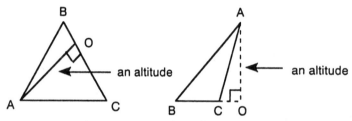

A line segment connecting a vertex of a triangle and the midpoint of the opposite side is called a **median** of the triangle.

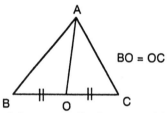

A line that bisects and is perpendicular to a side of a triangle is called a **perpendicular bisector** of that side.

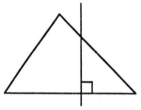

An **angle bisector** of a triangle is a line that bisects an angle and extends to the opposite side of the triangle.

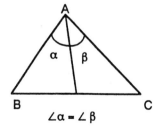

The line segment that joins the midpoints of two sides of a triangle is called a midline of the triangle.

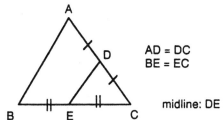

AD = DC
BE = EC

midline: DE

An exterior angle of a triangle is an angle formed outside a triangle by one side of the triangle and the extension of an adjacent side.

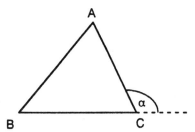

A triangle whose three interior angles have equal measure is said to be equiangular.

Three or more lines (or rays or segments) are concurrent if there exists one point common to all of them, that is, if they all intersect at the same point.

PROBLEM

The measure of the vertex angle of an isosceles triangle exceeds the measurement of each base angle by 30°. Find the value of each angle of the triangle.

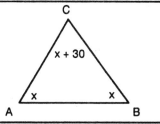

SOLUTION

We know that the sum of the values of the angles of a triangle is 180°. In an isosceles triangle, the angles opposite the congruent sides (the base angles) are, themselves, congruent and of equal value.

Therefore,

(1)   Let x = the measure of each base angle.

(2)   Then $x + 30$ = the measure of the vertex angle.

We can solve for x algebraically by keeping in mind the sum of all the measures will be 180°.

$$x + x + (x + 30) = 180$$

$$3x + 30 = 180$$

$$3x = 150$$

$$x = 50$$

Therefore, the base angles each measure 50°, and the vertex angle measures 80°.

PROBLEM

Prove that the base angles of an isosceles right triangle have measure 45°.

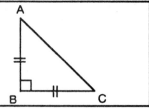

SOLUTION

As drawn in the figure, $\triangle ABC$ is an isosceles right triangle with **base angles** *BAC* and *BCA*. The sum of the measures of the angles of any triangle is 180°. For $\triangle ABC$, this means

$$m \angle BAC + m \angle BCA + m \angle ABC = 180° \tag{1}$$

But $m \angle ABC = 90°$ because $\triangle ABC$ is a right triangle. Furthermore, $m \angle BCA = m \angle BAC$, since the base angles of an isosceles triangle are congruent. Using these facts in equation (1)

$$m \angle BAC + m \angle BCA + 90° = 180°$$

or $$2m \angle BAC = 2m \angle BCA = 90°$$

or $$m \angle BAC = m \angle BCA = 45°.$$

Therefore, the base angles of an isosceles right triangle have measure 45°.

The area of a triangle is given by the formula $A = \frac{1}{2} bh$, where *b* is the length of a base, which can be any side of the triangle and *h* is the corresponding height of the triangle, which is the perpendicular line segment that is drawn from the vertex opposite the base to the base itself.

$$A = \frac{1}{2} bh$$

$$A = \frac{1}{2} (10) (3)$$

$$A = 15$$

The area of a right triangle is found by taking $\frac{1}{2}$ the product of the lengths of its two arms.

$$A = \frac{1}{2} (5) (12)$$

$$A = 30$$

Drill 3: Triangles

Angle Measures

1. In △ *PQR*, ∠ *Q* is a right angle. Find *m* ∠*R*.

(A) 27° (B) 33° (C) 54°

(D) 67° (E) 157°

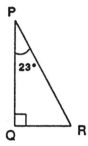

2. △ *MNO* is isosceles. If the vertex angle, ∠ *N*, has a measure of 96°, find the measure of ∠ *M*.

(A) 21° (B) 42° (C) 64°

(D) 84° (E) 96°

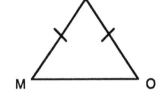

3. Find *x*.

(A) 15° (B) 25° (C) 30°

(D) 45° (E) 90°

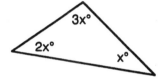

4. Find *m* ∠1.

(A) 40 (B) 66 (C) 74

(D) 114 (E) 140

5. △ *ABC* is a right triangle with a right angle at *B*. △ *BDC* is a right triangle with right angle ∠ *BDC*. If *m* ∠*C* = 36, find *m* ∠*A*.

(A) 18 (B) 36 (C) 54

(D) 72 (E) 180

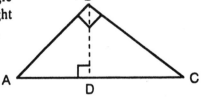

Similar Triangles

6. The two triangles shown are similar. Find *b*.

(A) 2 2/3 (B) 3 (C) 4

(D) 16 (E) 24

7.   The two triangles shown are similar. Find $m \angle 1$.

(A)   48   (B)   53   (C)   74

(D)   127   (E)   180

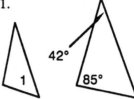

8.   The two triangles shown are similar. Find a and b.

(A)   5 and 10   (B)   4 and 8

(C)   4 2/3 and 7 1/3   (D)   5 and 8

(E)   5 1/3 and 8

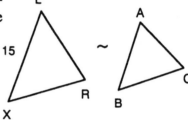

9.   The perimeter of $\triangle LXR$ is 45 and the perimeter of $\triangle ABC$ is 27. If $LX = 15$, find the length of AB.

(A)   9   (B)   15   (C)   27

(D)   45   (E)   72

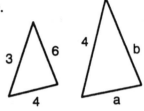

10.   Find b.

(A)   9   (B)   15   (C)   20

(D)   45   (E)   60

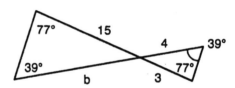

Area

11.   Find the area of $\triangle MNO$.

(A)   22   (B)   49   (C)   56

(D)   84   (E)   112

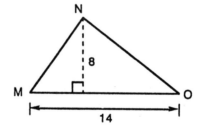

12.   Find the area of $\triangle PQR$.

(A)   31.5   (B)   38.5   (C)   53

(D)   77   (E)   82.5

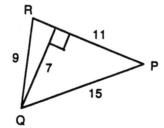

13.   Find the area of Δ *STU*.

(A) $4\sqrt{2}$ (B) $8\sqrt{2}$ (C) $12\sqrt{2}$

(D) $16\sqrt{2}$ (E) $32\sqrt{2}$

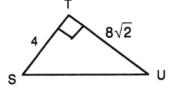

14.   Find the area of Δ *ABC*.

(A)   54 cm²   (B)   81 cm²   (C)   108 cm²

(D)   135 cm²   (E)   180 cm²

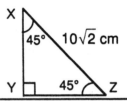

15.   Find the area of Δ *XYZ*.

(A)   20 cm²   (B)   50 cm²   (C) $50\sqrt{2}$ cm²

(D)   100 cm²   (E)   200 cm²

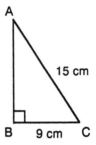

4.   Quadrilaterals

A **quadrilateral** is a polygon with four sides.

Parallelograms

A **parallelogram** is a quadrilateral whose opposite sides are parallel.

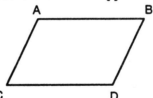

Two angles that have their vertices at the endpoints of the same side of a parallelogram are called **consecutive angles**.

The perpendicular segment connecting any point of a line containing one side of the parallelogram to the line containing the opposite side of the parallelogram is called the **altitude** of the parallelogram.

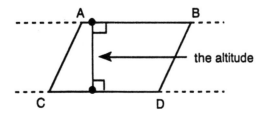

A diagonal of a polygon is a line segment joining any two non-consecutive vertices.

The area of a parellelogram is given by the formula $A = bh$ where b is the base and h is the height drawn perpendicular to that base. Note that the height equals the altitude of the parallelogram

$A = bh$

$A = (10)(3)$

$A = 30$

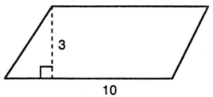

Rectangles

A rectangle is a parallelogram with right angles.

The diagonals of a rectangle are equal.

If the diagonals of a parallelogram are equal, the parallelogram is a rectangle.

If a quadrilateral has four right angles, then it is a rectangle.

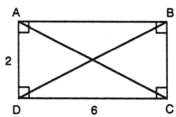

The area of a rectangle is given by the formula $A = lw$ where l is the length and w is the width.

$A = lw$

$A = (3)(10)$

$A = 30$

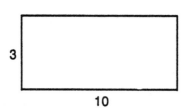

Rhombi

A rhombus is a parallelogram with all sides equal.

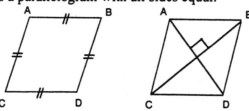

The diagonals of a rhombus are perpendicular to each other.

The diagonals of a rhombus bisect the angles of the rhombus.

If the diagonals of a parallelogram are perpendicular, the parallelogram is a rhombus.

If a quadrilateral has four equal sides, then it is a rhombus.

A parallelogram is a rhombus if either diagonal of the parallelogram bisects the angles of the vertices it joins.

Squares

A square is a rhombus with a right angle.

A square is an equilateral quadrilateral.

A square has all the properties of parallelograms, and rectangles.

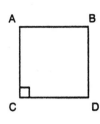

A rhombus is a square if one of its interior angles is a right angle.

In a square, the measure of either diagonal can be calculated by multiplying the length of any side by the square root of 2.

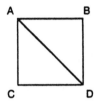

$$AD = AB\sqrt{2}$$

The area of a square is given by the formula $A = s^2$ where s is the side of the square. Since all sides of a square are equal, it does not matter which side is used.

$A = s^2$

$A = 6^2$

$A = 36$

The area of a square can also be found by taking $1/2$ the product of the length of the diagonal squared.

$A = 1/2\, d^2$

$A = 1/2\, (8)^2$

$A = 32$

Trapezoids

A **trapezoid** is a quadrilateral with two and only two sides parallel. The parallel sides of a trapezoid are called **bases**.

The **median** of a trapezoid is the line joining the midpoints of the non-parallel sides.

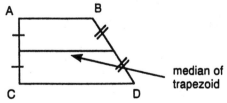

median of trapezoid

The perpendicular segment connecting any point in the line containing one base of the trapezoid to the line containing the other base is the **altitude** of the trapezoid.

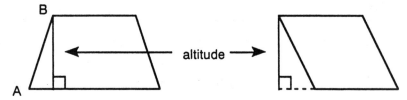

An **isosceles trapezoid** is a trapezoid whose non-parallel sides are equal. A pair of angles including only one of the parallel sides is called **a pair of base angles**.

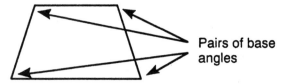

The median of a trapezoid is parallel to the bases and equal to one-half their sum.

The base angles of an isosceles trapezoid are equal.

The diagonals of an isosceles trapezoid are equal.

The opposite angles of an isosceles trapezoid are supplementary.

PROBLEM

Prove that all pairs of consecutive angles of a parallelogram are supplementary.

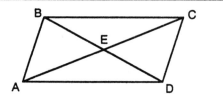

SOLUTION

We must prove that the pairs of angles ∠ *BAD* and ∠ *ADC*, ∠ *ADC* and ∠ *DCB*, ∠ *DCB* and ∠ *CBA*, and ∠ *CBA* and ∠ *BAD* are supplementary. (This means that the sum of their measures is 180°.)

Because *ABCD* is a parallelogram, $\overline{AB} \parallel \overline{CD}$. Angles *BAD* and *ADC* are consecutive interior angles, as are ∠ *CBA* and ∠ *DCB*. Since the consecutive interior angles formed by 2 parallel lines and a transversal are supplementary, ∠ *BAD* and ∠ *ADC* are supplementary, as are ∠ *CBA* and ∠ *DCB*.

Similarly, $\overline{AD} \parallel \overline{BC}$. Angles *ADC* and *DCB* are consecutive interior angles, as are ∠ *CBA* and ∠ *BAD*. Since the consecutive interior angles formed by 2 parallel lines and a transversal are supplementary, ∠ CBA and ∠ BAD are supplementary, as are ∠ ADC and ∠ DCB.

PROBLEM

In the accompanying figure, Δ ABC is given to be an isosceles right triangle with ∠ ABC a right angle and AB ≅ BC. Line segment $\overline{BD}$, which bisects $\overline{CA}$, is extended to E, so that $\overline{BD}$ ≅ $\overline{DE}$. Prove BAEC is a square.

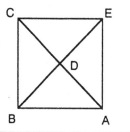

SOLUTION

A square is a rectangle in which two consecutive sides are congruent. This definition will provide the framework for the proof in this problem. We will prove that BAEC is a parallelogram that is specifically a rectangle with consecutive sides congruent, namely a square.

Statement		**Reason**	
1.	$\overline{BD}$ ≅ $\overline{DE}$	1.	Given.
2.	$\overline{AD}$ ≅ $\overline{DC}$	2.	$\overline{BD}$ bisects $\overline{CA}$.
3.	BAEC is a parallelogram	3.	If diagonals of a quadrilateral bisect each other, then the quadrilateral is a parallelogram.
4.	∠ ABC is a right angle	4.	Given.
5.	BAEC is a rectangle	5.	A parallelogram, one of whose angles is a right angle, is a rectangle.
6.	AB ≅ BC	6.	Given.
7.	BAEC is a square	7.	If a rectangle has two congruent consecutive sides, then the rectangle is a square.

Drill 4: Quadrilaterals

Parallelograms, Rectangles, Rhombi, Squares, Trapezoids

1. In parallelogram *WXYZ*, *WX* = 14, *WZ* = 6, *ZY* = 3*x* + 5, and *XY* = 2*y* − 4. Find *x* and *y*.

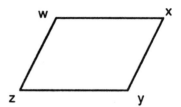

(A) 3 and 5   (B)   4 and 5   (C)   4 and 6

(D) 6 and 10 (E)   6 and 14

2. Quadrilateral *ABCD* is a parellelogram. If *m* ∠ *B* = 6*x* + 2 and *m* ∠ *D* = 98, find *x*.

(A) 12   (B)   16   (C)   16 2/3

(D) 18   (E)   20

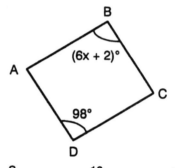

3. Find the area of parallelogram *STUV*.

(A) 56   (B)   90   (C)   108

(D) 162   (E)   180

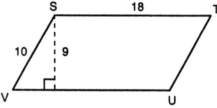

4. Find the area of parallelogram *MNOP*.

(A) 19   (B)   32   (C)   32√3

(D) 44   (E)   44√3

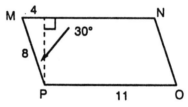

5. Find the perimeter of rectangle *PQRS,* if the area is 99 in².

(A) 31 in   (B)   38 in   (C)   40 in

(D) 44 in   (E)   121 in

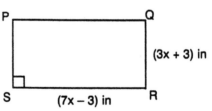

6. In rectangle *ABCD, AD* = 6 cm and *DC* = 8 cm. Find the length of the diagonal *AC*.

(A) 10 cm   (B)   12 cm   (C)   20 cm

(D) 28 cm   (E)   48 cm

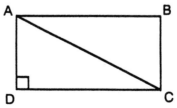

7. Find the area of rectangle *UVXY*.

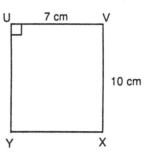

(A) 17 cm²   (B)   34 cm²   (C)   35 cm²

(D) 70 cm²   (E)   140 cm²

8. Find *x* in rectangle *BCDE* if the diagonal *EC* is 17 mm.

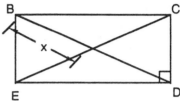

(A) 6.55 mm (B)   8 mm   (C)   8.5 mm

(D) 17 mm   (E)   34 mm

9. In rhombus *DEFG*, *DE* = 7 cm. Find the perimeter of the rhombus.

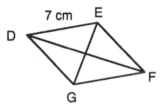

(A) 14 cm   (B)   28 cm   (C)   42 cm

(D) 49 cm   (E)   56 cm

10. In rhombus *RHOM*, the diagonal $\overline{RO}$ is 8 cm and the diagonal $\overline{HM}$ is 12 cm. Find the area of the rhombus.

(A) 20 cm²   (B)   40 cm²   (C)   48 cm²

(D) 68 cm²   (E)   96 cm²

11. In rhombus *GHIJ*, *GI* = 6 cm and *HJ* = 8 cm. Find the length of *GH*.

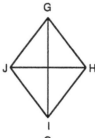

(A) 3 cm   (B)   4 cm   (C)   5 cm

(D) $4\sqrt{3}$ cm   (E)   14 cm

12. In rhombus *CDEF*, *CD* is 13 mm and *DX* is 5 mm. Find the area of the rhombus.

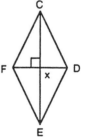

(A) 31 mm² (B)   60 mm² (C)   78 mm²

(D) 120 mm² (E)   260 mm²

13. Quadrilateral *ATUV* is a square. If the perimeter of the square is 44 cm, find the length of $\overline{AT}$.

(A) 4 cm   (B) 11 cm   (C) 22 cm   (D) 30 cm   (E) 40 cm

14. The area of square *XYZW* is 196 cm². Find the perimeter of the square.

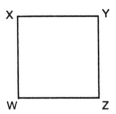

(A) 28 cm   (B) 42 cm   (C) 56 cm

(D) 98 cm   (E) 196 cm.

15. In square *MNOP*, *MN* is 6 cm. Find the length of diagonal $\overline{MO}$.

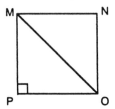

(A) 6 cm   (B) $6\sqrt{2}$ cm   (C) $6\sqrt{3}$ cm

(D) $6\sqrt{6}$ cm   (E) 12 cm

16. In square *ABCD*, *AB* = 3 cm. Find the area of the square.

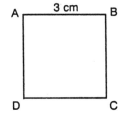

(A) 9 cm²   (B) 12 cm²   (C) 15 cm²

(D) 18 cm²   (E) 21 cm²

17. *ABCD* is an isosceles trapezoid. Find the perimeter.

(A) 21 cm   (B) 27 cm   (C) 30 cm

(D) 50 cm   (E) 54 cm

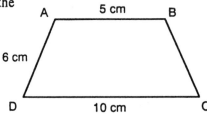

18. Find the area of trapezoid *MNOP*.

(A) $(17 + 3\sqrt{3})$ mm²

(B) 33/2 mm²

(C) $33\sqrt{3}/2$ mm²

(D) 33 mm²

(E) $33\sqrt{3}$ mm²

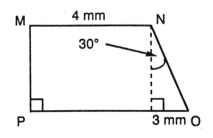

19.   Trapezoid *XYZW* is isosceles. If *m* ∠*W* = 58 and *m* ∠ *Z* = 4*x* − 6, find *x*.

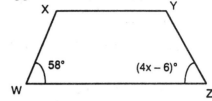

(A)   8   (B)   12   (C)   13

(D)   16   (E)   58

5. Circles

A **circle** is a set of points in the same plane equidistant from a fixed point called its center.

A **radius** of a circle is a line segment drawn from the center of the circle to any point on the circle.

A portion of a circle is called an **arc** of the circle.

Arc

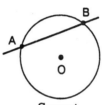

Secant

A line that intersects a circle in two points is called a **secant.**

A line segment joining two points on a circle is called a **chord** of the circle.

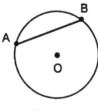

Chord

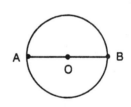

Diameter

A chord that passes through the center of the circle is called a **diameter** of the circle.

The line passing through the centers of two (or more) circles is called the **line of centers.**

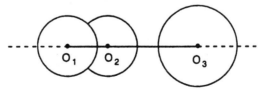

An angle whose vertex is on the circle and whose sides are chords of the circle is called an **inscribed angle**.

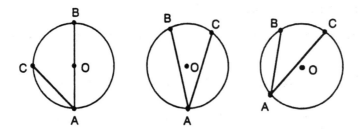

An angle whose vertex is at the center of a circle and whose sides are radii is called a **central angle.**

The measure of a minor arc is the measure of the central angle that intercepts that arc.

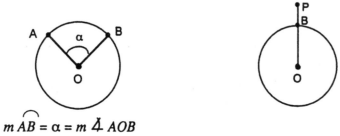

$$m \overset{\frown}{AB} = \alpha = m \angle AOB$$

The distance from a point P to a given circle is the distance from that point to the point where the circle intersects with a line segment with endpoints at the center of the circle and point P. The distance of point P to the diagrammed circle (above right) with center O is the line segment PB of line segment PO.

A line that has one and only one point of intersection with a circle is called a tangent to that circle, while their common point is called a **point of tangency.**

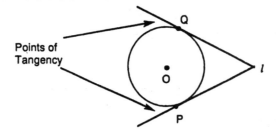

Congruent circles are circles whose radii are congruent.

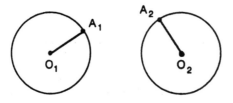

If $O_1A_1 \cong O_2A_2$, then $O_1 \cong O_2$.

The measure of a semicircle is 180°.

A **circumscribed circle** is a circle passing through all the vertices of a polygon.

Circles that have the same center and unequal radii are called **concentric circles.**

Circumscribed Circle   **Concentric Circles**

PROBLEM

A and *B* are points on circle *Q* such that △*AQB* is equilateral. If length of side *AB* = 12, find the length of arc *AB*.

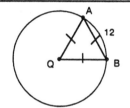

SOLUTION

To find the arc length of $\overset{\frown}{AB}$, we must find the measure of the central angle ∠ *AQB* and the measure of the radius $\overline{QA}$. ∠ *AQB* is an interior angle of the equilateral triangle △ *AQB*. Therefore, *m*∠ *AQB* = 60°. Similarly, in the equilateral △ *AQB*, *AQ* = *AB* = *QB* = 12. Given the radius, *r*, and the central angle, *n*, the arc length is given by *n*/360 · 2π*r*. Therefore, by substitution, 60/360 · 2π · 12 = $\frac{1}{6}$ · 2π · 12 = 4π. Therefore, length of arc $\overset{\frown}{AB}$ = 4π.

PROBLEM

In circle *O*, the measure of $\overset{\frown}{AB}$ is 80°. Find the measure of ∠ *A*.

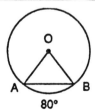

SOLUTION

The accompanying figure shows that $\overset{\frown}{AB}$ is intercepted by central angle *AOB*. By definition, we know that the measure of the central angle is the measure of its intercepted arc. In this case,

$$m\overset{\frown}{AB} = m \angle AOB = 80°.$$

Radius   and radius   are congruent and form two sides of $\triangle OAB$. By a theorem, the angles opposite these two congruent sides must, themselves, be congruent. Therefore, $m \angle A = m \angle B$.

The sum of the measures of the angles of a triangle is 180°. Therefore,

$$m \angle A + m \angle B + m \angle AOB = 180°.$$

Since $m \angle A = m \angle B$, we can write

$$m \angle A + m \angle A + 80° = 180°$$

or $2m\angle A = 100°$

or $m \angle A = 50°$.

Therefore, the measure of $\angle A$ is 50°.

Drill 5: Circles

Circumference, Area, Concentric Circles

1.   Find the circumference of circle A if its radius is 3 mm.

(A) 3π mm   (B) 6π mm   (C) 9π mm   (D) 12π mm   (E) 15π mm

2.   The circumference of circle H is 20π cm. Find the length of the radius.

(A)   10 cm   (B)   20 cm   (C) 10π cm   (D) 15π cm   (E) 20π cm

3.   The circumference of circle A is how many millimeters larger than the circumference of circle B?

(A)   3   (B)   6   (C) 3π

(D) 6π (E) 7π

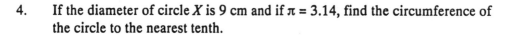

4.   If the diameter of circle X is 9 cm and if $\pi = 3.14$, find the circumference of the circle to the nearest tenth.

(A)   9 cm   (B)   14.1 cm (C)   21.1 cm (D)   24.6 cm (E)   28.3 cm

5.   Find the area of circle I.

(A)   22 mm²   (B)   121 mm²

(C) 121π mm²   (D)   132 mm²

(E) 132π mm²

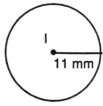

6.   The diameter of circle Z is 27 mm. Find the area of the circle.

(A) 91.125 mm²   (B) 182.25 mm²   (C) 191.5π mm²

(D) 182.25π mm²   (E) 729 mm²

7.   The area of circle B is 225π cm². Find the length of the diameter of the circle.

(A) 15 cm   (B) 20 cm   (C) 30 cm   (D) 20π cm   (E) 25π cm

8.   The area of circle X is 144π mm² while the area of circle Y is 81π mm². Write the ratio of the radius of circle X to that of circle Y.

(A) 3 : 4   (B) 4 : 3   (C) 9 : 12   (D) 27 : 12   (E) 18 : 24

9.   The circumference of circle M is 18π cm. Find the area of the circle.

(A) 18π cm²   (B) 81 cm²   (C) 36 cm²   (D) 36π cm²   (E) 81π cm²

10.   In two concentric circles, the smaller circle has a radius of 3 mm while the larger circle has a radius of 5 mm. Find the area of the shaded region.

(A) 2π mm²   (B) 8π mm²   (C) 13π mm²

(D) 16π mm²   (E) 26π mm²

11.   The radius of the smaller of two concentric circles is 5 cm while the radius of the larger circle is 7 cm. Determine the area of the shaded region.

(A) 7π cm²   (B) 24π cm²   (C) 25π cm²

(D) 36π cm²   (E) 49π cm²

12.   Find the measure of arc MN if $m \angle MON$ = 62°.

(A) 16°   (B) 32°   (C) 59°

(D) 62°   (E) 124°

13.   Find the measure of arc AXC.

(A) 150°   (B) 160°   (C) 180°

(D) 270°   (E) 360°

14. If arc *MXP* = 236°, find the measure of arc *MP*.

(A) 62°   (B) 124°   (C) 236°

(D) 270°   (E) 360°

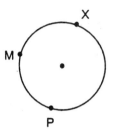

15. In circle *S*, major arc *PQR* has a measure of 298°. Find the measure of the central angle ∠ *PSR*.

(A) 62°   (B) 124°   (C) 149°

(D) 298°   (E) 360°

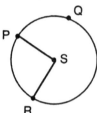

16. Find the measure of arc *XY* in circle *W*.

(A) 40°   (B) 120°   (C) 140°

(D) 180°   (E) 220°

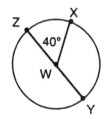

17. Find the area of the sector shown.

(A) 4 cm²   (B) 2π cm²   (C) 16 cm²

(D) 8π cm²   (E) 16π cm²

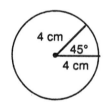

18. Find the area of the shaded region.

(A) 10   (B) 5π   (C) 25

(D) 20π   (E) 25π

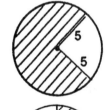

19. Find the area of the sector shown.

(A) $\dfrac{9\pi \text{ mm}^2}{4}$ (B) $\dfrac{9\pi \text{ mm}^2}{2}$ (C) 18 mm²

(D) 6π mm²   (E) 9π mm²

20. If the area of the square is 100 cm², find the area of the sector.

(A) 10π cm²   (B) 25 cm²   (C) 25π cm²

(D) 100 cm²   (E) 100π cm²

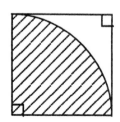

6. Solids

Solid geometry is the study of figures which consist of points not all in the same plane.

Rectangular Solids

A solid with lateral faces and bases that are rectangles is called a **rectangular solid**.

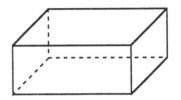

The surface area of a rectangular solid is the sum of the areas of all the faces.

The volume of a rectangular solid is equal to the product of its length, width and height.

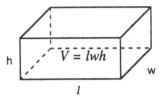

$V = lwh$

PROBLEM

What are the dimensions of a solid cube whose surface area is numerically equal to its volume?

SOLUTION

The surface area of a cube of edge length a is equal to the sum of the areas of its 6 faces. Since a cube is a regular polygon, all 6 faces are congruent. Each face of a cube is a square of edge length a. Hence, the surface area of a cube of edge length a is

$$S = 6a^2.$$

The volume of a cube of edge length a is

$$V = a^3.$$

We require that $A = V$, or that

$$6a^2 = a^3 \quad \text{or} \quad a = 6$$

Hence, if a cube has edge length 6, its surface area will be numerically equal to its volume.

Drill 6: Solids

1. Find the surface area of the rectangular prism shown.

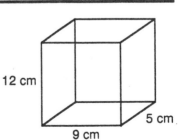

(A)   138 cm²   (B)   336 cm²   (C)   381 cm²

(D)   426 cm²   (E)   540 cm²

2.   Find the volume of the rectangular storage tank shown.

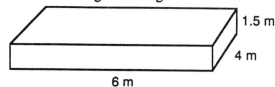

(A)   24 m³   (B)   36 m³ (C)   38 m³ (D)   42 m³ (E)   45 m³

3.   The lateral area of a cube is 100 cm². Find the length of an edge of the cube.

(A)   4 cm   (B)   5 cm   (C)   10 cm (D)   12 cm (E)   15 cm

7. Coordinate Geometry

Coordinate geometry refers to the study of geometric figures using algebraic principles.

The graph shown is called the Cartesian coordinate plane. The graph consists of a pair of perpendicular lines called **coordinate axes**. The **vertical axis** is the y-axis and the **horizontal axis** is the x-axis. The point of intersection of these two axes is called the **origin**; it is the zero point of both axes. Furthermore, points to the right of the origin on the x-axis and above the origin on the y-axis represent positive real numbers. Points to the left of the origin on the x-axis or below the origin on the y-axis represent negative real numbers.

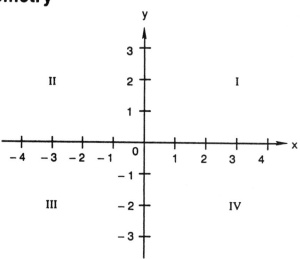

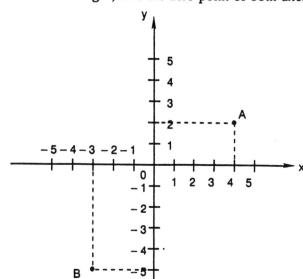

The four regions cut off by the coordinate axes are, in counterclockwise direction from the top right, called the first, second, third and fourth quadrant, respectively. The first

quadrant contains all points with two positive coordinates.

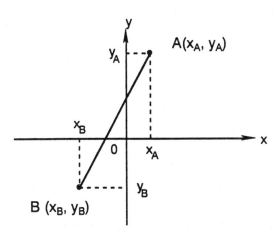

In the graph shown, two points are identified by the ordered pair, (*x, y*) of numbers. The *x*-coordinate is the first number and the *y*-coordinate is the second number.

To plot a point on the graph when given the coordinates, draw perpendicular lines from the number-line coordinates to the point where the two lines intersect.

To find the coordinates of a given point on the graph, draw perpendicular lines from the point to the coordinates on the number line. The *x*-coordinate is written before the *y*-coordinate and a comma is used to separate the two.

In this case, point *A* has the coordinates (4, 2) and the coordinates of point *B* are (− 3, − 5).

For any two points *A* and *B* with coordinates (X_A, Y_A) and (X_B, Y_B), respectively, the distance between *A* and *B* is represented by:

$$AB = \sqrt{(X_A - X_B)^2 + (Y_A - Y_B)^2}$$

This is commonly known as the distance formula or the **Pythagorean Theorem.**

PROBLEM

Find the distance between the point *A*(1, 3) and *B*(5, 3).

SOLUTION

In this case, where the ordinate of both points is the same, the distance between the two points is given by the absolute value of the difference between the two abscissas. In fact, this case reduces to merely counting boxes as the figure shows.

Let, x_1 = abscissa of A y_1 = ordinate of A

x_2 = abscissa of B y_2 = ordinate of B

d = the distance.

Therefore, $d = |x_1 - x_2|$. By substitution, $d = |1 - 5| = |-4| = 4$. This answer can also be obtained by applying the general formula for distance between any two points

$$d = \sqrt{(x_1 - x_2)^2 + (y_1 - y_2)^2}$$

By substitution,

$$d = \sqrt{(1-5)^2 + (3-3)^2} = \sqrt{(-4)^2 + (0)^2} = \sqrt{16} = 4.$$

The distance is 4.

To find the midpoint of a segment between the two given endpoints, use the formula,

$$MP = \left(\frac{x_1 + x_2}{2}, \frac{y_1 + y_2}{2}\right)$$

where x_1 and y_1 are the coordinates of one point; x_2 and y_2 are the coordinates of the other point.

Drill 7: Coordinate Geometry

1.   Which point shown has the coordinates $(-3, 2)$?

(A) A   (B) B   (C) C

(D) D   (E) E

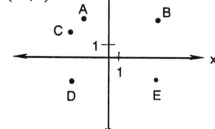

2.   Name the coordinates of point A.

(A) (4, 3)   (B) (3, -4)   (C) (3, 4)

(D) (-4, 3)   (E) (4, -3)

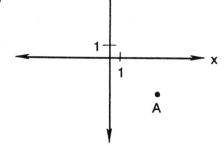

3. Which point shown has the coordinates (2.5, – 1)?

(A) M   (B) N   (C) P

(D) Q   (E) R

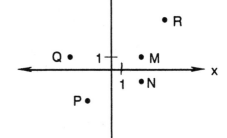

4. The correct *x*-coordinate for point *H* is what number?

(A) 3   (B) 4   (C) – 3

(D) – 4   (E) – 5

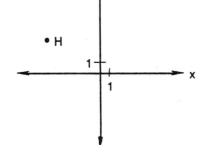

5. The correct *y*-coordinate for point *R* is what number?

(A) –7   (B) 2   (C) – 2

(D) 7   (E) 8

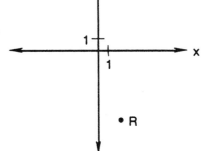

6. Find the distance between (4, – 7) and (– 2, – 7).

(A) 4   (B) 6   (C) 7   (D) 14   (E) 15

7. Find the distance between (3, 8) and (5, 11).

(A) 2   (B) 3   (C) $\sqrt{13}$ (D) $\sqrt{15}$ (E) $3\sqrt{3}$

8. How far from the origin is the point (3, 4)?

(A) 3   (B) 4   (C) 5   (D) $5\sqrt{3}$ (E) $4\sqrt{5}$

9.   Find the distance between the point $(-4, 2)$ and $(3, -5)$.

(A)   3   (B) $3\sqrt{3}$ (C)   7   (D) $7\sqrt{2}$ (E) $7\sqrt{3}$

10.   The distance between points A and B is 10 units. If A has coordinates $(4, -6)$ and B has coordinates $(-2, y)$, determine the value of y.

(A) -6 (B) -2 (C)   0   (D)   1   (E)   2

11.   Find the midpoint between the points $(-2, 6)$ and $(4, 8)$.

(A) $(3, 7)$ (B) $(1, 7)$ (C) $(3, 1)$ (D) $(1, 1)$ (E) $(-3, 7)$

12.   Find the coordinates of the midpoint between the points $(-5, 7)$ and $(3, -1)$.

(A) $(-4, 4)$ (B) $(3, -1)$ (C) $(1, -3)$ (D) $(-1, 3)$ (E) $(4, -4)$.

13.   The y-coordinate of the midpoint of segment $\overline{AB}$ if A has coordinates $(-3, 7)$ and B has coordinates $(-3, -2)$ is what value?

(A)   5/2   (B)   3   (C)   7/2   (D)   5   (E)   15/2

14.   One endpoint of a line segment is $(5, -3)$. The midpoint is $(-1, 6)$. What is the other endpoint?

(A) $(7, 3)$ (B) $(2, 1.5)$ (C) $(-7, 15)$

(D) $(-2, 1.5)$ (E) $(-7, 12)$

15.   The point $(-2, 6)$ is the midpoint for which of the following pair of points?

(A) $(1, 4)$ and $(-3, 8)$ (B) $(-1, -3)$ and $(5, 9)$

(C) $(1, 4)$ and $(5, 9)$ (D) $(-1, 4)$ and $(3, -8)$

(E) $(1, 3)$ and $(-5, 9)$

GEOMETRY DRILLS

ANSWER KEY

Drill 1–Lines and Angles

1.	(B)	5.	(D)	9.	(D)	13.	(B)
2.	(A)	6.	(C)	10.	(E)	14.	(E)
3.	(C)	7.	(B)	11.	(C)	15.	(A)
4.	(D)	8.	(A)	12.	(D)		

Drill 2–Regular Polygons

1.	(D)	4.	(A)	7.	(E)	10.	(B)
2.	(B)	5.	(D)	8.	(B)		
3.	(E)	6.	(C)	9.	(D)		

Drill 3–Triangles

1.	(D)	5.	(C)	9.	(A)	13.	(D)
2.	(B)	6.	(A)	10.	(C)	14.	(A)
3.	(C)	7.	(B)	11.	(C)	15.	(B)
4.	(E)	8.	(E)	12.	(B)		

Drill 4–Quadrilaterals

1.	(A)	6.	(A)	11.	(C)	16.	(A)
2.	(B)	7.	(D)	12.	(D)	17.	(B)
3.	(D)	8.	(C)	13.	(B)	18.	(C)
4.	(E)	9.	(B)	14.	(C)	19.	(D)
5.	(C)	10.	(C)	15.	(B)		

Drill 5–Circles

1.	(B)	6.	(D)	11.	(B)	16.	(C)
2.	(A)	7.	(C)	12.	(D)	17.	(B)
3.	(D)	8.	(B)	13.	(C)	18.	(D)
4.	(E)	9.	(E)	14.	(B)	19.	(A)
5.	(C)	10.	(D)	15.	(A)	20.	(C)

Drill 6–Solids

1.   (D)   2.   (B)   3.   (C)

Drill 7–Coordinate Geometry

1.   (C)   5.   (A)   9.   (D)   13.   (A)
2.   (E)   6.   (B)   10.   (E)   14.   (C)
3.   (B)   7.   (C)   11.   (B)   15.   (E)
4.   (D)   8.   (C)   12.   (D)

GLOSSARY: GEOMETRY

Acute Angle

An angle that is less than 90 degrees.

Acute Triangle

A triangle with all three angles under 90 degrees (i.e., all angles are acute).

Adjacent Angles

Angles with a vertex and side in common.

Altitude of a Parallelogram

A line segment between the opposite sides of a parallelogram, which is perpendicular to both sides.

Altitude of a Trapezoid

A line segment joining the two parallel sides of the trapezoid, which is perpendicular to each of these sides.

Altitude of a Triangle

The line segment from one vertex of the triangle to the opposite side such that it intersects the opposite side at a right angle.

Angle

What is formed by the intersection of two rays with a common endpoint. This intersection (endpoint) is the vertex of the angle. An angle is measured in terms of degrees.

Angle Bisector of a Triangle

A line segment from one vertex of the triangle to the opposite side, which bisects the interior angle of a triangle at the vertex.

Apothem of a Regular Polygon

The line segment joining the center of the polygon to the center of any side.

Arc of a Circle

A contiguous portion of a circle. An arc can be formed by the intersection of the lines forming a central angle and the circle. In this case, the measure of the arc equals the measure of the central angle.

Area

The space occupied by a figure.

Base of a Triangle

The unequal side of an isosceles triangle.

Bases of a Trapezoid

The two parallel sides of a trapezoid.

Bisect

Divide into two equal portions.

Center of a Circle

The point about which all points on the circle are equidistant.

Central Angle

An angle whose vertex is the center of a circle.

Chord of a Circle

A line segment joining two points on a circle. If it passes through the center of the circle, then the chord is a diameter.

Circle

The set of points in a plane at a fixed distance from a given point in that plane (the center of a circle).

Circumference

The length of a circle if it were to be "unwrapped." The circumference equals twice the length of the diameter of the circle.

Circumscribed Circle

A circle passing through each vertex of a polygon.

Collinear

Points that lie on a common line.

Complementary Angles

Angles whose measures sum to 90 degrees.

Concave Polygon

A polygon that does not contain all points on line segments joining all pairs of its vertices.

Concentric Circles

Circles with a common center.

Concurrent Lines

Lines with a point in common.

Congruent Angles

Angles of equal measure.

Congruent Circles

Circles with radii of the same length.

Consecutive Angles

Angles with vertices at adjacent sides of a polygon (i.e., the vertices have a common side).

Convex Polygon

A polygon containing all points on line segments connecting all pairs of its vertices.

Coordinate Axes

Two perpendicular lines (the x-axis and the y-axis) used for placing ordered pairs of reals relative to one another.

Coordinate Geometry

The study of geometry via algebraic principles.

Coplanar Lines

Lines in the same plane.

Cube

A six-faced solid in three dimensions in which each face is a square.

Decagon

A polygon with ten sides.

Degree

The unit of measurement for angles.

Diagonal of a Polygon

A line segment joining any two nonconsecutive vertices of a polygon.

Diameter of a Circle

The chord of a circle that passes through the center of the circle.

Equiangular Polygon

A polygon whose angles all have the same measure.

Equiangular Triangle

A triangle whose angles are all 60 degrees (an equilateral triangle).

Equidistant

The same distance from, or at a fixed distance from.

Equilateral Polygon

A polygon whose sides are all of equal length.

Equilateral Triangle

A triangle whose three sides all have the same length.

Exterior Angle of a Triangle

An angle supplementary to an interior angle of a triangle formed by extending one side of the triangle.

Hexagon

A polygon with six sides.

Horizontal Axis

The *x*-axis of the coordinate axes.

Hypotenuse

The longest side of a right triangle, it is the side facing the 90-degree angle.

Inscribed Angle

An angle whose vertex is on a circle and whose sides are chords of that circle.

Inscribed Circle

A circle within a (convex) polygon such that each side of the polygon is tangent to the circle.

Interior Angle of a Triangle

The smaller of the two angles formed by the intersection of two adjacent sides of a triangle (i.e., it never exceeds 180 degrees, while the larger angle always does).

Intersecting Lines

Lines that have a point in common.

Isosceles Right Triangle

A triangle with one 90-degree angle and two 45-degree angles.

Isosceles Trapezoid

A trapezoid whose nonparallel sides are of equal length.

Isosceles Triangle

A triangle with two angles of common measure.

Legs

The two shorter sides of a right triangle, these are adjacent to the right angle.

Line

A set of points of infinite length with the property that a line perpendicular to the given line at a certain point is parallel to any other line perpendicular to the given line at any other point. A line is said to be one-dimensional.

Line of Centers

A line joining the centers of circles.

Line Segment

The line portion that lies between two points.

Median of a Trapezoid

The line segment joining the midpoints of the nonparallel sides of a trapezoid.

Median of a Triangle

The line segment from one vertex of the triangle to the midpoint of the opposite side.

Midline of a Triangle

A line segment joining the midpoints of two adjacent sides of a triangle.

Midpoint

The unique point on a line segment that is equidistant to each endpoint of the line segment.

Minute

One sixtieth of a degree.

Nonagon

A polygon with nine sides.

Obtuse Angle

An angle whose measure exceeds 90 degrees.

Obtuse Triangle

A triangle with an obtuse angle.

Octagon

An eight-sided polygon.

Origin

The intersection of the two coordinate axes. The origin corresponds to the ordered pair (0, 0).

Pair of Base Angles of a Trapezoid

Two angles interior to the trapezoid, whose vertices have one of the parallel sides in common.

Parallel Lines

Lines in the same plane that do not intersect.

Parallelogram

A quadrilateral whose opposite sides are parallel.

Pentagon

A five-sided polygon.

Perimeter

The sum of the lengths of the sides of a polygon.

Perpendicular Bisector

A bisector that is perpendicular to the segment it bisects.

Perpendicular Bisector of a Side of a Triangle

A line segment that is perpendicular to and bisects one side of the triangle.

Perpendicular Lines

Lines that intersect, with the property that the angles whose vertex is the intersection are all right angles.

Plane

A set of points spanned by two intersecting lines and all the points between them. A plane is said to be two-dimensional.

Plane Figure

A figure in a plane (in two dimensions).

Plane Geometry

The study of plane figures.

Point

A specific location with no area. A point is said to be zero-dimensional.

Point of Tangency

The point at which a tangent intersects a circle.

Polygon

A closed figure with the same number of sides as angles.

Pythagorean Theorem

The rule that states that the square of the length of the hypotenuse of a right triangle equals the sum of the squares of the lengths of the two legs of that triangle.

Quadrilateral

A polygon with four sides.

Radii

Plural of radius.

Radius of a Circle

The line segment from the center of a circle to any point on the circle.

Radius of a Regular Polygon

The line segment joining the center of a polygon to any vertex.

Ray

The portion of a line that lies on one side of a fixed point.

Rectangle

A parallelogram with right interior angles.

Rectangular Solid

A solid with lateral faces and bases that are rectangles.

Reflex Angle

An angle whose measure exceeds 180 degrees but is less than 360 degrees.

Regular Polygon

A polygon that is both equiangular and equilateral.

Rhombus

A parallelogram with all four sides of equal length.

Right Angle

An angle measuring 90 degrees; it is formed by perpendicular lines.

Right Circular Cylinder

A three-dimensional solid whose horizontal cross sections are circles; these circles (for each horizontal location) have the same center and radius (i.e., can shaped).

Right Triangle

A triangle with one right angle.

Scalene Triangle

A triangle with no equal sides.

Secant of a Circle

A line segment joining two points on a circle.

Side of a Polynomial

Line segments whose endpoints are adjacent vertices of the polynomial.

Similar

Of the same shape, but not necessarily of the same size.

Solid Geometry

The study of figures in three dimensions.

Square

A rectangle with four equal sides. Alternatively, a rhombus with four right angles.

Straight Angle

An angle measuring 180 degrees, the two rays forming it form one line.

Supplementary Angles

Angles whose measures sum to 180 degrees.

Surface Area

The sum of the areas of all faces of a figure.

Tangent to a Circle

A line that intersects a circle at exactly one point.

Transitive Property

A relation, R, is transitive if, for all a, b, c the relations aRb and bRc imply aRc. For example, equality is transitive, since $a = b$ and $b = c$ together imply that $a = c$.

Transversal

A line that intersects two parallel lines.

Trapezoid

A quadrilateral with exactly two parallel sides.

Triangle

A three-sided polygon.

Vertex

A point at which adjacent sides of a polygon intersect.

Vertical Angles

Two angles formed by intersecting lines (not rays) and directly across from each other. They are also equal.

Vertical Axis

The *y*-axis of the coordinate axes.

Vertices

The points at which the adjacent sides of a polygon intersect.

Volume

Three-dimensional space occupied or displaced (i.e., if a three-dimensional solid were put into a full bathtub, its volume is the amount of water that would fall out).

REA's Test Preps
The Best in Test Preparation

- REA "Test Preps" are **far more** comprehensive than any other test preparation series
- Each book contains up to **eight** full-length practice tests based on the most recent exams
- **Every** type of question likely to be given on the exams is included
- Answers are accompanied by **full** and **detailed** explanations

REA publishes over 60 Test Preparation volumes in several series. They include:

Advanced Placement Exams (APs)
Biology
Calculus AB & Calculus BC
Chemistry
Computer Science
English Language & Composition
English Literature & Composition
European History
Government & Politics
Physics
Psychology
Spanish Language
Statistics
United States History

College-Level Examination Program (CLEP)
Analyzing and Interpreting Literature
College Algebra
Freshman College Composition
General Examinations
General Examinations Review
History of the United States I
Human Growth and Development
Introductory Sociology
Principles of Marketing
Spanish

SAT II: Subject Tests
Biology E/M
Chemistry
English Language Proficiency Test
French
German
Literature

SAT II: Subject Tests (cont'd)
Mathematics Level IC, IIC
Physics
Spanish
United States History
Writing

Graduate Record Exams (GREs)
Biology
Chemistry
General
Literature in English
Mathematics
Physics
Psychology

ACT - ACT Assessment

ASVAB - Armed Services Vocational Aptitude Battery

CBEST - California Basic Educational Skills Test

CDL - Commercial Driver License Exam

CLAST - College-Level Academic Skills Test

ELM - Entry Level Mathematics

ExCET - Exam for the Certification of Educators in Texas

FE (EIT) - Fundamentals of Engineering Exam

FE Review - Fundamentals of Engineering Review

GED - High School Equivalency Diploma Exam (U.S. & Canadian editions)

GMAT - Graduate Management Admission Test

LSAT - Law School Admission Test

MAT - Miller Analogies Test

MCAT - Medical College Admission Test

MECT - Massachusetts Educator Certification Tests

MSAT - Multiple Subjects Assessment for Teachers

NJ HSPT- New Jersey High School Proficiency Test

PPST - Pre-Professional Skills Tests

PSAT - Preliminary Scholastic Assessment Test

SAT I - Reasoning Test

SAT I - Quick Study & Review

TASP - Texas Academic Skills Program

TOEFL - Test of English as a Foreign Language

TOEIC - Test of English for International Communication

RESEARCH & EDUCATION ASSOCIATION
61 Ethel Road W. • Piscataway, New Jersey 08854
Phone: (732) 819-8880   **website: www.rea.com**

Please send me more information about your Test Prep books

Name _____

Address _____

City _____ State _____ Zip _____

Available at your local bookstore or order directly from us by sending in coupon below.

RESEARCH & EDUCATION ASSOCIATION
61 Ethel Road W., Piscataway, New Jersey 08854
Phone: (732) 819-8880   website: **www.rea.com**

VISA   MasterCard

☐ Payment enclosed
☐ Visa ☐ MasterCard

Charge Card Number

Expiration Date: _____ / _____
                         Mo   Yr

Please ship REA's **"SAT"** @ $17.95 plus $4.00 for shipping.

Name _____

Address _____

City _____ State _____ Zip _____

REA's

HANDBOOK OF ENGLISH

Grammar, Style, and Writing

All the essentials you need to know are contained in this simple and practical book

Learn quickly and easily
- **Rules and exceptions in grammar**
- **Spelling and proper punctuation**
- **Common errors in sentence structure**
- **2,000 examples of correct usage**
- **Effective writing skills**

Complete practice exercises with answers follow each chapter

REA *Research & Education Association*

Available at your local bookstore or order directly from us by sending in coupon below.

RESEARCH & EDUCATION ASSOCIATION
61 Ethel Road W., Piscataway, New Jersey 08854
Phone: (732) 819-8880   website: **www.rea.com**

VISA   **MasterCard**

Charge Card Number

☐ Payment enclosed
☐ Visa   ☐ MasterCard

Expiration Date: _____ / _____
                      Mo   Yr

Please ship **"Handbook of English"** @ $21.95 plus $4.00 for shipping.

Name _____

Address _____

City _____ State _____ Zip _____

"The ESSENTIALS" of Math & Science

Each book in the ESSENTIALS series offers all essential information of the field it covers. It summarizes what every textbook in the particular field must include, and is designed to help students in preparing for exams and doing homework. The ESSENTIALS are excellent supplements to any class text.

The ESSENTIALS are complete and concise with quick access to needed information. They serve as a handy reference source at all times. The ESSENTIALS are prepared with REA's customary concern for high professional quality and student needs.

Available in the following titles:

Advanced Calculus I & II
Algebra & Trigonometry I & II
Anatomy & Physiology
Anthropology
Astronomy
Automatic Control Systems /
   Robotics I & II
Biology I & II
Boolean Algebra
Calculus I, II, & III
Chemistry
Complex Variables I & II
Computer Science I & II
Data Structures I & II
Differential Equations I & II
Electric Circuits I & II
Electromagnetics I & II

Electronics I & II
Electronic Communications I & II
Fluid Mechanics /
   Dynamics I & II
Fourier Analysis
Geometry I & II
Group Theory I & II
Heat Transfer I & II
LaPlace Transforms
Linear Algebra
Math for Computer Applications
Math for Engineers I & II
Math Made Nice-n-Easy Series
Mechanics I, II, & III
Microbiology
Modern Algebra
Molecular Structures of Life

Numerical Analysis I & II
Organic Chemistry I & II
Physical Chemistry I & II
Physics I & II
Pre-Calculus
Probability
Psychology I & II
Real Variables
Set Theory
Sociology
Statistics I & II
Strength of Materials &
   Mechanics of Solids I & II
Thermodynamics I & II
Topology
Transport Phenomena I & II
Vector Analysis

*If you would like more information about any of these books,
complete the coupon below and return it to us or visit your local bookstore.*

RESEARCH & EDUCATION ASSOCIATION
61 Ethel Road W. • Piscataway, New Jersey 08854
Phone: (732) 819-8880   **website: www.rea.com**

Please send me more information about your Math & Science Essentials books

Name _____

Address _____

City _____ State _____ Zip _____

MAXnotes®

REA's Literature Study Guides

MAXnotes® are student-friendly. They offer a fresh look at masterpieces of literature, presented in a lively and interesting fashion. **MAXnotes®** offer the essentials of what you should know about the work, including outlines, explanations and discussions of the plot, character lists, analyses, and historical context. **MAXnotes®** are designed to help you think independently about literary works by raising various issues and thought-provoking ideas and questions. Written by literary experts who currently teach the subject, **MAXnotes®** enhance your understanding and enjoyment of the work.

Available **MAXnotes®** include the following:

Absalom, Absalom!
The Aeneid of Virgil
Animal Farm
Antony and Cleopatra
As I Lay Dying
As You Like It
The Autobiography of
    Malcolm X
The Awakening
Beloved
Beowulf
Billy Budd
The Bluest Eye, A Novel
Brave New World
The Canterbury Tales
The Catcher in the Rye
The Color Purple
The Crucible
Death in Venice
Death of a Salesman
Dickens Dictionary
The Divine Comedy I: Inferno
Dubliners
The Edible Woman
Emma
Euripides' Medea & Electra
Frankenstein
Gone with the Wind
The Grapes of Wrath
Great Expectations
The Great Gatsby
Gulliver's Travels
Handmaid's Tale
Hamlet
Hard Times
Heart of Darkness

Henry IV, Part I
Henry V
The House on Mango Street
Huckleberry Finn
I Know Why the Caged
    Bird Sings
The Iliad
Invisible Man
Jane Eyre
Jazz
The Joy Luck Club
Jude the Obscure
Julius Caesar
King Lear
Leaves of Grass
Les Misérables
Lord of the Flies
Macbeth
The Merchant of Venice
Metamorphoses of Ovid
Metamorphosis
Middlemarch
A Midsummer Night's Dream
Moby-Dick
Moll Flanders
Mrs. Dalloway
Much Ado About Nothing
Mules and Men
My Antonia
Native Son
1984
The Odyssey
Oedipus Trilogy
Of Mice and Men
On the Road

Othello
Paradise
Paradise Lost
A Passage to India
Plato's Republic
Portrait of a Lady
A Portrait of the Artist
    as a Young Man
Pride and Prejudice
A Raisin in the Sun
Richard II
Romeo and Juliet
The Scarlet Letter
Sir Gawain and the
    Green Knight
Slaughterhouse-Five
Song of Solomon
The Sound and the Fury
The Stranger
Sula
The Sun Also Rises
A Tale of Two Cities
The Taming of the Shrew
Tar Baby
The Tempest
Tess of the D'Urbervilles
Their Eyes Were Watching God
Things Fall Apart
To Kill a Mockingbird
To the Lighthouse
Twelfth Night
Uncle Tom's Cabin
Waiting for Godot
Wuthering Heights
Guide to Literary Terms

RESEARCH & EDUCATION ASSOCIATION
61 Ethel Road W. • Piscataway, New Jersey 08854
Phone: (732) 819-8880   **website: www.rea.com**

Please send me more information about MAXnotes®.

Name _____

Address _____

City _____ State _____ Zip _____

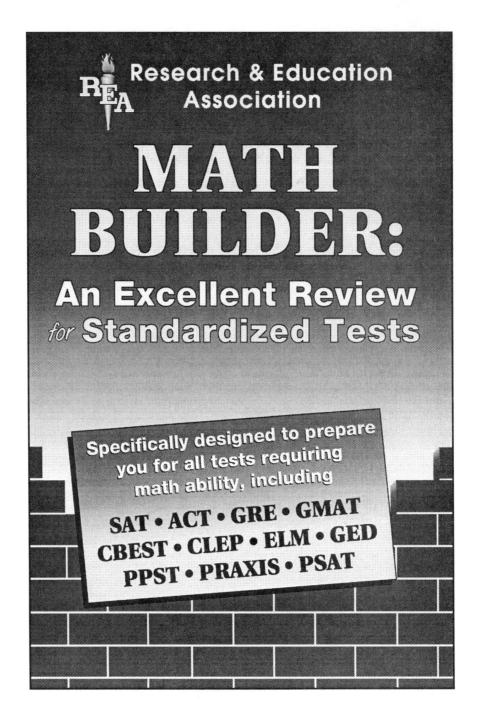

Research & Education Association

MATH BUILDER:
An Excellent Review
for Standardized Tests

Specifically designed to prepare you for all tests requiring math ability, including

SAT • ACT • GRE • GMAT
CBEST • CLEP • ELM • GED
PPST • PRAXIS • PSAT

Available at your local bookstore or order directly from us by sending in coupon below.

RESEARCH & EDUCATION ASSOCIATION
61 Ethel Road W., Piscataway, New Jersey 08854
Phone: (732) 819-8880   website: www.rea.com

VISA   **MasterCard**

Charge Card Number

☐ Payment enclosed
☐ Visa   ☐ MasterCard

Expiration Date: _____ / _____
                          Mo   Yr

Please ship **REA's MATH BUILDER** @ $16.95 plus $4.00 for shipping.

Name _____

Address _____

City _____ State _____ Zip _____

Available at your local bookstore or order directly from us by sending in coupon below.

RESEARCH & EDUCATION ASSOCIATION
61 Ethel Road W., Piscataway, New Jersey 08854
Phone: (732) 819-8880   website: www.rea.com

VISA   MasterCard

Charge Card Number

☐ Payment enclosed
☐ Visa   ☐ MasterCard

Expiration Date: _____ / _____
                              Mo   Yr

Please ship **REA's VERBAL BUILDER** @ $16.95 plus $4.00 for shipping

Name _____

Address _____

City _____ State _____ Zip _____

The High School Tutors®

The **HIGH SCHOOL TUTOR** series is based on the same principle as the more comprehensive **PROBLEM SOLVERS**, but is specifically designed to meet the needs of high school students. REA has revised all the books in this series to include expanded review sections and new material. This makes the books even more effective in helping students to cope with these difficult high school subjects.

If you would like more information about any of these books,
complete the coupon below and return it to us or go to your local bookstore.

RESEARCH & EDUCATION ASSOCIATION
61 Ethel Road W. • Piscataway, New Jersey 08854
Phone: (732) 819-8880   **website: www.rea.com**

Please send me more information about your High School Tutor books.

Name _____

Address _____

City _____ State _____ Zip _____